U-505

U-505

THE FINAL JOURNEY

JAMES E. WISE JR.

The Naval Institute Press wishes to thank the McCormick Tribune Foundation in Chicago, Illinois, for its continued support of this project. The foundation's benefactor, Col. Robert R. McCormick, the longtime editor and publisher of the *Chicago Tribune,* played an integral role in bringing the *U-505* to Chicago.

Naval Institute Press

Annapolis, Maryland

Naval Institute Press
291 Wood Road
Annapolis, MD 21402

Library of Congress Cataloging-in-Publication Data
Wise, James E., 1930–

U-505 : the final journey / James E. Wise, Jr.
p. cm.
Includes bibliographical references.
ISBN 1-59114-967-3 (alk. paper)
1. U-505 (Submarine) 2. World War, 1939–1945—Naval operations—Submarine. 3. World War, 1939–1945—Naval operations, German. 4. World War, 1939–1945—Regimental histories—Germany. 5. U-505 (Submarine)—Exhibitions. 6. Museum of Science and Industry (Chicago, Ill.)—Exhibitions. I. Title.

D782.U18W57 2005
940.54'51'0943—dc22

2005005568

∞ Print editions meet the requirements of ANSI/NISO z39.48-1992 (Permanence of Paper).
Printed in the United States of America.

27 26 25 24 23 22 21 20 9 8 7 6 5 4 3 2 1

Photo Credits: akg-images Ltd. (akg); DIZ GmbH (DIZ); Imperial War Museum (IWM); International Truck and Engine Corporation (formerly International Harvester Company) (ITEC); Library of Congress (LOC); the Mariners' Museum, Newport News, Virginia (MM); Archives, Museum of Science and Industry, Chicago (MSI); National Archives and Records Administration (NARA); Naval Historical Center (NHC); The Sherwin-Williams Company; Special Collections & Archives Division, Nimitz Library, U.S. Naval Academy; Steamship Historical Society of America Collection, Langsdale Library, University of Baltimore (SHSA); U-BOOT-ARCHIV; and U.S. Naval Institute (USNI). Illustration cut-away of *U-505* courtesy of John Batchelor. Photos donated or on loan from families and relatives of TG 22.3 veterans are so noted in the credit lines.

The following text is taken from a bronze plaque presented at the 1954 *U-505* dedication ceremony. It is fitting that this remembrance be continued as the *U-505* rests at her final port.

1815–1944

German Submarine
U-505

This prize of war is dedicated to the memory of the American seamen who went down to unmarked ocean graves helping to win victory at sea.

The *U-505* was boarded and captured on June 4, 1944, off Cape Blanco, French West Africa, by Task Group 22.3 of the U.S. Atlantic Fleet. This is the only German Submarine ever boarded and captured at sea, and the first foreign man-o'-war so captured by the U.S. Navy since 1815.

Task Group 22.3
Captain Daniel V. Gallery, USN

USS *Guadalcanal* CVE-60 (Flagship)	Captain Daniel V. Gallery, USN	USS *Pope* DE-134	Lieut. Comdr. Edwin H. Headland, USN
VC Squadron 8	Lieutenant Norman D. Hodson, USN	USS *Flaherty* DE-135	Lieut. Comdr. Means Johnston Jr., USN
		USS *Chatelain* DE-149	Lieut. Comdr. Dudley S. Knox, USNR
Escort Destroyer Division 4	Commander Frederick S. Hall, USN	USS *Jenks* DE-665	Lieut. Comdr. Julius F. Way, USN
USS *Pillsbury* DE-133	Lieut. Comdr. George W. Cassleman, USNR		

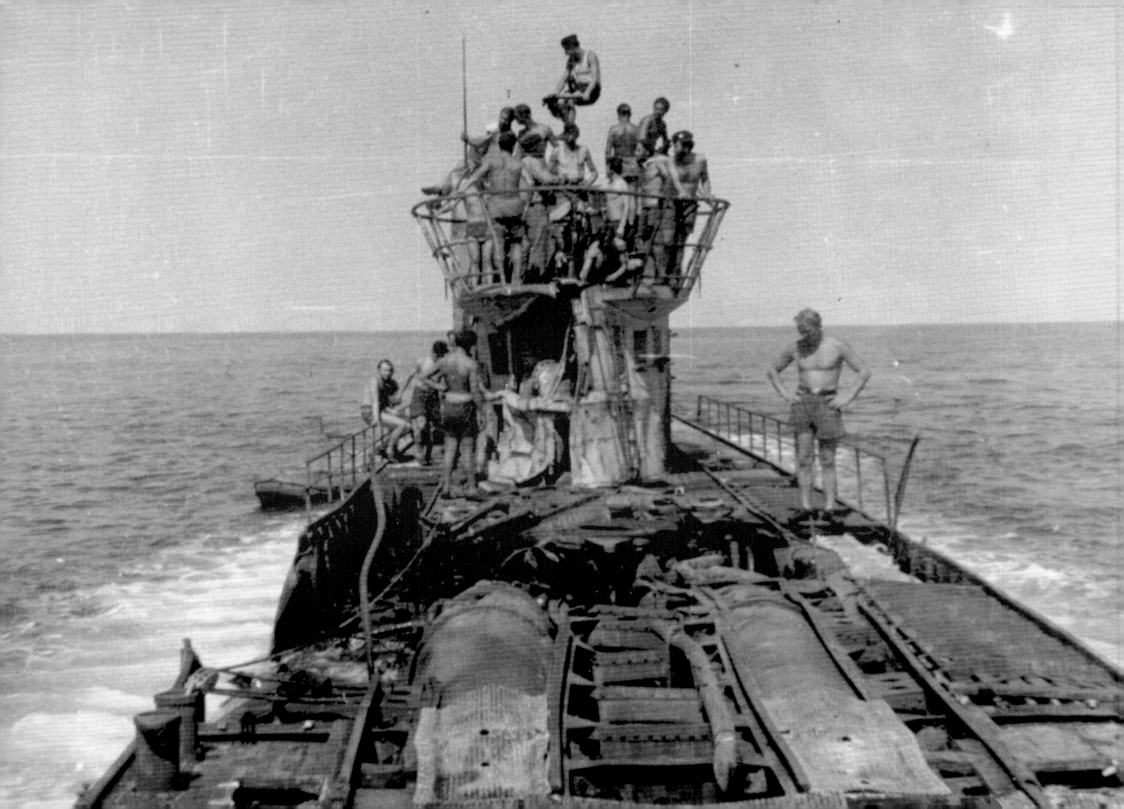

CONTENTS

Preface   ix

Acknowledgments   xi

List of Equivalent Commissioned and Enlisted   xii
  Ranks (World War II)

CHAPTER 1   The *U-505* Joins the War in the Atlantic   1

CHAPTER 2   The Battle of the Atlantic, 1939–1945   20

CHAPTER 3   U-Boat Hunter-Killer Groups   40

CHAPTER 4   Task Group 22.3   51

CHAPTER 5   The Last Patrol of the *U-505*   63

CHAPTER 6   The Battle and the Capture   72

CHAPTER 7   Bringing the *U-505* to Chicago   95

CHAPTER 8   Restoration—A Continuing Task   118

CHAPTER 9   The New *U-505* Experience   137

Appendix A   Operating and Living on Board the *U-505*   151

Appendix B   The Evolution of the Submarine   179

Works Consulted   201

PREFACE

"The New *U-505* Experience"

It was 1956 when I first visited the *U-505* while on leave in my hometown, Chicago. She had been put on static display outside the museum on September 25, 1954. I was at the time a naval aviator attached to an antisubmarine warfare (ASW) patrol squadron on the East Coast.

Looking back at my tour of the *U-505*, I realized it was my first experience in a submarine. And I think I can say in all honesty that at the time, few, if any, of my fellow ASW pilots were ever in a submarine. We would fly night and day, each pilot waiting for his radarman to call out a contact, and when he would respond, we would search for an underwater foe using somewhat the same tactics, radar systems, sonobuoys, and weaponry used in World War II.

I guess what surprised me most about the *U-505* was her interior spaces. To think that more than fifty men lived, worked, and fought in such confines boggled the mind. During the tour I learned about the Hunter-Killer Task Group (TG 22.3) that captured the boat under the steady hand of a remarkable naval officer, Captain Daniel V. Gallery.

Now, some fifty years after the *U-505* arrived in Chicago, the boat (submarines traditionally have been called boats rather than ships) has been moved to a new underground site on the north side of the east pavilion of the museum. During that half century, the U-boat had begun to deteriorate from erosive weather conditions and wear caused by the millions of visitors who toured her. "The New *U-505* Experience" will provide a permanent sanctuary for preserving one of the nation's unique historical landmarks for the education and enlightenment of current and future generations. Together with many new exhibits and an array of *U-505* artifacts collected from various sources over the years, the exhibit will vividly portray the impact of World War II undersea technology.

The museum's brochure "The Story of the *U-505*," first published in 1955, includes a preface written by Rear Admiral Gallery, who passed away in 1977. I think his words live on today and bear repeating.

NO TOMBSTONES ON THE SEA

The United States owes much to the sea. It carried our ancestors to freedom and a new way of life on a virgin continent. When our nation was new and weak, the sea was the bulwark that protected us from stronger nations, jealous of our democracy and growth. As we became stronger, our industry thrived and grew because the sea gave us access to the markets and resources of the entire world.

In both World Wars, after bloody battles against submarines, the sea was the highway over which we deployed our military might to fight the wars a long way from our home shores. Now that we are the world's greatest nation, we are utterly dependent on the sea's highways to bring strategic raw materials that keep the wheels of our mighty industry turning.

All over the country there are memorials to land battles of our seven wars. But where are the memorials to the two great Battles of the Atlantic, in which the fate of our nation hung in the balance? In these battles we fought to keep the vital sea-lanes open against the U-boats that torpedoed ships and left men, women, and children to their fate thousands of miles from shore. Nine thousand five hundred ships, totaling thirty-five million tons, are on the bottom now, sacrifices to the U-boat.

It is fitting that we have a memorial to the fifty-five thousand Americans who went down with those ships, fighting against great odds, to unmarked graves in the ocean's depths. This was the purpose in bringing the captured German submarine *U-505* to Chicago for installation at the Museum of Science and Industry as a permanent memorial to those Americans who thus lost their lives at sea.

The *U-505* is representative of the German underseas raiders that almost drove our ships from the sea. She was boarded and captured off the coast of Africa in 1944 and was brought back intact. She was the first enemy man-of-war captured in battle on the high seas since 1815 in the days of sailing ships. What more appropriate symbol of our victory at sea is there than an enemy submarine itself, beaten in mid-ocean battle, and installed in the Midwest a thousand miles from saltwater?

Even in the atomic age the submarine is still the greatest threat to our control of the seas. This captured sub now serves as a tribute to the heroism of our Navy men, as a memorial to the dead, and as a stern reminder to the living that control of the sea, so vital to our existence, has been won at a great price.

One final note. I had the privilege of meeting with and talking to Admiral Gallery in 1966 while serving on board the aircraft carrier USS *America* (CVA-60). He had come aboard to collect data for a new book he was writing (*Cap'n Fatso,* which was published in 1969 by W. W. Norton). The timing couldn't have been better for the still-rambunctious admiral. At the time, our ships were surrounded by harassing Soviet combatants, the "Six Day War" had begun, and the USS *Liberty* was attacked. Gallery was delighted to be back in the middle of near-wartime operations.

ACKNOWLEDGMENTS

There are many to thank for their assistance in this historic work. Aside from those who worked on the production and design of the book, others mentioned below made invaluable contributions to the story of the *U-505*. These include veterans of both the U.S. and German navies who did battle in June 1944 off West Africa. These veterans were interviewed at the Museum of Science and Industry (MSI) in March and April 1999. It is deemed appropriate that they be acknowledged. They and others include:

Robert Shenk, Ph.D., author and historian, and C. Herbert Gilliland, Ph.D., author and professor, for their invaluable assistance in this endeavor; Ronald Chambers (former director, Naval Institute Press); Hannah Cunliffe (researcher, London); Andy Zakrajsek (Director of Retail Businesses, MSI); Keith Gill (Curator of the *U-505*, MSI); Lindsey MacAllister (archivist, MSI); Richard Klarich (Capital Program Manager, MSI); Jack Green (Public Affairs Officer, Naval Historical Center); Jean L. Hort (Director, Navy Department Library); Glenn Helm (Head of Reference, Navy Department Library); Infinite Photo and Imaging, Inc., Gary Weir (Naval Historical Center); Jak P. Mallmann Showell (maritime author); Karl Oscar Springer (crewman, *U-505*); Karl Werner Reh (crewman, *U-505*); Freiter Wolfgang Gerhardt (crewman, *U-505*); Hans Goebeler (crewman, *U-505*); Horst Bredow (Director, U-BOOT-ARCHIV); Albert Rust (survivor, Liberty Ship *Thomas MacKean*); Edwin Harvey Headland (commanding officer, USS *Pope*/DE-134); Don Carter (signalman, USS *Guadalcanal*/CVE-60); D. F. Hampton (senior watch officer, USS *Guadalcanal*); Earl Trosino (chief engineer, USS *Guadalcanal*); Phil Thrusheim (coxswain, USS *Pillsbury*/ DE-133); Joseph Villanella (radarman, USS *Chatelain*/DE-149);Wayne M. Pickels (boatswain's mate, USS *Pillsbury*); Zenon B. Lukosius (engineer's mate, USS *Pillsbury*); U.S. Navy submariners Joe Hill and Jim Sisson (crewmen during the *U-505*'s war bond tour of U.S. port cities); Jack Dumford (communications officer, USS *Guadalcanal*); J. M. Ritzdorf (Avenger pilot, Composite Squadron 8); L. Watts and M. Chapman (sonarmen, USS *Chatelain*); as well as Pat Pascale, Fred Schultz, Tom Cutler, Jim Bricker, Donna Doyle, Susan Brook, Julie Olver, Mark Gatlin, Patti Bower, Linda O'Doughda, and Tim Wooldridge of the U.S. Naval Institute.

LIST OF EQUIVALENT COMMISSIONED AND ENLISTED RANKS (WWII)

German Navy	U.S. Navy
Offiziere	*Officers*
Grossadmiral	Admiral of the Fleet
Generaladmiral	No equivalent
Admiral	Admiral
Vizeadmiral (VA)	Vice Admiral
Konteradmiral (KA)	Rear Admiral
Kommodore (a Kapitän zur See holding a flag officer's position)	Commodore (a captain in a post usually held by a rear admiral)
Kapitän zur See (KzS)	Captain
Fregattemkapitän (FK)	Commander
Korvettenkapitän (KK)	Lieutenant Commander
Kapitänleutnant (KptLt)	Lieutenant
Oberleutnant zur See (Oblt.z.S.)	Lieutenant (junior grade)
Leutnant zur See (L.z.S.)	Ensign
Oberfähnrich zur See	Senior Midshipman
Fähnrich zur See	Midshipman

German Navy	U.S. Navy
Offiziere ohne Patent	*Warrant Officers, Chiefs, and Petty Officers*
Obersteuermann	Quartermaster of Warrant rank
Obermaschinist	Warrant Machinist
Oberbootsmann	Chief Petty Officer
	Chief Boatswain's Mate
Bootsmann	Petty Officer First Class
	Boatswain's Mate First Class
Mechaniker	Artificer's Mate First Class
	Torpedoman's Mate First Class
Oberbootsmannsmaat	Petty Officer Second Class
	Boatswain's Mate Second Class
Obermechanikersmaat	Artificer's Mate Second Class
	Torpedoman's Mate Second Class
Oberfunkmaat	Radioman Second Class
Bootsmannsmaat	Petty Officer Third Class
	Coxswain
Maschinistenmaat	Artificer's Mate Third Class
	Torpedoman's Mate Third Class
Funkmaat	Radioman Third Class

German Navy	U.S. Navy
Mannschaften	*Nonrated Personnel*
Stabsmatrose, Matrosenobergefreiter, Mechanikerobergefreiter, Funkobergefreiter	Seaman First Class
Maschinenobergefreiter	Fireman Second Class
Obermatrose, Matrosengefreiter, Mechanikergefreiter, Funkgefreiter	Seaman Second Class
Maschinengefreiter	Fireman Third Class
Matrose	Seaman Recruit (apprentice)

U-505

CHAPTER 1

The U-505 *Joins the War in the Atlantic*

The *U-505* was probably one of the unluckiest U-boats in Adolf Hitler's submarine service during World War II. Though her first one or two patrols showed no such signs, what occurred in the months that followed was pure bad luck. The first skipper had to cut short a promising patrol because of appendicitis. While under the command of a new captain, the boat suffered massive damage from an Allied air attack, which resulted in months of yard repairs. Mysterious equipment malfunctions (some of them apparently the result of sabotage) shortened so many subsequent patrols that the boat and her second captain became an object of contempt throughout the U-boat community. Finally, his morale crushed, this captain committed suicide during a bomb and depth charge attack. All of this happened long before an American hunter-killer group captured the *U-505* off the shores of West Africa—the worst luck of all.

The *U-505* is commissioned. Crew members stand at attention as her flag is flown for the first time following an address by Vizeadmiral Wolf. *MSI*

Characteristics of the *U-505*

The 750-ton *U-505* measures 252 feet in length, and her pressure hull diameter is 14.4 feet. She displaced 1,120 tons surfaced and 1,232 submerged. She had a range of 13,450 miles while cruising on the surface at 10 knots and 63 miles submerged at 4 knots. Her maximum surface speed was 19 knots and 7.5 submerged. Diving depth was 100 meters (328 feet), with a 2-1/2 times safety factor (e.g., the boat could survive to a depth of 250 meters, or 820 feet). Diving time was thirty-five seconds.

Weaponry consisted of twenty-two 20.9-inch-diameter torpedoes stowed on board, twelve in the pressure hull and ten in pressure-tight containers on deck. The torpedoes were fired through six 21-inch-diameter torpedo tubes (four in the bow, two in the stern). Mines could also be laid from the torpedo tubes. On deck, the *U-505* originally carried one 10.5-cm (4.1-inch) L/45 (Lafayette-type gun mounting) gun forward of the conning tower. At the time of her capture, she carried one 3.7-cm antiaircraft gun on the lower open bridge, and two 2-cm twin-barrel antiaircraft guns on the upper open bridge. Her deck weaponry was often modified during the war.

The *U-505* propulsion machinery included two 2,170-hp, nine-cylinder, supercharged, four-cycle diesel-electric engines that were cooled with salt water. Each was coupled to a dynamotor and to the shaft through appropriate clutches. Each engine had its own controls and instruments to give varied data the machinist mate needed to keep the engines operating. The temperature of each cylinder was also shown on a bank of vertical instruments, next to which was the engine order telegraph, repeaters for which were located throughout the boat, by means of which speed directions were signaled. Submerged, the boat was powered by two Siemens-Schuckert-Weake electric motors supplied from two banks of accumulators (batteries) with 62 + 62 cells, 740 W at 11.300 Ah.

German Type IXC submarine—*U-505*. The 750-ton boat measured 252 feet in length, displaced 1,120 tons surfaced and 1,232 submerged and had a range of 13,450 miles while cruising on the surface at 10 knots and 63 miles submerged at 4 knots. *MSI*

Note: All miles given here are nautical miles. One nautical mile equals 6,076 feet. A statute equals 5,250 feet. Speed is in knots. One knot equals one nautical mile per hour.

The *U-505*'s standard complement was forty-eight: four officers, fifteen petty officers, and twenty-nine ratings. After 1943, antiaircraft gunners were added to the crew which then totalled 59.

The IXC submarine (other variants were IXB, IXC/40, and IXD) was an oceangoing boat often used for mine laying because of her extensive range. Type IX model boats, modified to carry additional fuel, sometimes patrolled Pacific waters, operating out of the Japanese base at Penang, Malaya. For example, the *U-196* (IXD-2), under command of Kapitänleutnant Eitel-Friedrich Kentrat, made a seven-month cruise, one of the longest of the war. Another Type IX boat of note was the highly successful *U-123*, which was among the initial group of Operation Drumbeat U-boats that attacked merchant shipping off the East Coast of the United States in June 1942. Also of note was the *U-156*, which sank the passenger steamship *Laconia*, causing an Allied uproar that resulted in Admiral Karl Dönitz being charged as a war criminal at the Nuremberg trials following the war.

Film of the *U-505*'s engine room was included in the 2000 movie *U-571*, starring Matthew McConaughey.

U-181 (Type IXD2) on patrol in the Indian Ocean, summer 1944. Like all German U-boats operating in Japanese waters, the boats had to carry the swastika on both sides of the conning tower. This, together with white paint on the front of the bridge and white cross-stripes on the foredeck, were signs for Japanese aviators that this was a German U-boat. *Special Collections & Archives Division, Nimitz Library, U.S. Naval Academy*

A Type IXC U-boat, the *U-505* was built in Deutsche Werft AG in Hamburg, Germany, and launched on May 24, 1941. She was commissioned on August 26 of that year. The *U-505* was a large boat compared to her forerunners, such as the Type VIIC, which was the journeyman U-boat of the war. This extra size allowed the *U-505* and other Type IXs to carry more fuel than earlier boats, which in turn extended their range to more than ten thousand nautical miles. Like the other members of her class, the *U-505* was meant to operate far from her base as a "lone wolf" rather than in combination with other U-boats.

After her commissioning, the *U-505*, under command of Kapitän-leutnant Axel-Olaf Loewe, spent a month of intensive training in submarine warfare and undersea operations with the 25th and 27th U-Boat Flotillas in the Baltic Sea. There she conducted exercises in gunnery, torpedo practice, diving, evasive procedures, and tactical maneuvers.

Kapitänleutnant Axel-Olaf Loewe, first commanding officer of the *U-505*. *Special Collections & Archives, Nimitz Library, U.S. Naval Academy*

Opposite: Squared chart of British waters used by U-boat captains for grid references. As indicated on the chart, *U-505* transited from Kiel in the Baltic through the Kaiser Wilhelm Channel out into the North Sea and around England down to Lorient, a French port on the Bay of Biscay in occupied France. Operating from such French ports, the U-boats were much closer to the target-rich Atlantic. *U-BOOT-ARCHIV*

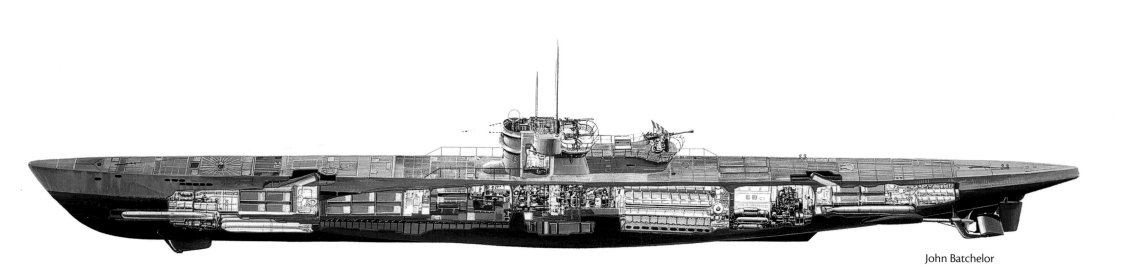

John Batchelor

U-505 Commanding Officers

Kapitänleutnant Axel-Olaf Loewe

Axel-Olaf Loewe was born on January 3, 1909 in Kiel to a family with strong naval connections. His father had been a gunnery officer on a battle cruiser during the Battle of Jutland in 1916, and two uncles had commanded U-boats during World War I (one of them went down with his ship and crew; the other survived).

Axel-Olaf Loewe entered the German Navy as an officer cadet of the Seaman Branch in 1928 and became an officer in 1932. Thereafter, he served aboard several cruisers. He had a post at the Naval Academy until the war broke out, but then was assigned to the German Armed Forces Supreme Command Staff from October 1939 to October 1940. After this, he underwent five months of U-boat training.

He completed five weeks of U-commander sea training on the *U-74* before being named Baubelehrung Commander (i.e., assigned as the commander of a U-boat about to be built). Loewe served as commanding officer of the *U-505* from August 26, 1941, to September 5, 1942, when he had to relinquish command because of illness. He was next assigned as Adviser W-Staff Commander-in-Chief for Submarines/Operations from December 1942 to July 1944. He then was transferred to the Reichs Ministry for Armaments and War Production under Albert Speer until April 1945, when he was assigned to I/Naval Anti-Tank Regiment. Upon Germany's capitulation, he was detained and then freed on December 30, 1945. After the war, Loewe first became a farmhand, then worked his way back up to manager of a sawmill, and eventually became an executive with a housing construction firm.

Axel-Olaf Loewe passed away in 1984.

Oberleutnant zur See Peter Zschech

Peter Zschech was born in Constantinople, Turkey, on October 1, 1918, where his father was a naval surgeon (Turkey was a World War I ally of Germany, and it hosted German forces in the country). Zschech entered the German Navy as an officer cadet of the Seaman Branch in 1936 and, when war broke out, he was initially assigned as watch officer on the German destroyer Z 7 *Hermann Schoemann* from August 1939 to April 1940. After this, he was transferred to destroyer Z 14 *Friedrich Ihn* for a seven-month tour before entering U-boat training. Upon completion of this training, Zschech was assigned as relief instructor at the torpedo school at Murwik. He transferred in August 1941 to the *U-124* as watch officer, serving under highly decorated Kapitänleutnant Johann Mohr.

Zschech attended the U-Commander's Course, 24th U-Flotilla, in August and September 1942 and was given command of the *U-505* on September 15, 1942. He was promoted to kapitänleutnant on April 1, 1943. Zschech became distraught during difficult circumstances aboard the boat, and he committed suicide in the control room of the *U-505* on October 24, 1943, while she was under attack by Allied antisubmarine forces. He was buried at sea.

Oberleutnant zur See
Reserve Officer Harald Lange

Harald Lange was born in Hamburg, Germany, on December 23, 1903. He graduated from the Murwik Naval Academy in 1925 and spent a tour of duty in the Reichsmarine, but then went into the merchant marine while remaining a naval reservist. In this civilian career, Lange sailed the Far Eastern trade routes on freighters.

On the outbreak of war in 1939, he found himself in naval uniform again. His first assignment was a two-month detail as watch officer on the magnetic minesweeper *Sperrbrecher II*. Lange was transferred in February 1940 to the 9th Patrol Boat Flotilla to serve as watch officer before being promoted to Patrol Boat-Commander, 9th Patrol Boat Flotilla, in June 1940. He then underwent U-boat training and was designated a Baubelehrung Commander during the period between November 1941 and June 1942.

Lange served as first watch officer on board the *U-180* for a year, during which period that U-boat patrolled into the Indian Ocean and back. Before completing the U-Commander's Course in late 1943, he was promoted to acting commander of the *U-180*. Lange reported on board the *U-505* as commanding officer on November 8, 1943, having reportedly been personally selected by Admiral Dönitz to provide stability to the troubled boat. Lange was still in command when the U-boat was captured on June 4, 1944, and he lost a leg during that engagement.

Lange was a prisoner of war for more than two years before being freed to return to Germany. After the war, he became a docks and warehouse manager for a fruit imports company. Harald Lange passed away in 1967.

Following her training, the *U-505* was outfitted at Stettin and then departed Kiel for her operational base of Lorient on the French coast. An uneventful first war patrol, this amounted to a transit of the *U-505* to join the famous 2nd U-Flotilla. In the March 1960 issue of the U.S. Naval Institute *Proceedings, U-505* crewman Maschinenobergefreiter Hans Joachim Decker remembered the occasion of the boat's arrival at Lorient:

As we came into the white-capped harbor on that cold, snowy afternoon, the off watch paraded on the afterdeck. The strains of a military march drifted out towards us as we closed the pier. We could see the faint glint of the band's brass and a rather large group of people from the 2nd Flotilla standing on the snow-tracked quay. In front of the knot of Flotilla officers, decked out in Navy blue greatcoats, stood our Flotilla chief, *Korvettenkapitän* Victor Schuetze, a great U-boat ace and holder of the Knight's Cross with Oak Leaves for his exploits while commanding *U-103*. After tying up, Loewe faced the burly Schuetze: "*U-505* reporting as ordered to the 2nd U-Flotilla." "*Heil* Crew," answered our chief. "*Heil, Herr Kapitän*," our Captain replied for us. Then from the dockside came, "We greet the *U-505* and its crew, hurrah, hurrah, hurrah!" How proud we were that day to receive this official welcome into the Flotilla! After all, it was the most famous and successful in the whole U-boat Arm.

. . . Lorient was quite a place in those days. Sixteen huge concrete bunkers with reinforced roofs twenty-two feet thick housed the U-boats in port. Rehabilitation camps *Prien* and *Lemp* with facilities unparalleled in the German *Wehrmacht* [army] and all just for us and our comrades, [and] a massive command center where the Grey Wolf himself, Admiral Dönitz, directed his boats to hunt and attack at sea. Lorient was the homeport for the 2nd and 10th U-Flotillas. Others were based at Saint Nazaire, La Pallice, Brest, and Bordeaux.

U-505 crewman Maschinenobergefreiter Hans Joachim Decker, 1942. *MSI*

After a short time in port, during which stores and fuel were loaded, the *U-505*, together with the *U-68*, departed Lorient on February 11, 1942, the *U-505* on her second war patrol and the *U-68* on her fifth. Cruising independently, they sailed for waters off Freetown, Sierra Leone, West Africa. At the time, German General Erwin Rommel and his Afrika Korps were engaged in a raging battle along the northern rim of the Sahara Desert, eager to take Egypt and control the whole of North Africa and the Suez Canal. With the Mediterranean almost closed to Allied shipping, except for some heroic convoys that fought their way through enemy-infested waters to supply Malta, most merchant ships had to sail around the tip of Africa to bring vital war supplies to British forces in Egypt. Thus, sea-lanes off Freetown offered easy pickings for prowling U-boats because of the heavy seaborne traffic and weak Allied antisubmarine defenses.

Karl Dönitz (in Grossadmiral uniform) was originally Commander-Chief-U-Boats, but halfway through the war took command of the entire German Navy. *USNI*

Loewe had ten torpedoes aboard, and if he could sink fifty thousand tons of enemy shipping, he was assured of being awarded an Iron Cross. At 4:30 PM on February 24, while the *U-505* cruised on the surface in calm seas, the watch crew sighted smoke 20 miles to the east of their position. The sighting turned out to be a southbound convoy, which had an air escort. Forced to submerge, Loewe lost contact with the ships and radioed headquarters, "My fault that we lost contact." On March 5 he got his first kill. At 6:30 PM his lookouts sighted a cargo ship 120 miles off Freetown. At six thousand yards, Loewe fired two torpedoes at the unsuspecting ship but missed. A third torpedo, however, hit the steamer amidships, and she stopped dead in the water. After waiting for the stricken ship's crew to man lifeboats and distance themselves from the ship, Loewe fired another torpedo as the ship settled, breaking her in half. The captain entered in his war diary, "5.3.42—Englische Frachter *Benmohr* 6000 gross registered tons (GRT)." Morale ran high among the crew with this first victory—they had proven themselves. The next morning their luck continued. At 9:30 AM, just fifty miles from where they encountered the *Benmohr*, they sighted a tanker heading for Freetown. Loewe fired two torpedoes at the ship as she entered a rainsquall. Two explosions were heard, and as the squall passed and the mist lifted, nothing remained but a cloud of smoke where the ship had been. Loewe recorded, "6.3.42—Engl. Tanker, Name unknown 8000 GRT." (The ship was the 7,587-ton Norwegian motor tanker *Sydhav*.)

During the rest of March, Loewe experienced several crash dives to escape patrolling Allied aircraft and withstood the attack of a British corvette, which rattled the boat with depth charges and tested the mettle of his crew. After escaping the encounter, Loewe recorded in his diary, "Baptism of fire, crew behaved excellently." The first week in April, the *U-505* scored two more successes, sending two freighters to the bottom: the 5,775-ton American steamship *West Irmo,* and the 5,759-ton Dutch freighter *Alphacca.* Loewe then sailed for Lorient, arriving there on May 7, 1942.

On this her second war patrol the *U-505* was credited with sinking twenty-five thousand tons of Allied shipping in eighty-six days at sea. The staff of Admiral Karl Dönitz, Commander, U-Boats, commented in the *U-505*'s war diary: "First mission of Captain with new boat, well and thoughtfully carried out. Despite long time in operations area, lack of traffic did not permit greater success."

After a brief refitting and repair period, Loewe was ordered to conduct a third war cruise in the Caribbean in early June 1942. The *U-505* easily transited the Bay of Biscay and headed for an area that promised many prizes. An earlier U-boat campaign against shipping off the coast of the United States had been fierce and devastating for the Allies. Since the United States was unprepared for the initial undersea assault, practically no antisubmarine defense capabilities existed, and patrolling U-boats sunk merchant ships almost at will, often within sight of coastal beaches. When the convoy system was eventually instituted and ASW aircraft and warships began to make the coastal hunting grounds perilous, Dönitz shifted his boats to the Caribbean. These waters had been untouched by the war, and shipping targets were plentiful.

Loewe scored early en route to his patrol area. On June 28, while the *U-505* was cruising several hundred miles east of the Caribbean, the port lookout sighted masts on the horizon. Loewe submerged the boat, and when the ship came within range, he fired a double shot. Both hit home. Loewe waited until the ship's crew was safely in lifeboats and then fired a third shot, and the 5,447-ton U.S. freighter *Sea Thrush* slipped slowly beneath the waves. The next day, Loewe added to his score with

the sinking of the 7,191-ton U.S. Liberty Ship *Thomas McKean*. In this instance, he sank the ship with a single torpedo and fire from his deck gun. Loewe did not sink another ship until July 22; this time it was the 110-ton three-masted Colombian schooner *Urios*.

American Liberty Ship *Thomas McKean* sinking after being torpedoed by *U-505*, June 29, 1942. *MSI*

But the *U-505*'s luck began to turn. Her first wartime skipper fell ill and requested that he return to Lorient. On his arrival there on August 25, Loewe was admitted to a hospital, where doctors removed an inflamed appendix. By the time the boat was ready to depart on her fourth patrol, Loewe was still not fully recovered, and on September 15, 1942, command of the *U-505* was given to Oberleutnant zur See Peter Zschech (promoted to Kapitänleutnant on April 1,1943), a twenty-four-year-old officer who had served under much-decorated Kapitänleutnant Johann Mohr in the *U-124*. When Zschech reported aboard the *U-505*, half of Loewe's original crew, including all of his officers, had been transferred to other U-boats. Many already had been lost in boats that had been destroyed by a steadily improving Allied antisubmarine capability. Still on board were sixteen of the original crew, among whom were four leading chief petty officers. Replacements had reported, and the boat was made ready for sea.

U.S. freighter *Sea Thrush* explodes after being torpedoed by *U-505* northeast of Puerto Rico on June 28, 1942. *MSI*

U-505 Emblems

2nd U-Flotilla

During World War II, U-boat flotillas commonly were named after submarine heroes of the previous great world war. The 2nd U-Flotilla, to which the *U-505* was attached, was called the *Saltzwedel* Flotilla after Oberleutnant zur See Reinhold Saltzwedel, who commanded five U-boats in World War I, sank 111 ships, and was awarded the "Blue Max" (Pour le Merite). The 2nd U-Flotilla emblem, above, was painted on the forward section of the conning tower of each of the flotilla's U-boats. The emblem was a blue victory rune (a letter from an early Germanic alphabet), through the upper part of which a U-boat passed from right to left.

Loewe's personal emblem was a shield displaying a springing lion that brandished an ax. The lion represented his family (Loewe = lion in German), while the ax was the emblem of his officer class (Crew of 1928). After the war, Loewe adopted the emblem as his family coat of arms.

Zschech retained the crew ax from the Loewe emblem when he took command of the *U-505* and added five Olympic rings, which symbolized his officer's class of 1936 (the year of the Berlin Olympics). Although the rings were painted on the front of the conning tower, the author has not located any photographs that display the emblem. *U-505* crewmen wore metal axe pins on their caps; these were made from parts of the Allied aircraft that attacked the boat in the Caribbean and was destroyed by one of its own bombs.

After assuming command of the *U-505* in 1943, the former merchant mariner Lange chose as his personal symbol a "scallop shell."

Early in the war, before Allied aircraft filled the skies, the U-boats could afford humanitarian actions. Here survivors from the U.S. Liberty Ship *Thomas McKean* approach the surfaced *U-505* for medical supplies and directions to the nearest land. *MSI*

Zschech was eager to make his mark with the crew and to engage the enemy. His crew, however, resented his often-eccentric behavior, especially when he ordered them to undergo infantry combat training while the boat was under repair. The *U-505* headed out to sea on her fourth operational cruise on October 4, 1942, covered with garlands and flowers, as was the custom when a U-boat departed on a war patrol. The traditional music of "For We Go Forth against England" blared from a speaker on the bridge. As the boat moved farther from shore, crewmen began to throw the decorative trappings over the side, since it was a maritime superstition that they should be removed before the crew lost sight of land. Zschech became outraged with the crew and ordered that the garlands remain where they were, ignoring the explanations of his leading petty officers. Many crewmen felt later that their bad luck was attributable to this incident.

Oberleutnant zur See Peter Zschech, second commander of the *U-505*, scans the horizon for targets. *MSI*

Zschech and his crew depart Lorient on patrol in early October 1942. A large battle-axe, part of the ship's emblem when commanded by Peter Zschech, is visible on the conning tower. *MSI*

On November 7, Zschech claimed his first victim when he sank the 7,173-ton British freighter *Ocean Justice* while patrolling southeast of Trinidad. Three days later, while the boat was cruising under low cloud cover, a Hudson two-engine bomber of Royal Air Force 53 Squadron flying out of Trinidad broke through the clouds and attacked the surprised Germans. At the controls was Flight Sergeant R. R. Sillcock, who was known for his stealth in attacking U-boats from just above sea level. This time, he dropped a perfect pattern of depth charges that enveloped the U-boat as she tried to escape. But one of the charges fell on the deck and discharged prematurely. The resulting blast critically damaged the Hudson, which crashed into the sea, killing its entire crew. On her part, the U-boat was dam-

U-505 heavily damaged by air attack in the Caribbean on November 10, 1942. *MSI*

Maschinenobergefreiter Hans Goebeler. *MSI*

aged so severely that Zschech ordered the crew to abandon ship. Obermaschinist Otto Fricke refused to obey the order, angrily asserting that he and his technical crew would remain on board and keep the boat afloat. Fricke and his crew were able to plug a large hole in the pressure hull with steel plating and stop numerous leaks in the port diesel engine. They manned bilge pumps and stemmed the flooding in the boat, which cleared the smoke-filled air that was choking the men as they worked to salvage the wreck.

Zschech watched his crew take matters into their own hands and frantically repair the boat. Many of the men had been wounded by flying pieces of metal, and several were severely burned. Miraculously, no one was killed. Maschinobergefreiter Hans Goebeler described the crippling damage to the boat in his book, *Steel Boats, Iron Hearts* (see Further Reading), as follows:

The wooden planks of the upper deck aft of the conning tower looked as if a bulldozer had plowed across them. In the center of the damage, an enormous hole gaped halfway across the entire topside hull of the boat, exposing a jumble of smashed and broken equipment below.... Fully half of the steel side plates of the conning tower were either gone or hanging limply, clanging against each other in time with the gentle rocking of the waves. One depth charge had exploded on the pressurized tubes where the spare torpedoes were stored, completely destroying one of the torpedoes except for the warhead section. If that torpedo warhead had gone off, none of us would have survived.

Eventually, the boat was able to dive to a depth of 130 feet. A message from Lorient ordered Zschech to rendezvous with the *U-154,* which provided some medication for the wounded. He was directed to meet with the *U-462,* a tanker, for further assistance. The boats rendezvoused on November 22 while the tanker was servicing the *U-68* and the *U-332.* Spare parts, fuel, and provisions were provided, and a doctor from the *U-462* boarded the *U-505* and tended to the wounded. Second Watch Officer Gottfried Stolzenburg, who was in need of immediate surgery, was transferred to the *U-462.*

The *U-505* began her long journey home, reaching Lorient on December 12, 1942. En route, the aggressive Zschech attempted to attack several Allied ships without success. Given the substantial damage the *U-505* had sustained, Zschech was probably imprudent even to try. Once back in port, the boat would require months of repair before being cleared for operational duty.

During her time in the repair yards, the boat was reconfigured to reflect a new strategy ordered by Admiral Dönitz. Because of increased Allied air patrols, especially in the Bay of Biscay, U-boats henceforth remained on the surface when attacked from the air and dueled the enemy with heavy antiaircraft (AA) fire. In addition, her conning tower was reinforced with steel plating; a lower extended platform (*wintergarten*) housed a four-barreled 3.7-cm Vierling AA gun; and two twin-barreled 2-cm AA cannons were mounted on her upper platform. The deck gun, now superfluous because U-boats could seldom remain on the surface, was removed. The departure procedure of the boat, which usually had her crew standing at attention on deck, had been changed. Like all departing crews at the time, Zschech's men now were lined up on deck wearing life jackets and kneeling. This was done to prevent personnel losses should the boat hit a mine as she departed.

Such posture was symbolic of the greatly changed conditions the U-boats were beginning to confront. The U-boat war had turned in favor of the Allies, and Zschech began the cruise wary of his fate and that of his crew. Many of his friends had disappeared during the previous several months, and the hunter had now become the hunted. Moreover, the boat's overall fortune had begun to change.

Mechanikerobergefreiter Wolfgang Gerhardt Schiller noted in his 1999 interview at the Museum of Science and Industry that from then on, the boat was haunted by bad luck.

About the situation of the sub I can only say the following. I lived through this bombing voyage, and after this nothing on the submarine worked anymore. Every time we would embark and start to submerge, something would happen and we came right back to the shipyard. So we made the attempt four or five times to get to the theater of operations, and for this reason the assumption naturally arose that the submarine was a bad-luck sub . . . problems continued to plague us as we tried to reach the Atlantic. Welding seams split during diving attempts. Various seals didn't hold. Rather than chancing a daylight transit of the Bay of Biscay, we had to return to base cruising close to the Spanish and French shorelines because we had big oil trails. We found that we could repair certain situations at sea. But as soon as an engine went out or a compressor malfunctioned or a bearing ran hot, we had to go back to the shipyard. Pretty soon workers at the yard were saying, "Here they come again."

Zschech finally sailed his pieced-together boat again from Lorient on July 1, 1943; this time, he was ordered to patrol the waters around the Azores. Within twenty-four hours, the boat was back in Lorient with a long list of discrepancies. These were disposed of quickly, and the boat left port again on July 3. Because of increased Allied air patrols over the Bay of Biscay, Zschech was forced to remain submerged about 75 percent of the time while transiting the bay. After four days he made a one-hour surface run for the open Atlantic at eighteen knots. The skies were clear, and no enemy ships or aircraft were sighted. On submerging, the crew's morale lifted since they would soon be in Atlantic waters.

Suddenly, the boat was rocked by a series of explosions; Zschech guessed that since he continued to be tracked as he maneuvered to escape, his attacker was most probably an aircraft using sonobuoys. He gradually distanced the boat from the barrage without suffering damage. However, the *U-505*'s Metox (aerial radar detection device) and sound gear went dead, which left her with no means of detecting attacking aircraft while surfaced and unable to hear propeller noises of surface ships while submerged.

The boat was stunned again by another attack, this one, Zschech surmised, by a surface warship. Diving to 240 feet and maintaining that depth, he found that his attacker tracked his every maneuver and guessed the *U-505* was trailing oil. In an attempt to thwart the enemy ship's sonar, Zschech fired decoys, which released bubbles to the surface. The ploy worked, and after about an hour he brought the boat to periscope level and sighted a destroyer a mile to the north. Looking astern, he could clearly detect an oil trail. He returned to Lorient for repairs on July 13.

After two weeks of yard work, the boat left Lorient the first week in August, only to return the next day. Zschech and his crew heard strange noises in the boat while submerged. Maintenance men swarmed over the boat but could find nothing wrong with the hull. Leaving port on August 14, Zschech took his boat deeper, and the noises returned. On surfacing, they found that the main air injection system had been crushed and was full of water. The *U-505* returned to the dockyard on August 15.

More bad luck followed: after departing Lorient on August 21, oil leaks forced Zschech to return to port the following day. While in port, repairmen found that vent gaskets had been eaten away and had to be replaced. French laborers who had earlier replaced the gaskets were reportedly accused of sabotage, arrested, and shot.

The crew was demoralized further when a Gestapo agent came aboard one day and accused the crew of not wanting to go to sea again. The men vigorously responded that they did want to go on patrol, but not in a defective boat.

On each return to port, Zschech heard of more losses of U-boats and close friends. Perhaps he began to wonder seriously if the next patrol would be his last. Finally, the *U-505* sailed from Lorient again on September 18, 1943. While crossing the Bay of Biscay—which, because of Allied air attacks, was becoming known as the "Valley of Death"—Zschech remained submerged except to recharge his batteries and to conduct a quick navigational fix. On her fifth day out, while surfacing to recharge her batteries, Metox radar picked up an approaching aircraft, and the *U-505* was forced to dive. Bad luck haunted the boat once again when the armature of the main ballast pump was disabled, perhaps because of the boat's hasty descent.

Zschech returned the boat yet again to Lorient, arriving on September 30. By then his despondency was clear to the crew, and they were convinced their skipper was unlucky and perhaps destined to lead them to a watery grave. The French Underground, taking advantage of the boat's plight, painted "*U-505*'s Hunting Grounds" in large white letters on the inside of a dock wall, as if this was one boat that would never get out of the dock.

While his boat was being repaired, Zschech brooded over his misfortune. He was patronized by his fellow commanders and left out of their conversations, so he took to drinking alone. Though probably not his fault, his many retreats back to Lorient caused others to wonder about his courage and competency to command.

Feeling the sting of such criticism, Zschech was determined that when he departed on his next patrol, nothing would make him abort his mission. When the *U-505* went to sea again on October 9, Zschech transited the Bay of Biscay submerged twenty-two out of twenty-four hours a day. He kept complete radio silence to the extent that headquarters had to query him regarding a required report on his reaching the Atlantic.

On October 24, while cruising at a depth of three hundred feet at reduced speed, Zschech's hydrophone operator reported distant exploding charges. Shortly thereafter, engine noises could be heard, and it seemed the boat would soon come under attack. Zschech, who had remained in his curtained cabin, finally appeared in the control room. He looked somewhat in a daze as he climbed into the conning tower. His first watch officer, Oberleutnant zur See Paul Meyer, called to him for orders, since the boat had clearly been pinpointed by the enemy's ASDIC (underwater sound locating device), and canisters could be heard breaking the surface above.

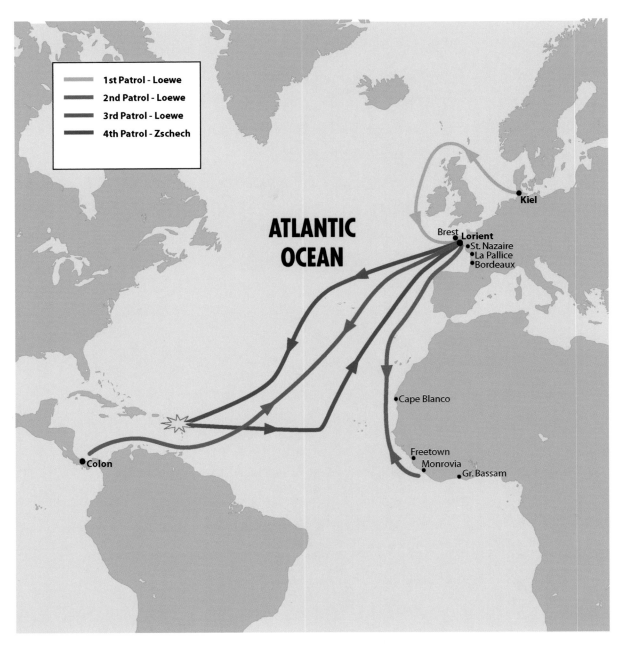

Legend:
- 1st Patrol - Loewe
- 2nd Patrol - Loewe
- 3rd Patrol - Loewe
- 4th Patrol - Zschech

ATLANTIC OCEAN

Kiel

Brest Lorient
St. Nazaire
La Pallice
Bordeaux

Cape Blanco

Freetown
Monrovia
Gr. Bassam

Colon

Illustration of tracks of Loewe and Zschech patrols. It is to be noted that between July 1 and September 30, 1943, Zschech had to abort numerous missions due to a variance of mechanical problems, which required a return to port for maintenance and repair. After the boat's near sinking in the Caribbean on November 10, 1942, the *U-505* seemed to be haunted by bad luck. By March of 1944 when the boat's new skipper, Oberleutnant zur See Harald Lange, sailed forth from Brest on the boat's last mission, one could say that the *U-505* was on her twelfth patrol. *Infinite Photo & Imaging*

Crewman Hans Goebeler described what followed: "Finally, Zschech came down the ladder . . . his expressionless face, illuminated by the fluorescent paint on the air ducts, was ghostly white. We all stared at him, anticipating some orders for maneuvers, but still he said nothing. Instead, he walked zombie-like through the forward hatch into the radio room. As he passed me, I could see his wide-open unblinking eyes shine in the half light."

Zschech came back through the hatch, stood in the control room, and remained speechless. Close-in explosives jarred the boat, which also took a hit from an aerial bomb. Gauges shattered, and lights were smashed as a hail of debris flew across the control room. As the explosions continued, another dull sound was heard, and Meyer noticed a sudden flash in the control room. As Zschech fell to the deck, Meyer thought the lurching of the boat had knocked out the captain. Meyer took command, proceeding to give orders, diving the boat, increasing her speed, and releasing chemical decoys.

Zschech lay motionless on the control room deck, and as a pool of blood began to spread around his head, the crew suddenly realized he had attempted to commit suicide. The critically wounded commander began making deep guttural sounds. Crewmen lifted him and placed him on his cot, where he finally succumbed ninety minutes later. (Zschech was one of two U-boat commanders to commit sucide while on patrol during the war.)

Hours later, after escaping the enemy assault, Meyer surfaced the boat and committed Zschech's body to the deep. His entry in the boat's diary was simple:

1952   Propeller noises in medium distance.

1954   Piston engine noises.

1956   Sonar noises.

1958   Depth charges very close.

1958   Captain fell out of ranks.

2100   Captain dead, First Watch Officer Meyer assumes command.

0406   Captain's body overboard.

When asked about Zschech during a 1999 interview, Maschinmaat Karl Oskar Springer remarked, "He was not a nice person. He was an imperious person; yes, quite taken with himself. He was arrogant; he never talked to us, unlike Oberleutnant zur See Lange, our next captain who always had a moment to chat with his crew. As I have said—I only knew him as a Petty Officer of course, but the noncommissioned officers simply could not stand him, although they had to be on board."

Meyer took the boat back to Lorient, arriving on November 7. The port that once swarmed with German naval officers, crewmen, and yard workers and was adjacent to a city that offered rest and respite from the loneliness of long war patrols and fierce combat was no more. During 1943, more than six thousand tons of Allied bombs had made a shambles of the German naval base and the city, sparing only the U-boat pens themselves, with their great concrete roofs.

CHAPTER 2

The Battle of the Atlantic, 1939–1945

The Allies had faced a terrible U-boat enemy in World War I. In that conflict, German submarines had sunk more than 5,000 commercial ships. They had also sent almost 250 Allied naval vessels to the bottom—including ten battleships. The second great war against the U-boat began on September 3, 1939. Unfortunately for the Allies, lessons learned during World War I were ignored in the years between, and Allied navies were compelled to meet the renewed challenge with inadequate and out-dated forces.

One critical lesson learned from the first war was the value of the convoy system. Unfortunately, few escorts were available for convoy duty at the beginning of World War II because the Royal Navy assigned most to escort army units being transported to France and for the protection of channel shipping. The Allies were to pay a high price for this lack of convoy support.

NARA

ASW air escort was still in its infancy, and what few surface escorts were available could accompany convoys only short distances into the Atlantic; there were additional ASW deficiencies. However, perhaps the most troubling was the overall British complacency toward the submarine threat. The dismissive attitude resulted from an over-reliance on an early form of "ASDIC" (an underwater sound locating device), which had been developed during the later stages of World War I and became fully operational in the late 1930s. The Royal Navy soon discovered that ASDIC was practically worthless when used in turbulent seas, or against surfaced submarines.

Admiral Dönitz, reasoning correctly that ASDIC would not be able to locate surfaced U-boats, early in the war ordered his boats to attack at night on the surface. Darkness allowed the U-boats to close the ships without being detected by lookouts, and the ASDIC upon which the escorts were forced to rely could not detect the U-boats either. Much to the dismay of the Royal Navy, this simple tactic worked spectacularly.

Still, the true measure of these major ASW deficiencies was not taken immediately, for when hostilities began, Germany itself was ill prepared for an all-out U-boat offensive. She had only fifty-seven commissioned U-boats (thirty-nine fully operational, eighteen engaged in sea trials or training), and these boats were handcuffed with operational restrictions. On the war's outbreak, Admiral Dönitz assumed unrestricted warfare would be in immediate effect. He ordered his U-boats to attack on the surface at night and to engage enemy ships during the day, submerged and at close range. The boats were to launch an aggressive offensive against British merchant shipping.

Adolf Hitler, however, insisted that U-boats operate under Prize Law because he hoped to work out favorable coexistence terms with Britain and France and did not wish to antagonize them unnecessarily or risk undue problems with neutral countries (especially the United States). Under Prize Law, U-boats could not destroy ships without first examining their papers and ensuring the safety of their crews. Unfortunately for the Germans, in early September 1939 the *U-30* misidentified the thirteen-thousand-ton British passenger liner *Athenia* for a warship and sank her. This led the British Admiralty to assume the Germans had adopted unrestricted submarine warfare at the start of hostilities.

British passenger liner SS *Athenia* shown sinking in September 1939 after being torpedoed by a German U-boat, *U-30*, commanded by Kapitänleutnant Fritz-Julius Lemp. The *Athenia* was the first Allied ship sunk in World War II. *IWM*

From the outset of the war, U-boat commanders steered clear of Allied convoys to prey on stragglers, or "independents." Merchant ships that had maximum speed capabilities in excess of fifteen knots (seventeen mph) and minimums under seven knots had to sail independently. Those whose maximum speed exceeded fifteen knots were considered capable of outrunning stalking U-boats. Most of them were. For example, during her six and a half years of troopship service during World War II, the *Queen Mary* (maximum speed thirty-five knots) traveled more than six hundred thousand miles transporting some eight hundred thousand military and civilian personnel—never threatened by U-boat attack. Ships that could make merely seven knots or less were considered to be risks to convoys, which usually maintained eight to nine knots. Slower speeds made the ships easy prey for U-boats.

As in the first great world conflict, the independent "runners" went to the bottom in great numbers. In 1939, 102 of these vessels met destruction at the hands of U-boats, while just four of the twelve merchant ships lost in convoys that year were attributed to U-boat attack. Dönitz suffered the loss of merely nine U-boats. The vulnerability of these ill-fated Allied independents was yet another lesson that had to be painfully relearned. Britain responded to the loss of the *Athenia* by arming its merchantmen.

The "Queens" (*Queen Mary* and *Queen Elizabeth*) along with the British liner *Aquitania* did most of the "heavy lifting" troop transport during World War II. They traveled unescorted since their speeds were so great that U-boats were not a menace. *Queen Mary*, shown here, traveled six hundred thousand miles transporting some eight hundred thousand military and civilian personnel during the war. *SHSA*

The most spectacular feat by a U-boat during the first year of the war was the sinking of the British battleship HMS *Royal Oak* while she lay anchored at Scapa Flow in Scotland's northern Orkney Islands. The *U-47*, commanded by Kapitänleutnant Gunther Prien, managed to slip into a nearly impregnable anchorage on a moonless night and, while surfaced, sent four torpedoes into the hull of the battleship. The *Royal Oak* sank within fifteen minutes, taking 786 of her crew with her. The British immediately moved their Home Fleet to anchorages on the west coast of Scotland.

The Germans next used surface ships, submarines, and Luftwaffe (German Air Force) aircraft to lay mines in the North Sea adjacent to the new British anchorages. The Royal Navy countered by laying undeclared minefields in the North Sea to sink German minelayers. This series of countermoves eventually led to Hitler's lifting the restrictions on his boats.

Initially, Admiralty officials organized hunting groups to search for prowling U-boats. Ships that could be used effectively as convoy escorts formed search-and-patrol groups in areas where undersea raiders could usually be located. Each group consisted of an aircraft carrier and a destroyer screen. Since carrier aircraft lacked radar, results were negligible. Indeed, the system quickly brought disaster. Just two weeks after the war started, the *U-39* nearly sank the carrier HMS *Ark Royal* with a spread of torpedoes that exploded prematurely. A few days later, the *U-29* sank the 22,500-ton carrier HMS *Courageous.* Following this loss, the Admiralty removed its fleet aircraft carriers from ASW patrols.

The Germans were likewise having their problems. Much to their frustration, they found their torpedo-firing systems and depth-keeping mechanisms to be unreliable. However, a few early spectacular successes by single U-boats served notice to the Allies that their undersea opponents were both skillful and courageous seamen.

While the first six months of the war turned out to be a series of skirmishes in which each side proved the other's strengths and weaknesses, the picture changed gradually in favor of the U-boat in mid-1940 with the fall of France and Norway. U-boats could now operate out of French bases at Brest, Lorient, St. Nazaire, La Pallice, and Bordeaux, dramatically reducing cruising time to western Atlantic waters. Previously, unable to use the English Channel because of British minefields, heavy seas, and air ASW patrols, the U-boats had been forced to circumnavigate Scotland to move into the Atlantic, burning fuel and limiting their time on station.

Type IX U-boat drydocked in the bombproof submarine pen at St. Nazaire, France, after the German surrender on May 13, 1945. The boat had just returned from a 110-day patrol in Japanese waters and was ready for general overhaul. *USNI*

Now, operating out of French bases, long-range U-boat groups, or "Wolfpacks," moved farther into the Atlantic, and Allied shipping losses mounted at an alarming rate. The deficient numbers and limited range of Allied ASW surface escorts had to be overcome.

In the dark days that followed the fall of France, the U-boats' wide-open access to Atlantic Ocean areas made Allied shipping even more vulnerable. One vital question arose: Could the U-boats sink merchant ships faster than the Allies could build them? Both sides closely watched this grim equation—called "tonnage warfare" by Dönitz, who had conceived the strategy and hoped thereby to starve the Allies—as an indication of who was winning the "Battle of the Atlantic." In May 1941, in response to this critical issue, U.S. President Franklin D. Roosevelt ordered two million tons of merchant shipping to be built as a part of the famous "lend–lease" program. Standardized designs allowed ships to be prefabricated in sections for quick assembly. Shipyards in Delaware, Mississippi, the Great Lakes, and along the West Coast began constructing thousands of freighters called "Liberty Ships." The first, the *Patrick Henry*, was built in 244 days. Once the design was mastered, aver-

With the Battle of the Atlantic heating up, President Roosevelt in 1941 ordered two million tons of merchant shipping to be built as a part of a lend–lease program. Construction began on thousands of freighters called "Liberty Ships." The first to be launched was the *Patrick Henry*, built in 244 days. By 1944 the average time for construction of Liberty Ships had dropped to 42 days. *MM*

age construction time for these ships decreased to forty-two days. On one occasion, a ship was constructed in just five days. In 1942, 646 freighters, which included 597 Liberties, were launched.

These ships took awhile to come on line, however, and in 1940 the Allies were in dire straits, trying desperately to save their supply line across the Northern Atlantic. That year became known as the "Happy Time" for German U-boat commanders; it was a castrophic period for the Allies. During the latter half of 1940, U-boats sank more than one million tons of Allied merchant shipping. One convoy (SC7) set out for Britain from Nova Scotia, Canada, in October with thirty-four slow and elderly ships. Seventeen eventually staggered into the British North Channel; the rest lay scattered on the ocean floor.

1940 became known as the "Happy Time" for German U-boat commanders. By September, Allied losses were catastrophic. One convoy set out for Britain from Nova Scotia, Canada, in October with thirty-four slow and elderly ships. Seventeen eventually staggered into the British North Channel. *NARA*

ULTRA and Enigma

Information obtained from Enigma radio-enciphering machines was given the special security classification of ULTRA. The Enigma device was an electro mechanically operated computer that generated random number groups. Using daily code changes and different codes, the Germans were convinced throughout World War II that their most secretive communications were protected from Allied intercept. British cryptanalysts, however, had constructed an effective deciphering machine known as "Colossus" early on in the war and thus had access to transmissions between German High Command and operational units until Germany surrendered in 1945.

The British were reluctant to share ULTRA information with American intelligence agencies when the United States entered the war, fearing that if the American navy overtly used it to coordinate hunter-killer attacks against U-boats in the Atlantic, the Germans might discover that their codes and ciphers had been compromised. That fear was addressed in 1943 with a new strategic reorganization (clarification of Allied command and control by the formation of the U.S. Tenth Fleet), in which U.S. hunter-killer groups henceforth covered the central southerly convoy routes, and British and American naval intelligence commands worked in tandem to unify their respective antisubmarine fleet units and to keep the Germans from getting suspicious. Using ULTRA intelligence and other technologies, the American hunter-killer groups were ultimately able to overwhelm the U-boats.

Credit for close coordination of British and American successes in defeating the Atlantic U-boat threat must go to two naval officers—Commander Kenneth A. Knowles, U.S. Navy, in charge of the Navy's N-21 "Atlantic Section" tracking room, Tenth Fleet, and Commander Rodger Winn, RNVR, Director,

Submarine Tracking Room—Admiralty Operational Intelligence Center. Their close relationship dispelled the British uneasiness about sharing ULTRA intelligence with U.S. intelligence specialists.

Commanding the U-boat tracking rooms where all sources of information on enemy submarines and Allied surface ship movements were combined, Winn and Knowles maintained a comprehensive intelligence

Commander Rodger Winn, RNVR, Director, Submarine Tracking Room-Admiralty. *MM*

During early 1941, the Allies did make one especially significant breakthrough, which would pay incalculable dividends as the Atlantic war went on. Messages from patrolling U-boats to headquarters at Lorient were transmitted in cipher and sent in brief transmissions. These signals eventually were sent in "spurt transmissions" to ensure greater security. However, the British were reading these transmissions early in the war. They had been working on the penetration of the German cipher system and the "Enigma" machine around which it was built—the original Enigma machines were built by Polish mathematicians—and they first broke the "ULTRA" code in March 1941. In May of that year they captured Kapitänleutnant Fritz-Julius Lemp's *U-110*, complete with the Kriegsmarine (German Navy) version of the Enigma code machine. The British Government Code and Cipher School at Bletchley Park (located outside of London) devoted one of its computers to naval work, and henceforth German signals usually could be decoded within thirty-six hours, often immediately.

Commander Kenneth A. Knowles, USN, Officer in Charge, U.S. Navy F-21 Atlantic Section Tracking Room, Tenth Fleet. *MM*

window of enemy operations in the Atlantic. The two first met during "Operation Drumbeat," the U-boat offensive along the U.S. East Coast in 1942 that proved disastrous for Allied merchant shipping. Knowles was subsequently invited to England to study under Winn, observing British ASW intelligence operations. Upon his return to America, Knowles reorganized the F-21 Atlantic Section, and the two men and their staffs shared "special intelligence," pooling their knowledge and technical resources to defeat the German U-boat fleet. The two intelligence organizations eventually established a means of secure communications, whereby British and American strategists could discuss sensitive operational matters without fear of intercept.

U-505 Enigma machine which encoded and decoded messages via a series of drums that could be selected for a prescribed pattern. This device was originally designed for business use, it was adopted by the German armed forces, which believed it foolproof. The British were able to obtain a working model before Poland fell and were able to decipher nearly all Enigma messages for the rest of the war except for one period of time when the Germans changed their number of coder reels. *MSI*

In addition to the threat of U-boat attacks, Allied convoys had to contend with Focke-Wulf 200C-1 "Condor" bombers like this one flying from French bases. Flying at high altitudes and out of range of merchantship antiaircraft guns, they found easy targets among the convoys. *NARA*

As the war progressed, more of these machines and some codebooks were confiscated from damaged and sinking U-boats, events that helped the decoders even more. With the exception of one ten-month "Blackout" period in 1942, controllers using these decoded messages were able to reroute convoys away from Wolfpacks and to better prepare escort destroyers for when and where an attack might occur. While using this information, however, the British simultaneously kept this great breakthrough completely hidden from the enemy. At the war's end, Hitler and his naval staff refused to believe the Kriegsmarine cipher system had been broken.

As for other events in 1941, the Italians operated a number of submarines out of Bordeaux, France, but these boats were slow and cumbersome and not capable of joining in Wolfpack operations. They subsequently were allocated to the Atlantic area south of 45 degrees north latitude. While patrolling those waters, they sank some two dozen Allied merchant ships. Also during this

period, the British added two new types of warships to their inventory: frigates and corvettes. These escort vessels were to play a major role in fighting an increasingly sophisticated enemy whose numbers at that point included heavier submarines with added weaponry.

Although U-boat successes continued throughout 1941, the U-Waffe (German Underseas Arm) suffered a stunning setback in early March. Late in February, Admiral Dönitz sent several of his most experienced U-boat commanders to patrol the northwestern Atlantic approaches. Four boats intercepted westbound convoy OB293 (Liverpool, England, to North America) on March 6. One was the *U-47*, commanded by Gunther Prien of Scapa Flow fame. The following evening, Prien attempted to slip through the escort screen under cover of a sudden rainsquall. HMS *Wolverine* sighted the U-boat through the heavy mist and destroyed the craft and her entire crew with a deadly depth charge attack.

A week later, convoy HX112 (Halifax, Nova Scotia, to the United Kingdom) came under attack from the remainder of the enemy undersea force. Two leading tonnage "aces," Kapitänleutnant Joachim Schepke in the *U-100* and Kapitänleutnant Otto Kretschmer in the *U-99*, were among the group. By the end of a two-day running battle, Admiral Dönitz had lost both commanders. Schepke's boat, in a duel with two destroyers, was fatally rammed by HMS *Vanoc*; Schepke perished with most of his crew. Then escort commander Captain Donald MacIntyre in HMS *Walker* blasted Kretschmer to the surface. Kretschmer was Germany's most brilliant tactician; his record of 266,629 tons sunk was not surpassed during the war. Kretschmer and most of his crew were rescued and returned to England as prisoners of war.

The loss of three top U-boat commanders within a week's time caused deep concern at headquarters. In an effort to reverse these losses, Admiral Dönitz decided to move his forces farther out into the North Atlantic, where Allied air and surface convoy protection was, as yet, nonexistent. He could thus gain a significant edge in "tonnage warfare" by concentrating his activity in an area that offered an opportunity for high tonnage sunk with minimal U-boat losses.

This area, known as the "Black Pit," provided relatively safe hunting grounds for prowling Wolfpacks. In addition to the constant threat of U-boat attacks, Allied merchant ships had to contend with long-range German bombers flying out of French air bases. Often called the "Scourge of the Atlantic," Focke Wulf Fw200C-1 Condor bombers, with a range of 2,200 miles, attacked convoys using forward-firing 20-mm cannon and payloads of 3,857 pounds of bombs. Allied countermeasures included equipping merchant ships with antiaircraft guns and the use of fighter aircraft rocketed from ships. Catapult aircraft merchant (CAM) ships were effective, but they were an expensive venture because the aircraft, usually Hurricanes, were lost with each launch. Once he engaged the enemy, the pilot

either had to ditch or bail out. Though the flights were, in effect, suicide missions, volunteer pilots were never lacking. (The CAM ship concept was said to have been the idea of British Prime Minister Winston Churchill.)

In April 1941, the size of the Black Pit narrowed. British long-range aircraft flying out of Iceland provided a measure of convoy protection. That same month, in the "destroyers for bases" deal, fifty older U.S. destroyers were turned over to the Royal Navy, and British escort of convoys was extended west to 35 degrees west longitude. The Royal Canadian Navy, strengthened by the addition of more escort vessels, increased its coverage of convoys sailing out of Halifax, Nova Scotia. On May 27, 1941, the first North Atlantic convoy, HX-129 (Halifax to the United Kingdom), was escorted all the way across the ocean. In addition, escorts at this time began being equipped with improved ASDIC, which made it more difficult for U-boats to remain undetected, day or night.

HMS *Audacity* was a "jeep" carrier that had been converted from the 467-foot, 5,600-ton German prize vessel, *Hanover*. She was commissioned in June 1941 and carried six Martlet fighters (the British version of the American Wildcat). While escorting a convoy, one of her aircraft shot down a German Condor bomber, the first aerial victory for a "jeep" carrier in the war. However, the *Audacity* herself was sunk by *U-751* on December 21, 1941, while escorting a convoy. *NHC*

When German U-boats first commenced long-range patrols, they were often met by German supply ships that roamed the Atlantic and Indian Oceans, where they could refuel the boats and replenish their stores. Once the British mastered the intercept of German naval communications, however, these supply ships were gradually dispatched by British warships. Dönitz was forced to turn to seventeen-hundred-ton submarine tankers, called "milch (milk) cows." By August 1941, Allied shipping losses had dropped to eighty thousand tons, while imports to Britain had risen to almost a million tons.

Another development had to do with ASW carrier forces. As we have seen, after the sinking of the *Courageous* at the beginning of the war, Royal Navy attack carriers were deemed too scarce and too valuable to be dedicated to convoy escort duty. Finally, however, after numerous discussions and situation assessments, the Admiralty agreed to convert several merchant hulls and naval auxiliaries into small carriers. HMS *Audacity,* a converted German prize, was the first to be commissioned and assigned ASW escort duty. While escorting convoy HG-76 (Gibraltar to the United Kingdom) in December 1941, *Audacity* aircraft assisted in sinking five U-boats. On December 21, the *U-751* ended the short career of the world's first ASW escort carrier. Nevertheless, British ASW measures had improved, and U-boat operations were becoming more difficult in the eastern and mid-Atlantic.

In late 1941, reports indicated that U.S. coastal lanes teemed with Allied merchantmen sailing independently without escort. Germany declared war on the United States on December 11, 1941. German Navy Chief Admiral Erich Raeder and Adolf Hitler met the next day and decided to order U-boats to attack Allied shipping in U.S. coastal waters. Admiral Dönitz was tasked with assigning U-boats to the new offensive, called "Operation Paukenschlag" (Drumbeat). Unexpected losses off Portugal and the Gibraltar Straits in November and December, together with Hitler's allocation of fifty U-boats to the Mediterranean for the North African campaign, compelled Dönitz to find boats in shipyards, refitting bases, and rotating U-boat groups. Within a month, five five-hundred-tonners were selected, all commanded by U-boat aces. Additional U-boats were released for Paukenschlag operations in the months to follow. According to U.S. Navy and British Admiralty records, however, the large number of merchant ship sinkings in the U.S. Eastern

Kapitänleutnant Rienhard Hardegen (shown wearing U-boat commander's white covered cap), commanding officer of *U-123*, a type IXB German U-boat, led the first U-boat contingent against American coastal shipping during World War II. In "Operation Paukenschlag" (Drumbeat), Type IXC U-boats crossed the Atlantic and wreaked havoc on U.S. coastal shipping from December 1941 to June 1942. Sinking nineteen ships during two coastal patrols, Hardegen was honored with the addition of an oak leaf cluster to his previously awarded Knight's Cross medal. *U-BOOT-ARCHIV*

Sea Frontier area during the first few months of Paukenschlag were wrought by no more than twelve boats operating at any one time.

Operation Paukenschlag recorded its first victim on January 12, 1942, when the *U-123*, under the command of Kapitänleutnant Reinhard Hardegen, torpedoed and sank the British passenger steamer *Cyclops* south of Nova Scotia. Aware that U.S. antisubmarine defenses would tighten soon after his initial Paukenschlag offensive began, Dönitz hoped to operate his boats for as long as possible where coastal shipping was densest. Initially, successes came quickly and were plentiful. The *U-123* sank nine ships for 52,586 tons; the *U-66* bagged five for 50,000 tons; the *U-130* sent four ships to the bottom for 30,000 tons; and two other boats shared in the sinking of an additional 35,000 tons.

During the early days of the campaign, tactics employed by Paukenschlag boats were highly effective, as merchant ship captains had not foreseen the possibility of night attacks. During the daylight hours, U-boats would lie on the bottom near shipping lanes. At night, they would surface and, primarily with their deck guns in order to save torpedoes, would attack ships that were silhouetted against shore lights. Because coastal communities continued their nighttime activities and were not officially informed of the devastation taking place offshore, no blackout orders were issued. As a result, merchantmen sailing at night became easy marks during the first three months of the offensive. Finally, on April 18, 1942, much to the consternation of tourist-minded business communities, the Eastern Sea Frontier belatedly enforced a darkening of waterfront lights. By the end of April, nearly five hundred thousand tons of Allied shipping had sunk to the bottom.

SS *Robert C. Tuttle* on fire off Cape Henry, near Norfolk, Virginia, after being torpedoed by *U-701*, June 1942. *NARA*

American steam tanker *Dixie Arrow* sinking following an attack off Cape Hatteras on the North Carolina coast by *U-71*, March 1942. *NARA*

Rear Admiral Adolphus Andrews, USN, Commander of the Eastern Sea Frontier, was responsible for offshore waters extending from the Canadian border to Jacksonville, Florida. He had to improvise quickly to face the sudden U-boat onslaught. *USNI*

Initially, American Admiral Adophus Andrews, Commander of the Eastern Sea Frontier, who was responsible for offshore waters extending from the Canadian border to Jacksonville, Florida, found himself nearly helpless against the sudden U-boat onslaught. Without naval air patrol forces, Admiral Andrews had to depend on the Army Air Forces' limited-range bombers to fly offshore patrols. Surface ASW units totaled ninety-one ships: sixty-five Coast Guard cutters, twelve converted yachts, and fourteen British armed trawlers.

In April, Admiral Andrews ordered a "Bucket Brigade" system as a defensive measure against the brazen U-boats patrolling within sight of eastern shores. Since attacks usually occurred at night, merchant ships were ordered to drop anchor in protected harbors. Patrolling U-boats felt the effect of this system almost immediately. Merchant ships passed lucrative hunting grounds such as Cape Hatteras only by day. Ships began to sail in groups, leaving long stretches of empty water between them.

To offset this new countermeasure, Admiral Dönitz switched to a frontal assault, whereby his boats would make simultaneous strikes on widely separated focal points on the U.S. coast. With milch cows available for at-sea replenishment in western waters, he was confident the plan would succeed. U.S. antisubmarine forces would have to scatter, thus disrupting their overall defensive capability. Sixteen to eighteen boats were positioned between Cape Sable and Key West. Much to the surprise of Dönitz and his staff, however, Paukenschlag U-boats sighted few targets. The unexpected had happened; the United States had adopted a coastal convoy system.

As the Eastern Sea Frontier area became more dangerous for U-boat operations, Dönitz moved his boats south into the Gulf of Mexico and the Caribbean Sea to commence a new operation, code named "Newland." Sinkings increased greatly in these areas before escort vessels were ordered in and a convoy system was instituted. By late spring 1942, defensive measures in U.S. waters had improved so much that Dönitz began shifting his boats back eastward to concentrate their operations in the unprotected Black Pit area of the mid-North Atlantic. Nevertheless, when U-boat operations off the U.S. Atlantic, Caribbean, and Gulf coasts came to a virtual standstill at the end of the year, the cost in ships, men, and materials had been enormous. More than four hundred ships (2.3 million tons) had been lost against six U-boats destroyed.

As the U-boats arrived back on station in the mid-Atlantic, they made their presence felt almost immediately. In May and June of 1942, they sank more than a million tons of merchant ships. Sinkings included both independent runners and ships sailing in convoy. Germany's U-boat building yards had turned out record numbers of new boats, which by mid-1942 increased Dönitz's inventory to three hundred boats. Moreover, German technologists had developed a radar detector called "Metox" that, because it warned of radar being employed by approaching planes, helped limit the effectiveness of radar detection of surfaced U-boats. They also installed a decoy device that, by discharging chemical bubbles, diverted sonar signals away from submerged boats.

Adding to Allied concerns was the inability to read Enigma messages starting in February 1942, when the Germans added a fourth rotor to their standard three-rotor Enigma machine. For almost ten months, the Allies experienced a blackout of vital enemy sig-

nals between U-boats and headquarters, making it difficult to direct convoys away from waiting Wolfpacks and to effectively position escorts. It is small wonder the Allies suffered heavy losses in the northern mid-Atlantic during the latter half of 1942. With no Allied air coverage in the Black Pit area, picket lines of U-boats found easy prey as merchant ships plied their way through the unprotected waters. Sinkings continued to mount, peaking in November, when seven hundred thousand tons of shipping were sent to the bottom.

In early 1943, Allied commanders met in Washington and adopted an ASW plan that gave control of the North Atlantic convoys to the British and Canadians while the United States covered Central Atlantic convoys. New technologies strengthened Allied ASW capabilities. By the time of this conference, the Enigma rotor problem had been resolved. Messages were decoded and information regarding U-boat positions was available once again to Allied controllers. Allied scientists had perfected a high-frequency radio direction finder (HF/DF), called "Huff Duff," that could locate the source of U-boat radio transmissions. These systems were installed both ashore and afloat to better pinpoint the source of U-boat communications. Allied aircraft and surface vessels were equipped with new microwave radar the Germans were unable to detect. A new depth-charge device, a twenty-four-barrel

In early 1943, Allied commanders met in Washington and adopted an ASW plan that gave control of the North Atlantic convoys to the British and Canadians while the United States covered Central Atlantic convoys. Aircraft, ships, and even blimps were employed in the Allied ASW effort. *NARA*

mortar called a "Hedgehog," which fired bomblets forward of an attacking ship, proved highly effective. More ocean escorts became available, and B-24 Liberator bombers began operating out of Newfoundland, Iceland, and Northern Ireland, further closing the Black Pit.

A month before the Washington conference, signs indicated that these dramatic new advances in Allied ASW were beginning to turn the tide in favor of the Allies.

On April 22, 1943, westbound Atlantic Slow Convoy ONS-5 (code-named "Marfleet"), which included forty-three ships escorted by Escort Group B7, two destroyers (HMS *Duncan* and *Vidette*), a frigate (HMS *Tay*), and four corvettes (HMS *Loosestrife, Pink, Snowflake,* and *Sunflower*), departed England for Halifax in deteriorating weather. Admiral Dönitz ordered forty-one U-boats to intercept the convoy; however, gale-force winds, heavy seas, storms, and fog, along with the tenacious counteroffensive of reinforced Allied surface escorts and air support from Iceland and Greenland, held the boats down as they maneuvered to attack. During two days of a fierce running engagement, twelve merchant ships were sunk, and six U-boats were destroyed. In addition, several boats were badly damaged and barely made it back to their homeports. British Coastal Command aircraft had earlier destroyed yet another boat, which had been patrolling ahead of the convoy, and two more U-boats were lost in a collision. The Allies considered the passage of ONS-5 a victory because so few Allied merchant ships were lost while being attacked by such a great force.

Dönitz also recognized the loss of nine U-boats as a stunning defeat. Writing in his war diary regarding the battle, he noted, "The enemy radar loca-

In 1943 a new depth-charge device, a 24-barrel mortar called "Hedgehog," which fired bomblets forward of an attacking ship, proved highly effective. Also, Allied scientists perfected a high-frequency radio direction finder (HF/DF) that could locate the source of U-boat radio transmissions. More ocean escorts became available and B-24 Liberators began operating out of Newfoundland, Iceland, and Northern Ireland, closing the "Black Pit" further. *NHC*

In April 1943, while one of eight ships escorting an eastbound convoy over the mid-ocean sector, U.S. Coast Guard Cutter *Spencer* made sound contact with the *U-175*, and after dropping numerous depth charges, so damaged the U-boat that she was forced to surface. Unable to withstand withering fire from the cutter, the skipper of the *U-175* finally ordered the boat to be abandoned. The four photos of the action depict the USCGC *Spencer* (A), its depth charging of the sub (B), the damaged sub surfacing (C), and three of the forty-one German crewmen who survived the destruction of their U-boat (D). (A, B, and D) *NARA;* (C) *USNI*

tion device . . . is together with enemy aircraft at present the worst enemy of the U-boat. . . . The location device is robbing the U-boat of its most important characteristic, its undetectability."

In addition to mounting U-boat losses in the North Atlantic, French-based U-boats, which had to transit the Bay of Biscay, began to suffer heavy losses both to bombers of the Royal Air Force Coastal Command and to U.S. B-24 bombers and PBY Catalina patrol aircraft. Before long, the number of U-boats lost in all areas grew to an all-time high. In May 1943 (known as "Black May"), forty-one U-boats were lost to Allied air and naval forces. Dönitz could not tolerate such losses, and thus ordered his North Atlantic boats south, away from North Atlantic waters.

In September 1943, the admiral would turn about and attack again on the main North Atlantic convoy routes. His boats now had an additional weapon on hand that he thought would be decisive when employed against a convoy screen. It was an acoustic torpedo. Dönitz was also continuing to improve the capability of his submarines. By January 1944, he would have built sev-

eral new boats that incorporated "snorkels" in their designs, long tubes that sucked in air from the surface. The snorkels enabled U-boats to run their diesel motors while at periscope depth and thus recharge their batteries while remaining submerged. These devices vastly reduced the chance of detection from the air.

Besides deploying these snorkel boats generally and backfitting some older boats with snorkels, in the spring of 1944, Dönitz would send a few snorkel-equipped boats on nuisance raids to the East Coast of the United States in hopes of sinking cargo vessels destined for the invasion of "Festung Europa" (Fortress Europe). The first snorkeler to reach U.S. waters was the *U-107,* which failed to sink a single ship. Next, the *U-233* was sent to mine the approaches to Halifax. The fifteen-hundred-ton boat was rammed and sent to the bottom off Sable Island by the destroyer escort USS *Thomas* (DE-102).

Finally, besides his other projects, the admiral was working on a submarine with a highly innovative design, the Walther boat. This new design, with its revolutionary propulsion system, could have prolonged the U-boat war and actually posed a serious threat to Allied shipping. These boats were designed so that oxygen for their diesel engines and for breathing could be supplied from hydrogen peroxide, which allowed the boats to remain submerged indefinitely. In addition, they were capable of traveling at high speeds for long distances underwater.

The Walther boats would never see action before the end of the war, though, and the snorkel boats were not deployed until early 1944. Nor did the acoustic torpedo by itself bring significant tactical victory. The U-boats suffered staggering losses in the North Atlantic until February 1944, when Dönitz again ordered his boats to withdraw south, this time to an area west of the Azores

A snorkel extends above a sub's conning tower. The shaft would pull in air from the surface while expelling diesel fumes. It allowed a submerged U-boat to run on its diesel engines while charging its electric batteries at periscope depth. As a result, the boats didn't have to fully surface to recharge their batteries, thus lessening the chances of detection by the enemy. However, the snorkel did nothing to change the U-boat's role from the defensive to the offensive during the war. The technology was never perfected and the device did not generate much interest, since the first boat to be fitted with the snorkel, *U-264,* was lost in February 1944 to British escorts *Woodpecker* and *Starling. NHC*

where they would be less likely to be attacked by shore-based aircraft. He also ordered that U-boats not to attack convoys except under especially favorable conditions.

Dönitz refused to believe he was beaten; he labeled his moving of the U-boats a tactical withdrawal. He recognized that his boats lacked the firepower to counter the array of Allied weaponry, and he was determined to resume the battle in North Atlantic waters once his surviving boats had been rearmed sufficiently. However, even in the central Atlantic his boats had begun to face a daunting enemy: the developing ASW forces of the United States.

Dönitz also had high hopes for the highly innovative Walther boat. The boats were designed so that oxygen for the diesel engines could be supplied from hydrogen peroxide, which allowed them to remain submerged indefinitely. However, the Walther boats never saw action before the end of the war. *NARA*

Back in the Washington conference of spring 1943, with the United States having been made responsible for the central Atlantic, Admiral Ernest King, Commander in Chief of the U.S. Fleet, realized that new organizational measures were needed. On May 1, 1943, he ordered the Joint Chiefs of Staff to "set up immediately in the Navy Department an antisubmarine command to be known as the Tenth Fleet. The headquarters of the Tenth Fleet will consist of all existing antisubmarine activities of the U.S. Fleet Headquarters which will be transferred intact to the Commander, Tenth Fleet." Thus, the Tenth Fleet was born.

Tough, conscientious Rear Admiral Francis "Frog" Low, Assistant Chief of Staff in charge of ASW under Admiral King, was selected to head this new "paper" fleet organization. This secret organization was designed to give operational cohesiveness to the American antisubmarine effort. Pos-

Rear Admiral Francis S. Low, USN, a tough, conscientious, intelligent, hardworking officer, was made Chief of Staff of the newly established (May 1, 1943) antisubmarine command "Tenth Fleet." The headquarters of the new "paper" fleet consisted of all existing antisubmarine activities of the U.S. Fleet headquarters. All would be transferred intact to the Commander Tenth Fleet (Admiral King). Functions of the fleet included destruction of enemy submarines, protection of Allied and neutral merchant shipping, control of convoys and shipping, and control and correlation of antisubmarine warfare training and materiel development. *NARA*

Back in the spring of 1943, Admiral Ernest J. King, USN, Commander in Chief, U.S. Fleet, realized that new organizational measures were needed to give operational cohesiveness to the American antisubmarine effort. Within a month he established a new antisubmarine command to be known as the Tenth Fleet. Henceforth, all American forces involved in ASW operations would report to Rear Admiral Francis "Frog" Low, Assistant Chief of Staff in charge of ASW under Admiral King. *USNI*

sessing no assets of its own, the Tenth Fleet would borrow ships and planes from other American organizations and unite them under one command to fight the U-boats.

Hence, in both 1943 and 1944, when he moved his boats south from the well-protected North Atlantic routes, Admiral Dönitz's submarines had to confront the newly organized American ASW force. This force featured an increasingly effective kind of tactical organization that ultimately destroyed fifty-four U-boats and hastened the end of the Battle of the Atlantic—the U.S. Navy's new hunter-killer groups.

Operation Pastorius

In June 1943 Hitler tried to insert spies into the United States when two U-boats—the *U-202* and the *U-584*—dropped off eight German saboteurs along the East Coast: four at Amagansett, Long Island, and four at Ponte Vedra, Florida. All eight were German born, had lived in the United States, and were familiar with American customs and manners. Most returned to their homeland in loyalty to a new triumphant Germany at the beginning of the war, and some of these men were trained by the German Abwehr (secret service branch of the German Navy) as spies and saboteurs to be returned to the United States.

The main objectives of the saboteurs were the American light metals industries and rail transportation. Targets included plants of the Aluminum Company of America at Alcoa, Tennessee, the lines of the Chesapeake and Ohio Railroad, and railroad stations in New York and New Jersey.

The Germans code-named the mission "Operation Pastorius." All agents landed safely. They immediately buried their explosives in beach areas, to be retrieved after the men had spent ninety days preparing for acts of sabotage. Shortly after the group landed at Amagansett, a Coast Guardsman discovered the leader, George John Dasch, and his three companions. After threatening to kill the guard, Dasch had a change of heart and gave the frightened young man $260 if he would forget what he had seen. The Coast Guardsman accepted the money, returned to his station, but then reported the incident, and the saboteur's presence was then made known to the FBI. Following this incident, Dasch and his men traveled to New York City and checked into hotels near the Pennsylvania Station. They were to meet up with the four other saboteurs at a given site at the end of the ninety-day period. In the meantime, several of them returned to where they had previously lived in the States to visit relatives and friends.

Dasch had had misgivings about the mission even before they came ashore, and the encounter with the Coast Guardsman made him even more concerned. Finally, deciding that the mission would fail, he called the FBI office in New York City and told agent Dean F. McWhorter that he had recently arrived from Germany and had important information to give to J. Edgar Hoover. Since Dasch would not reveal what the information was, and the FBI office received numerous crank calls, McWhorter simply made a record of the call after Dasch hung up.

Several days later, Dasch checked into the Mayflower Hotel in Washington, D.C., and called the Washington FBI office. He asked to speak directly to Mr. Hoover, and he told agent Duane L. Traynor that he was the leader of a group of German saboteurs. Traynor knew of the Amagansett incident and told Dasch to stay in his room and wait for them. FBI agents arrived and quickly took Dasch into custody.

During subsequent interrogation, Dasch revealed the nature of their mission, how they had been transported by U-boats, the identity of the other saboteurs, and where they could be found. Within a week's time, all of the other saboteurs were in federal custody.

President Franklin D. Roosevelt decreed that the saboteurs were not to be handed over to a civil court. They were guilty of high treason, he said, and therefore should receive the death penalty. The eight were tried before a military commission of seven U.S. Army general officers appointed by the president. J. Edgar Hoover, other Justice officials, and numerous high-ranking military officers attended the trial, which was held in the Department of Justice building in Washington. During the proceedings, the eight prisoners were kept in the cleared women's section on the second floor of the district jail.

All eight were found guilty. The prosecutor, Attorney General Francis Biddle, and Hoover appealed to the president to commute the death sentence of Dasch and another member of his group, Earnest Peter Burger, for their assistance in stopping the conspiracy. Subsequently, Dasch's sentence was commuted to thirty years and Burger's to life imprisonment—each sentence to be served in a federal penitentiary.

The remaining six were executed in the District of Columbia jail. Their remains were buried in the district's Potter's Field at Blue Plains, just south of the city. Like the hundreds of remains surrounding them, their names and mission have, for the most part, been forgotten.

Instead of serving out their sentences, Dasch and Burger were repatriated at the war's end.

| George John Dasch | Ernest Peter Burger | Richard Quirin | Heinrich Harm Heinck | Edward Kerling | Herbert Hans Haupt | Werner Thiel | Herman Otto Neubauer |

Eight German saboteurs who were dropped off by U-boats along the American coast in June 1943, four at Amagansett, Long Island, and four at Ponte Verde, Florida. Their leader, George Dasch, having misgivings about the success of their mission, turned himself in to the FBI and the other seven were quickly apprehended. Six were executed and Dasch and another cooperative agent, Ernest Burger, were imprisoned and repatriated after the war. *NARA*

CHAPTER 3

U-Boat Hunter-Killer Groups

As early as 1935, Admiral J. M. Reeves, Commander in Chief, U.S. Fleet, predicted that convoys would have to be protected by carrier aircraft if they were to survive the attacks of U-boats and enemy aircraft. Five years later, Rear Admiral William F. Halsey, Commander, Aircraft Battle Force, alerted high-ranking naval officials that if war came, all six fleet carriers in the Navy inventory would be required to deploy. This would leave the Navy without carriers to train new pilots and to transport planes to U.S. bases overseas. Halsey forcefully promoted the procurement of merchant vessels to be converted to small carriers.

In January 1941, the Office of the Chief of Naval Operations ordered the purchase of two diesel-powered C-3 freighter hull merchant ships for conversion to ASW carriers. The ships would have full-length flight decks for operation of Navy torpedo bombers and fighter aircraft. The Navy estimated it would take more than a year to complete the conversions. President Franklin D. Roosevelt gave the Navy just three months to have the first ship in the water.

NARA

In March 1941, the Navy purchased the merchant hull *Mormacland*. On June 2, a few days before the three-month deadline, the converted ship was commissioned the *Long Island*. The vessel was 492 feet long, had a beam of 69 feet, 6 inches, and displaced 14,953 tons with a full load. Her flight deck was 419 feet long; she had one elevator to the hangar deck below, and one catapult forward on the port side; her top speed was seventeen knots.

The *Long Island* initially operated out of Norfolk, Virginia, conducting exercises to prove the feasibility of aircraft operations from converted cargo ships. After escorting a convoy to Newfoundland, she departed in May 1942 for the West Coast, where she provided carrier pilot training. In July, the ship sailed to the South Pacific and participated in the Guadalcanal Campaign. On returning to San Diego, she was used once again to train carrier pilots. After the war, she transported sailors and Marines home from the Pacific during "Operation Magic Carpet."

Following the commissioning of the *Long Island*, in March 1942 Congress approved the conversion of additional merchant hulls. A month later, the British Admiralty requested that the United States convert and transfer to the Royal Navy six more escort carriers for convoy protection. The competition for converted merchant hulls became so intense that four oilers of the *Cimarron* class were converted (the *Sangamon, Suwanne, Chenango,* and *Santee*) in August and September 1942. They participated in "Operation Torch," the invasion of North Africa, that November. Escort carriers were designated "aircraft carriers, escort" (AVG) until August 20, 1942, and "auxiliary aircraft carriers" (ACV) until the CVE designation was established on July 15, 1943. Eventually, these vessels were categorized as *Sangamon*-class carriers, and four CVEs constituted the class. They were ordered to the Pacific Fleet and fought their way through the Pacific, making their mark at the battle off Samar. Between 1943 and 1945, seventy-six CVEs were commissioned. They were divided into four classes: *Bogue, Sangamon, Casablanca,* and *Commencement Bay.*

USS *Long Island* (CVE-1), delivered to the Navy in March 1941, was the U.S. Navy's first escort carrier, having been converted from the ten-thousand-ton freighter USS *Mormacland.* This photo shows clearly how the merchant hull supports the flight deck. This carrier had no island; it was conned from wings on either side of the flight deck. *USNI*

The USS *Bogue* (CVE-9), screened by four old flush-deck destroyers, led the first U.S. ASW escort group. Groups like this were called "The Woolworth Brigade" because of their jeep-like appearance, i.e., a converted merchant ship surrounded by less than "greyhound"-looking destroyer escorts. The *Bogue* displaced 7,800 tons, was 495 feet in length (the flight deck was 436 feet long), and had a turbine-geared propulsion system and a top speed of seventeen knots. At fifteen knots she had a range of 26,300 miles. She carried two 5-inch/38-caliber dual purpose, ten 40-mm antiaircraft twins, and twenty-seven 20-mm antiaircraft guns. Her aircraft complement was sixteen fighters (F4F, FM-1, or FM-2) and twelve torpedo bombers (TBF or TBM).

Composite squadrons (VCs), consisting of F4F-4, FM-1, and FM-2 Wildcat fighters and TBF-1 and TBM-1C Avenger torpedo bombers, flew from the deck of the *Bogue* during her wartime cruises. The Wildcats had a maximum speed of 318 mph at 19,400 feet, with a cruising speed of 155 mph. Each carried six fixed forward-firing .50-caliber machine guns. The Avenger had a maximum speed of 271 mph at 12,000 feet, with a cruising speed of 145 mph. It had two fixed forward-firing .50-caliber machine guns, a dorsal ball turret that housed a .50-caliber machine gun, and a ventral .30-caliber machine gun. It could carry two thousand pounds of bombs, torpedoes, or depth charges in its bomb bay.

The *Bogue*'s first U-boat kill, the *U-569*, was during "Black May" of 1943 while the group was

The *Bogue* and Her Escorts

Having been credited with twelve submarine kills, the *Bogue,* together with the task groups that operated in 1943 and 1944, was awarded the Presidential Unit Citation, the highest American award given to an operational unit. Not only were these task groups credited with twelve U-boat kills during that period, but the carrier also lost none of her aircraft to enemy fire, and no convoy she escorted lost a ship while under the *Bogue*'s protection.

On May 13, 1944, the USS *Francis M. Robinson* (DE-220), one of the destroyer escorts operating with the *Bogue,* made an underwater contact northwest of the Cape Verde Islands. The American ship delivered a fierce hedgehog and depth charge attack, sending the boat to the bottom, thinking she was a German U-boat. It was the Japanese submarine *RO-501* (formerly the *U-1224*), however, which Germany had just given to Japan. Manned by a Japanese crew, she was on her delivery voyage. Not until after the war did the American crewmen learn that they had sunk a Japanese submarine with her entire crew.

escorting a United Kingdom-to-Haifax convoy (ON-184). Moving farther south the following month, the *Bogue* located the Wolfpack "Trux," which was forming off the Azores. Her planes sent the *U-217* and the *U-118* to the bottom of the ocean. Other hunter-killer groups, organized around the USS *Core* (CVE-13), the USS *Card* (CVE-11), and the USS *Santee* (CVE-29), soon joined the *Bogue* in the Atlantic. By the end of August 1943, the groups had sunk sixteen U-boats. Escort carrier aircraft specifically targeted German milch cows to eliminate the refueling and resupplying of U-boats at sea, thus shortening their patrol cruises.

On June 23, some 850 miles west of Cape Verdes, an Avenger from the *Bogue* picked up a large Japanese submarine (the *I-52*) that had left Singapore two

Bogue hunter-killer aircraft attack and sink *U-118* on June 12, 1943, south of the Azores. *U-118* had been surprised on the surface, and attempts to man and fight her guns were futile. Note the two men crouching by the conning tower. *NARA*

The USS *Core* (CVE-13), here sporting a wartime camouflage pattern (there were a variety of such patterns), had considerable success against the U-boats, particularly in mid- to late-1943. Such *Bogue*-class escort carriers regularly carried twenty-eight aircraft and approximately one thousand men. *NARA*

months earlier with a cargo of rubber, wolfram, molybdenum, and quinine. The boat had picked up a German pilot and was headed for Bordeaux. The VC-69 aircraft illuminated the Japanese submarine with a flare and drove her down with a vigorous air attack. Tracking her with sonobuoys (expendable floats that carried hydrophones for listening underwater and radio transmitters to relay submarine sounds to searching aircraft), the Avenger made a midnight bombing attack, and the sonobuoys relayed a series of breaking-up noises. At dawn, surface escorts picked up various pieces of debris, including numerous bales of crude rubber. No survivors were sighted.

Although the *Bogue* sank only one U-boat during her July to September 1944 cruise, that particular incident was unique in the history of the ship's ASW operations. On July 26, the *U-1229* departed Trondheim, Norway, to place an espionage agent ashore in Maine. The spy, a former New York bartender named Oscar Mantel, was to have been put ashore at Winter Harbor with $2,000 in U.S. currency to begin his activities. Avengers some three hundred miles southeast of Cape Race sighted the snorkel-equipped U-boat on the surface on August 12. The boat was immediately depth-charged and strafed with rockets. After a brief period at snorkel depth, the U-boat commander surfaced the vessel and ordered the

On October 20, 1943, *Core* aircraft attacked and disabled another U-boat, the *U-378*. *NARA*

U-185 is shown going under after being attacked by *Core* hunter-killer aircraft, August 24, 1943. *NARA*

Bogue aircraft attack an unidentified U-boat in the mid-Atlantic. *NARA*

crew to abandon ship. A five-hundred-pound bomb hit finally sent the boat to the bottom. Forty-two survivors were recovered, among them the hapless German spy. Mantel eventually was interned at the Army prisoner of war camp in Alva, Oklahoma, and sent back to Germany after the war.

In 1943, several antisubmarine technical advances further threatened the survival of prowling U-boats. Escort vessels were now fitted with supersonic echo-ranging equipment and a fast-sinking depth charge that could be set to explode at six hundred feet. Hunter-killer aircraft carried new five-hundred-pound depth bombs and an acoustic homing torpedo named "Fido" (a U.S. Navy acoustic antisubmarine torpedo). A newly developed airborne microwave radar (of ten centimeter wavelength) had also come into play.

USS *Card* (CVE-11), shown in 1945. The *Card*'s Task Group sent eleven U-boats to the bottom. Escort carriers were usually accompanied by four or five destroyer escorts. *USNI*

Second in overall U-boat kills to the *Bogue* was the *Card* (CVE-11) a *Bogue*-class carrier that destroyed eleven U-boats during the war. During her first cruise, her screening destroyers consisted of the USS *Barry* (DD-248), the USS *Borie* (DD-215), the USS *Goff* (DD-247), and the USS *Dupont* (DD-152). Departing Hampton Roads, Virginia, on July 27, 1943, the group refueled at Bermuda, then headed for a reported concentration of U-boats west of Flores Island in the Azores. On August 7, one of the *Card*'s Avengers sighted two surfaced U-boats 320 miles to the west. The boats were sailing in parallel, the *U-66* refueling from a milch cow, the *U-117*. The pilot dove on the boats, strafing and dropping depth bombs. The *U-66* slipped away, submerged, and escaped, but one of the Avenger's bombs ruptured the afterdeck of the *U-117*, and she was unable to submerge. With the arrival of two reinforcing Avengers, the milch cow was sunk, with her entire crew, in short order. The *Card* group sank two more boats in August and four in October 1943.

A sinking by one of the *Card*'s escorts, the destroyer *Borie*, in November, has been called the most spectacular surface battle since the days of John Paul Jones.

The USS *Borie* was an old "four-stacker" of World War I vintage. The flush-deck destroyer had been commissioned in March 1920 and early on had seen service in the Black Sea and the Asiatic and Atlantic Fleets. In July 1943, she joined the *Card* hunter-killer group. Skippered by Lieutenant Charles Hutchins, the youngest destroyer commanding officer in the U.S. Navy at the time, the *Borie* sailed with the *Card* from Casablanca as escort for a westbound convoy.

When approaching the Azores, underwater contacts began to be reported, and the *Card*'s aircraft and destroyers, along with convoy escorts, commenced air and sea searches for the enemy. The *Card*'s aircraft sank the *U-584*, which was cruising with the *U-91* on the surface; the *U-91* submerged and escaped. Because of pilot reports, Captain A. J. Isbell, commanding officer of the *Card*, thought the escaping sub was a milch cow and ordered the *Borie* to search for her. At 8:10 PM, radar contact was made, and the *Borie* made several depth charge runs, during which the destroyer crew heard a loud explosion that rattled the ship. This, together with a strong odor of oil in the air, convinced the crew they had been successful. Though no surface debris was found after three hours of searching, Hutchins, certain they had sunk the *U-91*, radioed the *Card*, "Scratch one pig boat." In fact, the *U-91* had long departed the area, and the *Borie* actually had been battling the *U-256*, which managed to limp back to Germany severely damaged.

Above: Card Avenger scores a direct hit on *U-117* on August 7, 1943, west of the Azores. *U-117*, a "milch cow" refueling vessel, was attempting to refuel the *U-66*, seen at the left. *NARA*

Right: Caught on the surface charging her batteries, *U-664* was attacked by a Wildcat and two Avengers from the *Card* on August 9, 1943. Following a fierce air barrage of strafing and bombing, the sub's crew abandoned the boat, which upended and sank. The *Borie*, an old "four stacker" destroyer of the *Card* group, picked up forty-four survivors. Note the "smiling" Saw Fish emblem on the sub's conning tower. *NARA*

At 2:00 o'clock the next morning, the *Borie* picked up another contact and released depth charges. A leading fire controlman and gun director stationed immediately above the bridge first sighted the conning tower of a U-boat near a marker flare the ship had dropped. Because of damage caused by the *Borie*'s depth charges, the *U-405* tried to escape in the darkness on the surface. Turning on her twenty-four-inch searchlight and using radar bearings, the destroyer was able to keep the *U-405* illuminated during a one-hour running surface battle. Amid continuous gunfire and torpedo near misses, the two adversaries fought until the *Borie* rammed the U-boat and became lodged across her bow. The crews opened fire at point-blank range with machine guns, shotguns, rifles, and pistols. By the time the two separated, the *Borie* had sustained serious underwater damage but continued to chase the U-boat, keeping her under constant fire.

Finally, the *U-405* slowed and stopped dead in the water. Crewmen began to throw life rafts over the side and abandon the boat. As they drifted toward the destroyer, they fired flares into the night air, which appeared to elicit white stars in the distance, perhaps from another U-boat. Fearing an attack by other boats, Hutchins withdrew to return to the *Card* task group, but the *Borie* was unable to locate the carrier group because of severe damage that caused a loss of electrical power and loss of her radar, a shutdown of her boilers, and a dense fog that engulfed the ship. Through the ingenuity of the crew, a message using the ship's auxiliary radio generator reached the *Card*. It read simply, "Commenced sinking."

The task group found the foundering ship, and at 4:30 PM Hutchins ordered her abandoned. Climbing into life rafts, the crew left the ship. Though no crew members were lost in the battle with the *U-405,* twenty-seven men died during the abandonment of the ship and a harrowing rescue operation. Almost all the losses occurred as the men attempted to board the screen destroyers in a worsening sea state. The derelict *Borie* continued to remain afloat. Since the group was in seas where U-boats concentrated and the ship was beyond salvage, it was decided to sink her and clear the area. Three bombs from the *Card*'s aircraft sank the tough "old-timer." When the task group returned to Norfolk, it received the Presidential Unit Citation, and Commander Hutchins was awarded

An artist's rendering of the USS *Borie* (DD-215) shown ramming the *U-405* in the North Atlantic on November 1, 1943, after a furious night surface engagement. The U-boat sunk, and the *Borie* had to be abandoned the following day due to severe damage inflicted during the engagement. The destroyer suffered no losses during the battle but lost twenty-seven crewmen during transfer operations in heavy seas. *USNI*

the Navy Cross. Two additional Navy Crosses, two Silver Stars, and a Legion of Merit were awarded to *Borie* crew members.

The third leading scorer of U-boat kills would be another *Bogue*-class escort carrier, the USS *Croatan* (CVE-25), which departed Hampton Roads on August 6, 1943, with a screen of flush-deck destroyers. Nicknamed "Old Crow," the carrier reached the Azores but had little success in locating U-boats, which usually concentrated in that area. Nevertheless, two of her aircraft sighted the *U-134,* which was en route to her home base after shooting down a U.S. Navy blimp (airship), the *K-74,* off Key West in July.

The *K-74*'s radar screen had picked up the U-boat at midnight on July 18, 1943. Ignoring lighter-than-air doctrine, which forbade attacks on surfaced U-boats, the pilot of the airship flew over the U-boat, hoping to score a hit with one of its bombs. With a speed of just forty-seven knots, the blimp could not avoid the hail of gunfire from the U-boat, which punctured the balloon and

started fires in the fuselage. As the airship drifted over the boat, the pilot tried to release a bomb, but the release gear failed, and the craft settled into the water. All ten men on board the blimp survived the *U-134* attack, although one man was subsequently lost to sharks.

The U-boat continued on her journey until detected by the two aircraft from the *Croatan*. Neither aviator could score a hit on the boat during a fifty-five-minute battle after which the *U-134* submerged and escaped.

The *Croatan* began to be besieged by a host of problems. Two of her Wildcats crashed during recovery operations. Then a main fuel pump gave way, and the ship was forced to reduce speed to ten knots. She lost her surface-search radar, and her catapult broke down, making it impossible to launch aircraft. A disenchanted carrier crew headed for Casablanca with their destroyer screen to effect repairs. In April 1944, the Old Crow escort group scored its first success when three of its destroyer escorts—the USS *Snowden* (DE-246), the USS *Barber* (DE-161), and the USS *Frost* (DE-144)—sank the German milch cow *U-488* west of the Cape Verde Islands. With the sinking of the *U-488*, only one refueler, the *U-490*, remained out of a fleet of ten. Admiral Dönitz noted in his official war diary that "until submerged refueling were possible . . . refueling will be carried out only in urgent cases from combatant boats." The *Croatan* task

An unprecedented battle between the American blimp *K-74* and a German U-boat, *U-134*, during the evening hours of July 18, 1943, is captured in this artistic rendering of the encounter. Gunfire from the U-boat punctured the blimp's air bag and set the craft on fire. It subsequently crashed into the sea off Key West, Florida. *NARA*

group would sink two more boats, including the *U-490* (the last of the milch cows) and the *U-154,* in June and July of 1944.

The *Croatan* bagged her last three U-boats in April 1945. Two of the boats, the *U-1235* and the *U-880,* were sunk during "Operation Teardrop." In early 1945, rumors circulated of a German U-boat attack on major U.S. East Coast cities and ports using robot rocket bombs similar to the V-1s and V-2s used against Britain. Fearful that the Eastern Seaboard had become too complacent, Navy officials held a press conference that dealt with that possibility. As it happened, the rumors rang somewhat true, because Dönitz was planning a final attack on the Eastern Sea Frontier that would employ six snorkel boats. However, only conventional weapons were to be used, since the German Navy had no secret weapons or rocket bombs. Navy escort groups were ready for the intruders, though. Operation Teardrop would destroy almost the entire German force long before it reached U.S. shores.

Two barriers of carrier escort groups were spread north to south across the Atlantic. The first barrier consisted of two forces. The Northern Force, centered around the escort carrier *Mission Bay* (CVE-59), covered approaches north of latitude 48 degrees, 30 minutes. The Southern Force, led by the *Croatan,* protected the southern sector. To the east of the barrier was a picket line of twenty destroyer escorts spread along the thirtieth meridian.

The second barrier, which was positioned south of the Flemish Cap and southeast of the Grand Banks, consisted of the *Core* and the *Bogue* and a similar picket line of destroyer escorts. On April 15, one of the *Croatan*'s screen destroyers, the

USS *Stanton* (DE-247), made contact with the *U-1235*, which had surfaced because heavy seas prevented use of her snorkel. As the U-boat submerged, the USS *Frost* joined the *Stanton*, and the two destroyer escorts commenced hedgehog and depth charge attacks, resulting in a huge underwater explosion that was heard as far away as the *Croatan*, 12 miles distant. The *U-1235* had gone down north of Flores Island in the Azores and 520 miles east of the Flemish Cap.

Shortly after the *U-1235* was destroyed, the *Frost* made contact with another boat, the *U-880*. The *Stanton* quickly joined in the chase, and after a fierce hedgehog barrage, the U-boat exploded and broke up in the dark seas below. Prior to relieving the first barrier force, the *Croatan*'s screen destroyer escorts, the USS *Carter* (DE-112) and the USS *Neal A. Scott* (DE-769), located the *U-518* at a depth of 150 feet. It took only one pattern of hedgehog missiles to destroy the U-boat, which was on her seventh patrol.

Although not as productive of U-boat kills as the carrier escorts mentioned above, another CVE arguably would become the most famous of them all. The USS *Guadalcanal* (CVE-60), a *Casablanca*-class carrier, entered the Atlantic foray in the spring of 1944. The ship was in Seattle, being prepared for commissioning, when she was ordered to the Atlantic for antisubmarine duty. Captain Daniel V. Gallery, skipper of the ship, recalled, "When I got word we were going to the Atlantic I was bitterly disappointed because I figured I'd done my stint in the Atlantic and that the Battle of the Atlantic was won by now anyway. So I figured we were just going to the backwater of the war now and we ought to be going to the Pacific." Little did Captain Gallery know that he would later make naval history when his force, Task Group 22.3, joined the U-boat hunt in Atlantic waters.

Only four U.S. hunter-killer ships were lost during the U-boat war in the Atlantic. However, three of these went down after Gallery's task group entered the war, and one of them was a CVE. Between 1943 and 1945, the destroyer *Borie* (DD-215) and two destroyer escorts, the *Fiske* (DE-143) and the *Frederick C. Davis* (DE-136), were sent to the bottom by U-boats, and the *Block Island* (CVE-21) was sunk by the *U-549* on May 29, 1944. This sinking of a carrier escort occurred just a few days before the *Guadalcanal*'s historic achievement, and it took place not too very far away.

The USS *Block Island* (CVE-21) was sunk in late May 1944 by three torpedoes from the *U-549* while patrolling the waters around the Cape Verdes Islands. She was the only U.S. carrier lost in the Atlantic during the war. Overall, her task group destroyed seven U-boats, including the *U-549*, which, quickly after her attack on the *Block Island*, was sent to the bottom by two of the carrier's destroyer escorts. *USNI*

CHAPTER 4

Task Group 22.3

As each new crewman reported aboard the *Guadalcanal* at the Astoria, Oregon, shipyard, he was given the following memo:

1. The motto of this ship will be "Can Do," meaning that we will take any tough job that is given to us and run away with it. The tougher the job, the better we'll like it.

2. Before a carrier can do its big job of sinking enemy ships, several hundred small jobs have got to be done and done well. One man falling down on a small job can bitch the works for the whole ship. So learn all you can about your job during this pre-commissioning period. Pretty soon we will be out where it rains bombs and it will be too late to learn.

Note: This ship will be employed on dangerous duty. We will either sink the enemy or get sunk ourselves depending on how well we learn our jobs now and do our jobs later.

ANYONE WHO PREFERS SAFER DUTY SEE ME AND I WILL ARRANGE TO HAVE HIM TRANSFERRED.

D. V. Gallery
Captain, USN

Captain Gallery after making the first landing aboard the newly commissioned escort carrier USS *Guadalcanal* (CVE-60). *NARA*

The *Guadalcanal* was commissioned on September 25, 1943, at Vancouver, Washington, with Captain Dan Gallery aboard as skipper. The *Guadalcanal* steamed north for a brief shakedown cruise into Puget Sound but soon took on ammunition and headed south. In company with another escort carrier, the *Mission Bay* (CVE-59), the *Guadalcanal* then landed her aircrew off San Diego, California. The two ships exercised with their planes en route to Panama. The "Can Do" subsequently made her way through the Panama Canal to Norfolk, where "Captain Dan" was designated Commander, Task Group 22.3. When the *Card* (CVE-11) returned to Norfolk, Gallery huddled with her commanding

officer, Captain Arnold Isbell, to collect as much information as possible about stalking and destroying what remained of the U-Waffe in the Atlantic.

The *Guadalcanal* was somewhat bigger than such earlier escort carriers as the *Bogue.* She displaced two thousand more tons, her flight deck was fifty feet longer, and her propulsion system consisted of two shaft-geared turbines. The ship also had additional oil storage capacity and could carry up to thirty-four aircraft, six more than the *Bogue.*

Task Group 22.3 departed Norfolk on January 3, 1944. The group consisted of the Can Do, four flush-deck screen destroyers—the USS *Alden* (DD-211), the USS *John D. Edwards* (DD-216), the USS *Whipple* (DD-217), and the USS *John D. Ford* (DD-228)—and VC-13, a veteran air group under the command of Lieutenant Commander Adrian H. Perry. Her air complement included nine Wildcats and twelve Avengers. The task group met with high winds and heavy seas as it headed out, and two Wildcats tied down on the flight deck were damaged so severely they had to be off-loaded at Bermuda.

Bad luck seemed to follow the force as it approached a reported U-boat fueling rendezvous point some five hundred miles west of the Azores. On January 10, Lieutenant (junior grade) James F. Schoby, flying an Avenger, was lost as he tried to land on a pitching deck. (Schoby had been awarded the Distinguished Flying Cross for sinking the *U-487* the previous July.) Fortunately,

The *Guadalcanal* was commissioned on September 25, 1943, at Vancouver, Washington. Here she rides down the ways from the shipyard where she was built into the Columbia River. *NARA*

Rear Admiral Daniel V. Gallery

Rear Admiral Daniel V. Gallery, USN. *USNI*

Born in Chicago, Illinois, on July 10, 1901, Daniel Vincent Gallery attended St. Ignatius High School in Chicago prior to his appointment in 1917 to the U.S. Naval Academy. As a midshipman, he was a member of the highly successful Naval Academy wrestling team, and, upon graduation, he wrestled for the United States in the 1920 Olympic Games in Antwerp, Belgium.

Gallery had duties afloat until 1927, when he volunteered for naval air. He was ordered to Naval Air Station, Pensacola, Florida, for flight training and received his "wings" as a naval aviator later that year. He became the commander of a patrol plane detachment in Iceland shortly after World War II began; his planes patrolled far to the west to help guard North Atlantic convoys. In 1943, Gallery was detached from this duty, and, shortly afterward, he took command of the "baby flattop" USS *Guadalcanal* (CVE- 60). He staged the first boarding and capture at sea of an enemy naval vessel since 1815—the capture of the German submarine *U-505* off Cape

Commander Gallery, commanding officer of the U.S. Navy Fleet Air Base at Reykjavik, Iceland, in 1942, shown with American and British officers in front of a pair of "palm trees" crafted by Gallery's chief metalsmith. It was during this tour that he began to think about capturing an abandoned U-boat. *USNI*

Blanco, French West Africa, in June 1944. In 1954, his prize was hauled out of the water and installed on concrete cradles alongside the Museum of Science and Industry in Chicago as a memorial to the Americans who had lost their lives defending the country at sea.

Captain Gallery assumed command of the USS *Hancock* (CV-19) in 1945, in time to be present during the surrender ceremonies in Tokyo Bay. Following operational duty in the Pacific, he became Assistant Chief of Naval Operations (Guided Missiles), serving from 1946 to 1949. He hoisted his flag on the USS *Coral Sea* (CVB-43, later CVA-43) as Commander, Carrier Division Six, on March 10, 1951, and became Commander, Hunter-Killer Force, on March 21, 1952.

Gallery commanded the nationwide Naval Air Reserve Training Command, headquartered at Naval Air Station, Glenview, Illinois, between November 18, 1952, and November 1955, serving also from October 1954 as Commandant, Ninth Naval District, Great Lakes, Illinois. On December 6, 1956, he assumed command of the Caribbean Sea Frontier, with additional duty as Commandant of the Tenth Naval District, with headquarters in San Juan, Puerto Rico. While in San Juan he was Commissioner of Little League Baseball for Latin America and organized the Tenth Naval District Steel Band (also known as "Admiral Dan's Pandemaniacs"), which played on instruments made out of oil drums at World's Fairs in Brussels and New York. From mid-May to August 1957 he was tasked with further additional duty as Commander, Antilles Defense Command. He served briefly in the Bureau of Naval Personnel, Navy Department, prior to his retirement, effective October 1, 1960.

Rear Admiral Gallery had more than six thousand hours' flying time in all types of naval aircraft, including single-seat jets, and he was the proud holder of the "green" card issued by the Navy to specially qualified instrument pilots. His hobbies included baseball and writing. His writings appeared in several national magazines, and he wrote several books, including *Clear the Decks, Twenty Million Tons Under the Sea, Now Hear This*, and *Cap'n Fatso*. Besides his autobiographi-

cal accounts, he was most successful with humorous short stories.

Gallery was a great friend of novelist Herman Wouk, and was Wouk's primary naval consultant for *The Winds of War* and *War and Remembrance*.

Rear Admiral Gallery's three brothers were in the Navy. Rear Admiral William O. Gallery and Rear Admiral Philip D. Gallery were both Naval Academy graduates. Another brother, Reverend John I. Gallery, former pastor of Saint Christina's Parish in Chicago, served as a Naval Reserve chaplain during World War II.

Dan Gallery's many decorations included the Distinguished Service Medal, the Bronze Star, the Presidential Unit Citation (Antisubmarine Task Group 22.3), and Commander of the British Empire (Honorary). Further information about Gallery can be found in *Admiral Dan Gallery: The Life and Wit of a Navy Original* by C. Herbert Gilliland and Robert Shenk (see "Works Consulted").

Admiral Gallery passed away on January 16, 1977.

The Tenth Naval District Steel Band was a product of leisure hours in the semi-tropical land of Puerto Rico, where Admiral Gallery was stationed from 1956 to 1960. Inspired by the steel bands of Trinidad, Rear Admiral Gallery organized his own group of steel drum musicians and took them to the World's Fair in Brussels. The steel band remained a Navy institution for almost forty years. *MSI*

his turret gunner was rescued. Within hours, another Avenger landed on the ship's catwalk. The aircraft had to be pushed over the side to make room for yet another aircraft, which was low on fuel. With these losses the squadron was down to seven Wildcats and ten Avengers.

On January 16, eight Turkeys (the nickname for Avenger torpedo bombers) were on patrol under a heavy overcast. Just before sunset, two of the aircraft—piloted by Ensigns Bert J. Hudson and William M. McLane—sighted three surfaced U-boats (the *U-544*, the *U-129*, and the *U-516*) that were conducting a refueling operation. The milch cow *U-544* was fueling the *U-516*. On sighting the onrushing enemy aircraft, the *U-129* submerged quickly. Both pilots attacked the remaining boats with rockets and depth bombs. Hudson sank the *U-544*, but the *U-516* was able to make home port, despite being badly damaged. Captain Gallery recalled what happened next in his book *Twenty Million Tons Under the Sea*.

As soon as we got word of the kill we recalled all planes. But curiosity is a strong human emotion, this was our first kill, and that oil puddle with the Germans paddling around in it was only 40 miles from the ship. I had detached destroyers to pick up survivors, but every one of our pilots felt it was essential to the war effort for him to fly over there and take a gander at the scene. We put out some peremptory orders on the radio to "get the hell back here and land." But the boys later claimed there was a lot of static. . . . By the time my pilots came wandering back from their rubberneck trip, the sun had gone down, and under that solid overcast, darkness was rapidly closing in on us.

The first four lads got aboard OK, but the fifth one landed too far to the starboard and wound up with his right wheel down in the gallery walkway and his left wing and tail sticking out over the deck, fouling the landing area. We still had three planes in the air and the darkness was getting blacker every minute. I had the feeling then and there that we had had it.

Shortly after returning to the *Guadalcanal*, Avenger pilots of Composite Squadron 13 relive the sinking of the *U-544* with Captain Gallery. *NARA*

The Guadalcanal was a larger escort carrier than earlier ones since she displaced two thousand more tons, had a longer flight deck, and could carry more aircraft. The large aircraft on the ship's deck are torpedo bombers (Avengers); the small ones further aft are fighters (Wildcats). *USNI*

Ordinarily, getting that plane back on deck and out of the landing area should have been about a five-minute job. But we were a new ship, the pressure was on us for the first time, and we got butterfingered. After we had fumbled around for about ten minutes, the plane took a sickening lurch, swung its left wheel over the coaming of the flight deck, and came to rest nose down in the walkway with its tail now sticking out at right angles across the deck into the landing area. My farmer boys messed around with it for five more minutes, getting nowhere, and then I said, "The hell with it—shove it overboard."

This was easier said than done. We heaved and we hauled, we grunted and we cursed, we pried with 4 x 4 beams, we pumped hydraulic jacks, and we even rammed into it with tractors. We couldn't move the damn plane. . . . We lit the ship up like a waterfront saloon on a Saturday night and I made the following pitch to the boys in the air by radiophone: "That tail doesn't stick out very far into the landing area. If you land smack on the centerline your right wing will clear it. So just ignore that plane on the starboard side . . . come on in and land."

Three very dubious "Rogers" came back out of the darkness. For the next half hour those three lads made the most hair-raising passes I've ever seen made at a carrier's deck, except maybe for dive-bombing attacks. Our landing signal officer gave them wave-off after wave-off trying to get them to settle down. It was easy enough for us on deck to make believe that the wreck wasn't there but the boys in the air just didn't have enough imagination. They kept edging over too far to port coming up the groove.

Finally, one of them reluctantly drifted over pretty close to the centerline and the LSO gave him a desperate "cut," even though he was way too fast. He hit wheels

USS *Gallery*

USS *Gallery* (FFG 26). The USS *Gallery* was commissioned on December 5, 1981, and was named after three brothers, Daniel, Philip, and William Gallery, all of whom served in World War II and subsequently reached the rank of Rear Admiral. Rear Adm. Daniel Gallery is known for his capture of the German submarine *U-505*. Rear Adm. William Gallery was a naval aviator and served with distinction in the Pacific. Rear Adm. Philip Gallery was one of the heroic destroyer men of World War II. *MSI*

first, bounced into the air, rolled over on his back and plunged into the sea to port. A plane guard destroyer fished all three men out of the water unhurt.

That was enough of that business. We turned on the searchlights of all ships, pointed them down at the water, and ordered the other two planes to ditch alongside destroyers. The "cans" fished everybody out of the water, we blew out the light, and got the hell out of that area.

The task group subsequently replenished at Casablanca and sailed for Norfolk, arriving on February 16, 1944. Gallery determined that such an incident would not happen again while he was in command. En route to Norfolk, he exercised the deck crew night and day in an attempt to clear the flight deck of the wrecked Avenger. Finally, he allowed a worn-out crew to push the Avenger over the side before reaching port.

Task Group 22.3 departed Norfolk on March 7 with a different air group and destroyer screen. VC-58, commanded by Lieutenant Commander R. K. Gould, was comprised of nine Wildcats and twelve Avengers. The Can Do's surface escorts were the USS *Pillsbury* (DE-133), the USS *Pope* (DE-134), the USS *Forrest* (DD-461), the USS *Flaherty* (DE-135), and the USS *Chatelain* (DE-149). The group sailed without incident to Casablanca.

Departing Norfolk on its second patrol, the *Guadalcanal* welcomed aboard a new Composite Squadron (VC-58) and a different group of surface escorts: USS *Pillsbury* (DE-133), USS *Pope* (DE-134), USS *Forrest* (DD-461), USS *Flaherty* (DE-135), and USS *Chatelain* (DE-149). Shown here is the *Guadalcanal* refueling the *Forrest* while under way. *NARA*

On August 8, 1944, the Task Group made contact with the *U-515* northwest of Madeira and attacked it with rockets and depth charges. Forced to surface and face a fierce barrage of fire from Task Group air and surface units, U-boat captain Kapitänleutnant Werner Henke ordered the boat abandoned. Screen destroyers picked up forty-five survivors, including Henke. *MSI*

During the transit, Gallery ordered his pilots to conduct flight operations around the clock. Escort carrier commanders were hesitant about putting their aircraft in the air at night because of the many inherent dangers in conducting such operations. The pilots took Gallery's order in stride, and gradually they became proficient in night operations. Gallery would later speak proudly of his ship's "breaking the ice on night operations for CVEs," and would attribute some of their U-boat kills to such regular night operations.

The Can Do got under way from Casablanca on March 30 in support of convoy GUS-37 bound for the United States. On April 8, the task group made contact with the *U-515* northwest of Madeira. Squadron aircraft and all destroyers but the *Forrest* closed on the submerged U-boat and attacked with rockets and depth charges throughout the night. Losing depth control on the afternoon of April 9, the U-boat was forced to surface amid the waiting ships and was immediately devastated by point-blank rocket and strafing fire. As Wildcat fighters riddled the boat with bullets, her captain, German U-boat ace Kapitänleutnant Werner Henke, ordered abandon ship, and the boat shortly thereafter went to the bottom. The destroyers rescued forty-five survivors, including Henke. The enemy crew was transported to the *Guadalcanal* and held as prisoners of war.

Interrogations provided little information about the U-boat and her operational activities. Although Henke was steadfast in his refusal to answer Gallery's questions, Gallery did learn through one of his men who stood guard over the

Kapitänleutnant Werner Henke, recipient of the "Knight's Cross of the Iron Cross," is shown after being transferred from a destroyer escort to the *Guadalcanal. U-BOOT-ARCHIV*

prisoners that Henke had sunk the British liner *Ceramic* in December 1942. The liner sank with the loss of 377 lives, including women and children. Henke had been accused by the British press of machine-gunning survivors in the water and was portrayed as brutal and inhumane. He became Britain's number one war criminal and was threatened with death if apprehended.

To get Henke to talk, Gallery played a little ruse. Ordering Henke to his cabin, Gallery showed him an official dispatch purportedly received from the Commander in Chief, Atlantic Fleet. It read: "British Admiralty requests you turn over crew of *U-515* to them when you refuel at Gibraltar. Considering crowded condition your ship authorize you to use your discretion." Lying alongside the document was a statement on legal paper with the ship's seal that said: "I, Captain Lieutenant Werner Henke, promise on my honor as a German officer that if I and my crew are imprisoned in the United States

instead of England, I will answer all questions truthfully when I am interrogated by Naval Intelligence Officers. Signed _____ Kapt. Lt. / Witness: D. V. Gallery, Capt. USN, J. S. Johnson, Cdr, USN."

Henke was reluctant to sign the paper and parried with Gallery about its legality under the Geneva Convention and international law. Finally, to save himself and his crew, he signed. Gallery had copies of the document distributed to Henke's crew, along with similar documents for their signatures. Seeing Henke's agreement, they all signed, and some of them talked freely afterwards.

When the prisoners arrived in the United States, Henke was sent to Fort Hunt, an interrogation center south of Washington, D.C. He refused to abide by the agreement, and the interrogators carried the ruse a step further. They told Henke he was being shipped to Canada, a move Henke knew would mean transfer to Britain and death. In the early evening of June 15, 1944, while walking in the prison's exercise compound, he made a rush for the surrounding barbed wire fence and started climbing it. When ordered to halt, he did not comply, and was shot and killed.

Before reaching Norfolk, the task group made an additional kill. On the night of April 10, it caught the *U-68* on the surface in broad moonlight three hundred miles south of the Azores and sank her with rockets and depth charges. The Can Do and her team reached Norfolk on April 26 with, as Captain Gallery boasted, "two pelts in our belt." This was indeed an achievement, especially during a time when U-boats were becoming difficult to find.

Standard operating procedure called for hunter-killer groups to hold departure conferences before taking to sea. These sessions were attended by the skippers of the task groups and staff members of the various Navy commands involved in antisubmarine warfare. They discussed communications plans, search procedures, surface and air operations, intelligence, and other related matters. When Commander Gallery took the floor, he proposed that when a surfaced U-boat was crippled and abandoned by her crew, instead of sending the submarine to the bottom with additional firepower, an attempt should be made to capture the boat as a prize and bring her back to the United States. He went on to relate his experience with the *U-515*, stating that after the crew had scrambled off, there was ample time to have sent over a prize crew to take control of the stricken U-boat. Thereafter, Gallery ordered each of the commanding officers of his destroyer screen to organize a boarding party, to be prepared to lower a whaleboat, and to keep a towline handy throughout the coming cruise.

Perhaps the seed for this rather audacious action had been planted while then-Commander Gallery had commanded the U.S. Navy Fleet Air Base at Reykjavik, Iceland (January 1942–May 1943). The primary mission of his fleet of Navy PBY (Catalina) patrol bombers had been to support the efforts of the Royal Air Force (RAF) and Royal Navy to escort convoys through the mid-ocean gap, where U-boats preyed on poorly protected convoys.

Flying fourteen-hour patrols, these lumbering seaplanes helped keep the Wolfpacks down, forcing them to use their precious batteries and to lose distance on convoys. One morning, the *U-570* surfaced to air out the boat on her first cruise. Unknowingly, she had surfaced about a half-mile from an RAF patrol plane, and within minutes the U-boat was the victim of a full depth charge load. Though the boat did not suffer fatal damage, she was crippled and could not submerge. Much to the surprise of the RAF pilots, the German crew scrambled onto the sub's deck, waving their hands and lifting a white sheet to indicate their surrender. The bomber radioed for assistance, and a tug was sent out to take the U-boat in tow. As the vessels neared the south coast of Iceland, the towline broke, and heavy seas washed the boat ashore on a sandy beach. The British later towed the U-boat to England, repaired her, and commissioned her in the Royal Navy as HMS *Graph*.

Gallery and his officers subsequently discussed capturing a U-boat with a PBY. It all seemed far-fetched, but as the officers' club bar stayed open late in

When the *Guadalcanal* departed Norfolk on her next cruise on May 15, 1944, her destroyer screen remained the same except that the *Forrest* was replaced by the USS *Jenks* (DE-665). *USNI*

Iceland in those days, weird plans were being hatched nightly. Now, in mid-1944, Captain Dan's experience with the *U-515* made capture of a U-boat seem quite possible, as his task group prepared once again to meet its undersea enemy.

After undergoing repairs, taking aboard replenishments, and refueling, the *Guadalcanal* and her escorts departed Norfolk on May 15, 1944. Her destroyer screen remained the same, with one exception: the *Forrest* was replaced by the USS *Jenks* (DE-665), the first DE to be launched in the Ohio River. She also had aboard a new air group, VC-8, under the command of Lieutenant N. D. Hodson, a veteran pilot who had flown with Fighter Squadron 6 off the USS *Enterprise* (CV-6) at Midway. He had since been awarded two Distinguished Flying Crosses while operating in an ASW mode off the *Card*. VC-8 consisted of twelve Avengers and nine Wildcats.

Soon after reaching the open seas, Gallery commenced around-the-clock flight operations. All pilots were checked out in night carrier takeoffs and landings. This capability had proved so successful during the previous cruise that Gallery made it standard procedure for pilots flying from the Can Do's deck.

The task group reached the Cape Verde Islands without incident and scoured the area for three weeks without any contacts. The group next searched the route from Biscay to Freetown, with no luck. At the time, U-boats transiting north and south chose island routes and hugged the African coast. The group finally returned to the Cape Verde Islands to continue search operations.

On May 30, 1944, the task group set a course for Casablanca to refuel. On the following day, however, the group was contacted by the Tenth Fleet and informed that a submarine was about three hundred miles north of their position and that they were to close the contact in all haste. Gallery immediately responded by organizing his forces to pursue a possible fleeing U-boat. The Tenth Fleet had picked up the U-boat by Huff Duff in March, and thereafter had been attempting to keep track of her, though it was difficult since she had sunk no ships during her month-long patrol. Finally, on May 27, she was picked up again off Portuguese Guinea. Tenth Fleet analysts tracked her as she moved north along the twentieth meridian (longitude), heading toward Cape Blanco, and then told Gallery about her.

On May 31, Gallery ordered Task Group 22.3 to head toward Casablanca for refuling and to search up the twentieth meridian on the way. Hodson's fliers patrolled 125 miles ahead of the force and 100 miles to the east and west. The U-boat was not aware of the search force that was fast approaching her position. VC-8 aircraft began to report a number of radar contacts and sonobuoy noises during their patrols.

On June 4—a clear Sunday morning—Gallery, while sitting in his skipper's chair on the bridge, heard the squawk box blare, "Frenchy to Bluejay—I have a possible sound contact!" (Frenchy was the code name for the *Chatelain;* Bluejay was Gallery). Although such reports were not unusual, Gallery radioed two of his escorts to assist Frenchy. The contact turned out to be the *U-505*. The battle was about to begin.

CHAPTER 5

The Last Patrol of the U-505

On November 18, 1943, Oberleutnant zur See Harald Lange came aboard as the new commanding officer of the *U-505*. Lange was an experienced seaman, being a merchant ship officer by trade, and having served aboard minesweepers and patrol boats at the beginning of World War II before transferring to the U-boat service in 1941. After submarine training and completion of a commanding officer's program, he was assigned as first watch officer, then acting commanding officer, of the *U-180* prior to receiving orders to take command of the *U-505*. Above all, Lange was a mature officer who at forty-one years of age was noted for his leadership and personnel skills. He was selected specifically to take over a boat and crew that had been traumatized by a series of morale-shattering events. It was not long before the crew responded to his calm, steady hand, and Lange gained their respect and loyalty.

This artist's conception of the *U-505*, drawn days after its capture, shows how the boat possibly appeared during Lange's tour. When Loewe commanded the boat, she had a deck gun forward of the conning tower. *MSI*

Oberleutnant zur See Harald Lange took command of the *U-505* in November 1943. He may have been personally selected by Admiral Dönitz to take over this boat and crew, which had been traumatized by a series of morale-shattering events. In his short time aboard, his calm, steady hand gained the respect and loyalty of the crew. *MSI*

On December 21, Lange departed Lorient, but he was soon forced to return to port because of a leak in the cable lead-in for the multiple hydrophones. Repairs were made, and the *U-505* sailed again on Christmas Day 1943. As the boat transited the Bay of Biscay, encountering heavy rains and a roiling sea, the hydrophone operator picked up distant explosive noises. A surface battle was taking place in the bay between British and German forces. The British cruisers HMS *Glasgow* and HMS *Enterprise* were attacking German torpedo boats and destroyers escorting the *Alsterufer* (a blockade-runner). During the encounter, the Germans lost destroyer *Z27* and torpedo boats *T25* and *T26*. Lange was ordered by headquarters to close the area of battle and rescue survivors.

Arriving on December 29, the *U-505* picked up *T25* survivors along with crewmen of the *U-106*, which *T25* had rescued. Many of the men were sick from swallowing diesel fuel and seawater and were half frozen from swimming in a bitterly cold sea. Finding no additional survivors, the *U-505* was ordered to Brest, home base of the Fifth Torpedo Flotilla. As the boat came alongside the dock in one of the huge bunkers, a torpedo boat sailor eager to get ashore slipped from a ladder and fell on the U-boat's helmsman, knocking him down. As a result, the boat swerved and hit the concrete bay, bending the shaft of the forward dive plane. Since a new shaft could only be found at Bordeaux and the *U-505* was unable to dive, a new shaft was sent to Brest where repair work on the boat lasted more than two months. Although the boat was now damaged once again, and for several days the crew had been forced to endure extra-cramped spaces, inconvenience, and nauseous odors from having almost double the normal number of people aboard (many of whom were seasick), the successful rescue operation had lifted the morale of the crew. They felt the boat had gained some stature from her participation in the operation. At last they had arrived at a home base (Brest) in good stead; in fact, dignitaries and a brass band awaited their arrival.

Lange and his crew pose for a photo before leaving on the last patrol of the *U-505*. *Special Collections & Archives Division, Nimitz Library, U.S. Naval Academy*

Lange sailed from Brest on March 16, 1944, in company with two Type VIIC boats, *U-373* and *U-471*. His assigned area of operation was the ocean approaches to Freetown on the west coast of Africa. It was to be the last patrol for the U-boat. Lange quickly cleared the Bay of Biscay and in a little over a month reached the waters off Freetown, where he patrolled the coastal areas, often entering ports in search of merchant targets. Failing to sight a single ship, in late May he decided to return to Brest, frustrated that no sinking pennants would be flying from his aerial periscope as he entered port. As he sailed north, however, he was continually harassed by patrolling Allied aircraft and had to spend much of the time submerged. However, because the boat had no snorkel, she could not recharge her batteries without surfacing, and the more time on the surface, the more danger. Given the constant enemy air coverage, Lange believed he was in the area of a U.S. hunter-killer group.

Since he was far out to sea, Lange decided to distance himself from the enemy force by sailing east toward Africa. He ran as often as possible on the surface during daylight hours to recharge his batteries, believing his adversary would not think him foolish enough to risk detection and thus would ease its vigilance. Although his thinking proved to be correct, the course he had chosen would soon bring him into contact with U.S. Task Group 22.3.

As it happens, a crewman was keeping a diary of this last cruise. Hence, we are able to provide a detailed account of the *U-505*'s last patrol up to the events of June 4. Here, however, we do not see things as usual from an official, operational viewpoint. Instead, in this account we look through the eyes of an ordinary crew member discussing his simple human concerns. As the days pass, we hear of an unbearable heat and sweat in a boat submerged at the tropics; we read of a deep yearning for the sight of green forests and gardens; we hear of an enlisted sailor's envy of the butter cream served with the officers' pastry; and we listen to a variety of other complaints, occasional delights, and frequent anxieties.*

16.3 [March   Sailed (from) Brest 1830 hrs. 235
  16, 1944]   until 24.3.44, then 210—25.3 180

14th day

It is fourteen days today that we departed from the base. Throughout the entire period we have seen neither the sky nor the sun. The days go by slowly. We have finally crossed the dangerous area of maximum air threat— the Bay of Biscay. Hence was our transit: we hardly had time to breathe some fresh air and charge our batteries, and down below we went again. For the past three days we have been experiencing rough seas, sea state 3–6, high swell and wind. The crockery is flying all around the inside of the boat, and

---

*This excerpt from a *U-505* personal diary is reprinted with the permission of the Naval Historical Center, Washington, D.C., holder of the original document. The author was most likely Oberfunkmaat Gottfried Fischer, the only *U-505* sailor killed during the battle that led to the capture of the submarine. This identification is based on an entry of May 7, 1944, in which the author refers to himself as the leading radioman. At that time, the leading radioman aboard the *U-505* was Fischer. Identification of the probable author was made by Dave Kohnen, the *U-505* Exhibit Developer at the Museum of Science and Industry, Chicago, Illinois.

an escape breathing apparatus nearly hit my head. It is a relief to submerge in this kind of weather. Miraculously, even though we had pudding, apple compote and other sweets, everything stayed inside me. Small wonder, after all, our ancestors were all seafarers!

1 April

Tonight, while we ran on the surface, the sea was exceptionally vicious. Sea state 6–7. The boat rolls and pitches even at depth of 7–20 meters [22–63 ft]. And then we sit (or rather stand) in our radio room and monitor our equipment, and fret whether the enemy has already detected us. It is tiresome work. We are on a south-westerly heading of 120. The warmer climate is already beginning to make itself felt. How is it going to get once we cross the equator in a few days?

3 April

Mom's birthday. It's 1230h and I've just wolfed down a cutlet, which would not have gone down well had we been on the surface. What are you having today? A decent birthday dinner, I hope. Grune Klosse [literally, green dumplings, a

U-505 crewman sleeve rating patch for specialty in communications (radioman). *MSI*

regional German specialty]. We were treated with fresh rolls today, as if to mark the occasion. 3 per person. Have the flowers I have asked for been delivered? We've spent the past two nights on the surface. During that time, with heavy seas going, I was unable to eat anything at all. . . . It is always lunch I have to skip, because we've turned the day into night and vice versa. So, when it is noon at home, we're submerged and we call it midnight over here. Due to the heavy seas, which meet us head on, we've made only slow progress. Even though we run on the surface 12 hours every day. Our area of operations is still unknown, we don't know whether we're bound for America or Africa. The

Crew members of a U-boat crowd the conning tower area while surfaced to enjoy fresh air and perhaps a brief tropical shower. The heat inside was often stifling, the air dull and sultry. Sweat poured down the bodies of the men. Nearly everyone had ailments—headaches, fevers, and colds. Yet they endured and performed their duties. *MSI* mystery should be solved within the next few days, once we get our instructions by wireless.

Easter Sunday, 2100hrs

We have just finished our coffee break. Plum Cakes were made to celebrate the holiday. In spite of the Sunday feeling the atmosphere is a bit tense. The officers and senior petty officers had butter cream with their pastry. And I thought there were supposed to be no exceptions on a U-boat on combat patrol. 3 days ago we rendezvoused with *U-123*. Since it was on its way back, they took on board everybody's letters to their families. Since two days our threat receiver is down. Troubleshooting. To wrap up the day I spent nearly 4 hours repairing [the equipment] and sweating.

We have been on a 180 heading for a few days now. The sea has calmed down but the heat has become intense.

14 April

It is 4 weeks today that we've left base. What a thankless task, and we have got another 3 months to go. We have been assigned our area of operations by wireless today. The West-African Gold Coast. We're on a heading of 210 with the [Cape Verde] Islands just on our beam. Unfortunately we're not going anywhere close to the equator. I would have loved to take part in a crossing the line ceremony, even though I'm certain that Neptune would not have shown mercy with us. Fortunately, we were able to fix our threat receiver again—after 4 long

night shifts. Rations have been reduced drastically. We have already gone three evenings without sausage. They say that provisions have to last for a total of 17 weeks, even though we only took on provisions (including fresh groceries) for 14 weeks. That's how it is being a poor U-Boots-Schwein, as they call us. Yesterday we logged our 200th hour of surface transit during this patrol.

15 April

All quiet, course 240. On the wireless we caught part of the armed forces' situation report. We heard about the air raids on central Germany. I hope everything is all right back home. Our position is 14 North, another 10 days until we reach the area of operations. Sea state: 3–3.

17 April

Yesterday we had the first passive sonar contact since a long time. Periscope depth. However, the swell is too heavy to see anything. It was mid-day, about 1300h. Today, in the course of the afternoon we picked up detonations at a very great distance from the boat. Probably flak or light bombs.

25 April

We've reached our area of operations. It took us 5 weeks to get here. The age of the boat is telling again. The door on one of the torpedo tubes does not close properly. Of all things this has to happen now and here. Yesterday the echo sounder broke down. Just our luck. Repaired it and fitted new neon lighting-tube. For a few days now we have been "enjoying" the tropical heat. Everybody is perspiring freely. Even in the bunks it takes only a few minutes until everything is soaked wet. From sweat mind you! Water temperature is 29 C [84 F]. The temperature inside the boat is 35–40 [95–105 F]. And this is only the beginning. The heat is so intense that I sometimes wish I could shed my skin.

30 April

The heat is so unbearable that I'm not really in the mood to write anything. I avoid all unnecessary movement within the boat. Thus I spend most of my off-watch time in my soaked-through bunk. The day before yesterday we sighted our first steamer. After a very swiftly executed interception maneuver, the ship turned out to be a neutral Portuguese. He was lit up like a Christmas tree.

3 May

The day before yesterday I had my second glimpse of daylight through the periscope since we left base. The first time, 8 days ago—it was about 1800h—it had been a brilliant day. My eyes hurt from the unaccustomed brightness. We reached 3° north latitude, and only a mere 200 nm separate us from the equator. We won't get there, though. Instead, we'll hang around close to the shore and prey on passing steamers. Unfortunately, with the exception of the neutral ship, nobody has done us a favor to show up yet. Just now we've gone up to periscope depth again to survey the area. We're at 7–20m again [periscope depth] and the Commanding Officer announces over the intercom that anybody who wishes to see two young sharks should come to the bridge. Indeed, when I looked through the periscope I saw two of those cute animals that had somehow latched on to the 2cm gun and were fooling around, enjoying a free ride. What a nice diversion!

7 May—Middle of Tour!

A few minutes ago the CO announced over the loudspeaker that we have completed half of our war patrol. He stressed that it wasn't easy for anyone to hang around in these waters, hugging the coast and waiting for the eventual enemy vessel to appear. The day before yesterday the bridge ordered all communications equipment be switched off because of a severe thunderstorm. Almost instantly the CO ordered the leading radioman [petty officer] of the watch to strip to his trousers and come up onto the conning tower. And so, on 4 May in the evening between 2200 and 2230, I stood outside on the conning tower for the very first time on this patrol. I breathed the fresh and humid air of Africa and let the rain wash down my body. What a feast!! The patrol is winding down now. In 14 days we will leave our area of operations and begin our journey home.

12 May

We're standing in closer to shore again. We had ventured further out during the moonlit nights. The day before yesterday we spotted a steamer while running at periscope depth. We planned to intercept him with flank speed on the surface after dawn and put a torpedo into him. Unfortunately we were forced underwater by a destroyer or something even bigger. Else there's nothing new to report. I've got a nice little inflammation on my thumb, which I believe needs to be punctured.

15 May

Sent off our situation report by wireless this morning at 0100h. The signal was received well with good strength. Not bad, given the distance between the African west coast and Germany. And considering how small our U-boat transmitter is. I split my scalp on a metal ventilator during a crash dive. Well, these things happen. 6 more days until we begin our journey back home. Thus we could be back the end of June or early July.

19 May

The heat inside the boat is unbearable. Sweat is pouring down my body as I write. In the radio room it never gets below 38 C [100 F]. The stale and fetid air makes it all even worse. We have only one consolation: in 5–6 days the heat will become less. The day after tomorrow we will head back home.

23 May

Today we finally set course for home. I had a contact [on threat receiver] at around 0400 today. Submerged. We surfaced again after 1 1/2 hours and immediately picked up a radar emission. Submerged again. After that: 2 acoustic contacts. Probably a Hunter-Killer-Group made up of destroyers and patrol craft. Periscope depth. Propeller noise faded after one hour. Continue transit.

30 May

We've spent the Whitsuntide holiday more or less happily. One of our leading seamen has proven his talent as a baker by producing a little cake for each of us. He used empty tin cans as forms. Otherwise the holidays were like every other day at sea. No radio, no music from the record player, no light, and very little air. Today was a particularly dismal day. Within minutes of surfacing during the evening hours we picked up radar emissions. We had no choice but to go down again. We went through that routine four times. In the end we remained on the surface and manned the antiaircraft guns. After a short while we picked up a second radar emission. Submerged again. Probably a surface antisubmarine group working together with aircraft. Now we tried out something which, I believe, is not commonly done. At a distance of about 100nm from the shore, shortly after noon, we surfaced and raced eastward, away from the radar emissions, for half an hour. The enemy was certainly unprepared for this, because we remained undetected. Now the CO wants to continue the transit underwater throughout the entire 31st of May, and surface again only in the small hours of the 1st of June. Therefore we are conserving air and electricity. All off-duty personnel are confined to their bunks. Even so we will be gasping for air during last few hours. It really is a comforting thought that we'll be back home in 4–5 weeks. I can't wait to see the sights of green forests and gardens again, of which we have been deprived for so long.

Sunday, 4 June

Forenoon, 1100h. Submerged. I hope that we are through the worst of it. We spent 4 hours on the surface today, and we'll try to remain on the surface the entire night tomorrow. We had to conserve air during the past few days, because every time we only had a few minutes on the surface. 10 contacts in 4 days is quite a lot. We are at Latitude 22° north. . . .

The chronological narrative ends at 11:00 AM on June 4. At noon of that same day, the hydrophone operator picked up faint underwater noises, and Lange brought the boat to periscope depth. Climbing into the conning tower and raising the periscope slowly, he sighted a destroyer and distant carrier. He slammed down the scope, yelled "Destroyer!" and ordered an immediate dive. As the ship lost buoyancy, he fired a T5 acoustic torpedo from a stern tube toward a distant aircraft carrier. He released decoys, but it was too late, as depth charges were already exploding around the boat.

Everything seemed to happen in seconds: the stern torpedo room flooding was out of control; the boat soon filled with seawater and surpassed her maximum depth. The *U-505* seemed destined to sink in the dark depths. Lange knew only one way to save his crew, and that was by surfacing the boat. He gave the order, and the *U-505* began to rise slowly to the surface. As she broke water, she met a hail of gunfire from U.S. carrier aircraft and escort destroyers.

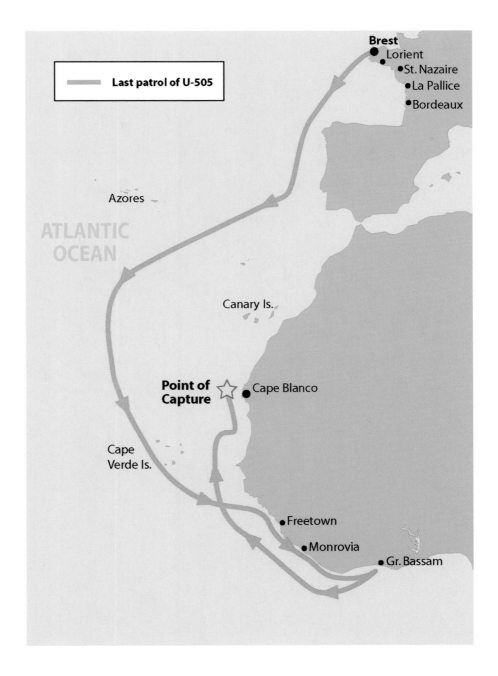

Track of the *U-505*'s last patrol. The U-boat was at sea for 81 days and traveled 7,977 miles before her capture on June 4, 1944. *Infinite Photo & Imaging*

CHAPTER 6

The Battle and the Capture

When the destroyer escort *Chatelain* reported "possible contact," the destroyer escort commander aboard the *Pillsbury*, Commander Frederick S. Hall, USN, took charge of the remaining escorts. His title was Commander Escort Division Four (ComCortDiv 4). The Can Do (*Guadalcanal*) streamed her "foxer" gear (a noise-making device towed astern to foil acoustic torpedoes), headed away from the contact so as not to interfere with the escort attack, sounded General Quarters (all hands to their battle stations), and ordered the ready hunter-killer group of one Wildcat and one Avenger to stand by for takeoff. Wildcat fighters flown by Ensign John W. Cadle Jr. and Lieutenant Wolffe W. Roberts were already in the air and were notified of the contact and told to assist the *Chatelain*.

NARA

At 11:12 AM, the *Chatelain* reported the contact as a submarine. Four minutes later she fired a barrage of hedgehogs with no effect. The sub was maneuvering and preparing to go deep. Before she could submerge further, pilots Cadle and Roberts sighted the sub running just under the surface. They advised the *Chatelain* to change course, and then they fired bursts of machine-gun fire into the water to indicate the position of the sub. Following the directions of the pilots, the destroyer made sonar contact and fired a spread of twelve six-hundred-pound depth charges, all set to explode shallow. Ensign Cadle shouted, "You've struck oil, Frenchy [the code name for the *Chatelain*]; sub is surfacing."

Within minutes the sub surfaced in plain view of the entire task group and some eight hundred yards from the *Chatelain*. Depth charge plumes were rising all around her as she broke the surface, with white water pouring off her rusty sides. The sub had been taken completely by surprise. Hearing noises in the seas above, Oberleutnant zur See Lange upped periscope in swelling seas to find enemy warships and aircraft surrounding him. His crewmen, who were having lunch at the time, left their tables and scrambled to their action stations.

The *Chatelain, Jenks, Pillsbury,* and the attacking planes opened fire with 3-inch shells, .50-caliber slugs, and 20- and 40-mm explosive bullets. At one point, seeing the sub turning and believing she might be firing a torpedo, the *Chatelain* attacked the *U-505* with her own torpedo, which went wide. During the attack, Captain Gallery restrained the *Guadalcanal, Pope,* and *Flaherty* from firing because the other escorts and aircraft had the sub under continuous fire.

At 11:24 AM, the *Guadalcanal* launched her ready hunter-killer group (a Wildcat and Avenger), with orders not to use any weapons that could sink the

Attacked by American destroyers and aircraft, the *U-505*'s captain surfaced the boat and ordered "Abandon ship and sink the boat." All the German crew members obeyed. Here some of the crewmen and a couple of rafts are visible in the water to the stern of the circling U-boat. *NARA*

sub unless she started to submerge. A delay in launching this group was necessary because the original contact had placed the sub in a perfect position to fire torpedoes at the carrier, and Gallery wanted to get outside of torpedo range before turning into the wind. He suspected the sub already had fired a salvo of torpedoes at his ship. The loss of the *Block Island* just six days earlier was still very much on his mind. According to Signalman Second Class Frank P. Denardo aboard the *Chatelain,* after the ship had fired her hedgehogs, "We noticed she [the sub] had fired a torpedo at the carrier. We immediately altered course to intercept the torpedo with our ship, to save the carrier. I remember watching the torpedo come at our port side, and nothing happened. I rushed to starboard and watched it go by. It was set for the carrier and not us." Later statements by prisoners confirmed the firing of an acoustic torpedo at the carrier.

As Gallery and men aboard the carrier and the other two escorts looked on, the three destroyer escorts and the two aircraft already aloft continued to attack the sub. Soon her crew emerged from the conning tower and deck hatches to abandon the stricken vessel. At 11:27 AM, ComCortDiv 4 ordered all hands to cease firing. The sub at this point appeared to have a jammed rudder and was running in a tight circle to starboard, fully surfaced, and the U.S. forces assumed that most, if not all, of her crew had escaped the boat.

German crewman Mechanikerobergefreiter Wolfgang Gerhardt Schiller vividly recalled the moment of attack and his escape from the boat.

On Sunday, June 4th, in the early morning around six, it was ordered "Torpedomen to battle stations!" Later, when the commander surfaced with the submarine and put up the periscope, he immediately got cover fire from aircraft. He retracted the periscope, reversed course, came out with the periscope again, and was always announcing at each moment, "Destroyer!" Consequently he said, "Dive!" We reached fifty, sixty meters, then the depth charges came. After the depth charges had fallen, we got the message from the sternpost, "Rudder taken out—water breach!" The commander gave the order (which I heard in the speaking tube), "Surface—every man off boat!" When I told that to my mates, everyone took off to midship. I was pretty much the last one who came out of the bow torpedo room toward the central control room. There were many people who all wanted to get up this ladder. I saw a fur jacket lying on the way to the control room, and because I didn't know how cold the water was or the temperature outside, I put it on. And then when I got to the conning tower, a crew member held me back and had me wait until enemy aircraft had passed overhead. He let me go then and when I came up, I saw a plane flying at us from the starboard side. I didn't know at that point whether it would fire. I jumped sternward . . . down from the conning tower and made a headlong dive and was in the water. The sub cruised in a circle, so I got away from the boat pretty quickly.

ComCortDiv 4 ordered the *Jenks* and the *Chatelain* to pick up survivors and ordered "Away boarders," thereby sending the *Pillsbury*'s boarding party toward the sub. A half hour later, the Can Do headed back toward the scene of action to get her own boarding parties aboard the boat, having meanwhile recovered the aircraft that had assisted in the attack. The carrier boarding parties left the ship at 12:30 PM. Maschinmaat Mate Karl Springer related his exit from the battered sub and his finding the body of the only German crewman to be killed in the battle, Gottfried Fischer.

I had just got off duty and was at my battle station, which was the forward battery main switch, next to the commander's quarters, when I heard the commander say, "Every man off the sub!" And then it hit the fan. I got out pretty early, because I was right near the conning tower hatch. The commander first, then the radioman second class came out second. He and others practically flew out with me, we had so much excess pressure . . . because the pipes were all shot. And as I came out of the conning tower hatch I saw "Gogi" lying topside. I just picked him up and said to him, Gottfried was his name, "Gogi, come on!" and then I saw that he had been shot dead. I went down on the deck and tried to get forward to the front of the conning tower, where a big inflatable raft was stowed. We got it out and then they stopped shooting! Thank God! We inflated the raft, which was filling with water,

The boat from the *Pillsbury* approaches the *U-505,* which still is under way, though abandoned by her crew. Boarding personnel faced the risk that the *U-505* might blow up at any moment in accordance with the usual German abandonment tactics of setting nine-minute scuttle charges. *MSI*

got in and maneuvered it away from the sub. Apart from the early firing at the boat by the aircraft and ships around us, and our frantic scramble to clear the sub, our escape went smoothly. We were first picked up by a destroyer and then brought over to the aircraft carrier. Before we were transferred to the carrier, the destroyer men searched us thoroughly. We heard later that the Americans had had bad experiences with Japanese military who would surrender carrying hidden explosives. Once on board the carrier we were ordered to strip after which we were sprayed with fresh water.

We had a difficult time after capture. On the aircraft carrier we were housed in a shaft under the flight deck where there were big exhaust systems of the engines.

Meanwhile, the *Pillsbury* had lowered her whaleboat, which began to pursue the sub as she circled around. But in the struggle to come alongside the runaway sub, the bow diving plane of the *U-505* put a hole in the *Pillsbury* so that two main compartments, including one engine room, were flooded to the waterline, forcing her to haul clear and go dead in the water. Meanwhile, however, someone from the *Pillsbury*'s boarding party, commanded by Lieutenant (junior grade) Albert L. David, was able to jump from the plunging whaleboat onto the heaving deck of the sub, the whaleboat's bowline in hand. From the carrier's bridge, according to Gallery, "it looked for all the world like a cowboy roping a wild horse." When the first man leaped aboard, Gallery grabbed the TBS and broadcast to the *Pillsbury*, "Heigho Silver—ride 'em cowboy!"

The *Pillsbury* stands by the *U-505,* which is still under way. It was during this period that the destroyer escort was holed by the U-boat's bow diving plane. *NARA*

Statement of Commanding Officers of the *U-505*

USS *Guadalcanal* at Sea, June 15, 1944

On June 4, about 1200, I was moving underwater on my general course when noise bearings were reported. I tried to move to the surface to get a look with the periscope. The sea was slightly rough and the boat was hard to keep on periscope depth. I saw one destroyer [to the] West, another [to the] Southwest, and a third at 160 degrees. [At] about 140 degrees I saw, far off, a mass that might belong to a carrier. Destroyer #1 (West) was nearest to me, at about 1/2 mile. Further off I saw an airplane, but I had no chance to look after this again because I did not want my periscope seen. I dove again and quickly, with noise, because I couldn't keep the boat on periscope depth safely. I suppose that I must have been seen by the airplane because if these heavy boats are rolling under the surface they make a large wake.

I had not yet reached the safety depth when I received two bombs at a distance and then close after them two heavy dashes, from depth charges perhaps. Water broke in; light and all electrical machinery went off and the rudders jammed. Not knowing exactly the whole damage or why they continued bombing me, I gave the order to bring the boat to the surface by [compressed] air.

When the boat surfaced, I was the first on the bridge and saw now four destroyers around me, shooting at my boat with .50-caliber and antiaircraft. The nearest one, now [at about] 110 degrees, was shooting with shrapnel into the conning tower. I got wounded by numerous shots and shrapnel in both knees and legs and fell down. At once I gave the order to leave the boat and to sink her. My chief officer, who came after me onto the bridge, lay on the starboard side with blood streaming over his face. Then I gave a course order to starboard in order to [help] make the aft part of the conning tower [shield an area from] the destroyer to get my crew out of the boat safely. I lost consciousness for I don't know how long, but when I awoke again a lot of my men were on the deck and I made an effort to raise myself and haul myself aft. By the explosion of a shell I was blown from the first antiaircraft deck down onto the main deck; the explosion hit near the starboard machine gun.

I saw a lot of my men running on the main deck, getting pipe boats [individual life rafts] clear. In a conscious moment, I gave notice to the chief that I was still on the main deck. How I got over the side I don't know exactly, but I suppose by another explosion. Despite my injuries I somehow managed to keep afloat until two members of my group brought me a pipe boat and hoisted me into it; my life-jacket had been punctured with shrapnel and was no good. During all this time I could not see much because in the first seconds of the fight I had been hit in the

Oberleutnant zur See Harald Lange, last captain of the *U-505. U-BOOT-ARCHIV*

face and eye with splinters of wood blasted from the deck; my right eyelid was pierced with a splinter.

When I sat in the pipe boat I could see my boat for the last time. Some of my men were still aboard her, throwing more pipe boats into the water. I ordered the men around me to give three cheers for our sinking boat.

After this I was picked up by a destroyer, where I received first-aid treatment. Later, on this day, I was transferred to the carrier hospital and here I have been told by the Captain that they captured my boat and prevented it from sinking.

Harald Lange
Oberleutnant zur See d.Res.

Before the German crew abandoned the *U-505*, they opened a six-inch strainer in the Control Room, and water began rushing in. Zenon Lukosius of the *Pillsbury* boarding party found the cover (here shown chained to the strainer) and dogged it back in place, helping to save the boat. *MSI*

The "cowboy" found Gottfried Fischer, dead, on the deck. The boarders had no idea how many men might still be below setting demolition charges. Though only the bow and conning tower were visible above the water (the boat was down by the stern), without hesitation, Lieutenant David, Torpedoman Third Class Arthur K. Knispel, and Radioman Second Class Stanley E. Wdowiak plunged down the conning tower hatch to capture and save the boat. They found no one below and immediately went to work closing valves.

Lieutenant David called to the men on deck for help, and Motor Mechanist's Mate First Class Zenon B. Lukosius jumped through the hatch down into the boat. His help proved invaluable, because he found and replaced the cover of a strainer (six inches in diameter) that was allowing a large stream of water to pour into the boat. Not knowing at what moment the submarine might either blow up or sink, the four men quickly turned to and seized all the important-looking papers they could find, passing them to boarding party members on the deck.

At about 12:40 PM, boarding parties from the *Guadalcanal* arrived. One boat literally arrived with a bang, being picked up by the sea and deposited bodily on the deck of the sub. This crash caused some concern to even the most stouthearted men from the *Pillsbury,* down below, who had no idea

Capping the Sea Strainer

Excerpts from an interview with Motor Machinist's Mate Zenon B. Lukosius of the USS *Pillsbury* (DE-133), who along with seven shipmates led by Medal of Honor recipient Lieutenant (jg) Albert L. David, was first to board the abandoned U-boat. Lukosius actually prevented the boat from sinking when he was able to cap an open sea strainer.

When they ceased firing, I was still in the engine room, and when the call came "Forty Boarding Party Away," I left my station, went up on top, got in a whaleboat, and we headed for the submarine. She was far down enough in the water where we could get alongside and jump from our boat to the top of her rail and down the conning tower hatch. We were surprised that the lights were still on and the motors were still running. I was going toward the engine room, and to my left I could see water coming in through a sea strainer. The cover was off, and water was flowing in. That's how they were going to scuttle the submarine. With the right amount of water they were going to tilt the boat where she was going to slide down. I asked one of the Germans I met later, "Hans, why didn't you open up the valve more, because when I went down, the water was just coming over the edge, and I could pick the cover up?" He told me he didn't open it further because he knew if he opened the valve all the way, he couldn't have reached the top of the sub before she went down. . . .

I found and put the cover on the sea strainer, and there was enough room that I could slip the wing nuts on and tighten the cover, which stopped the flow of water. But other valves were open, and we had to find them and shut these down. If Hans had fully opened this particular valve, water would have gushed in, and there's no way I could have put the cover on unless I knew where the valve was to shut it off. He told me that within another five minutes, there would have been enough water coming through the strainer that it would have tilted the sub so that there would be no saving it.

MSI

what was happening on deck. The *Guadalcanal* boarding parties, under the command of Navy Commander Earl Trosino (who relieved David) and Lieutenant D. E. Hampton, immediately set to work looking for demolition charges that might have been set, closing valves and watertight doors, rigging gasoline-driven billy pumps (for dewatering spaces), and assisting in the removal of official-looking papers, two Enigma machines, codebooks, and what appeared to be messages. Trosino later commented that he felt at home on any sea vessel, since he had spent most of his life as a chief engineer in Sun Oil tankers. Shortly thereafter, Gallery got a message from Trosino: "We must be towed to stay afloat."

Boarding party members from the *Pillsbury* and the *Guadalcanal* are shown on the bow of the U-boat preparing for the towing of the boat; one of them is signaling with semaphore flags. Other crewmen are inside the U-boat shutting down valves and moving equipment. The conning tower hatch had to be kept closed to keep waves of water from pouring into the U-boat. *NARA*

Boarders Away!

Excerpts from an interview with Phil Trusheim, coxswain of the *Pillsbury* boat crew.

My job was to take the boarding party to the submarine in a whaleboat. Three of us stayed on the boat while nine men went down through the conning tower hatch, led by Lieutenant (jg) David. In about ten minutes all kinds of stuff started coming out of the tower hatch, and we put them all in the whaleboat—things like guns, binoculars, and a bunch of what we were told were important papers and documents. One of the items was a decoder machine. We recognized it because we knew that all subs had them. They got a lot of codebooks and radio data in the radio room. Then, after it was all over, they said they had found thirteen or fourteen charges that the Germans had forgot to set. But we didn't know their status at that time.... It took almost an hour before the boarding party came out from the carrier to relieve our guys. I guess we were there about two hours before we headed back to the *Pillsbury*.

The *Pillsbury* boarding party goes down into the sub while coxswain Phil Trusheim keeps the boat handy. *NARA*

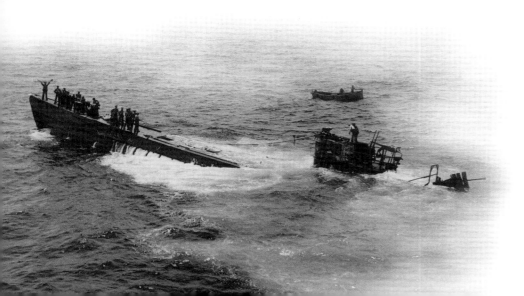

Interrogations

Excerpts from an interview with Commander Earl Trosino, chief engineer of the *Guadalcanal*

One afternoon after they transferred the prisoners from the destroyer to the *Guadalcanal,* Gallery brought the prisoners into his room one by one. Our interpreter (the ship's physician, Doctor Monat), the executive officer, and myself were in the room. He would ask them questions and they would say, "Heil, Hitler. I am a soldier of the German Reich. You will not betray your country; I will not betray mine!" And Dan would say, "Get 'im the hell out of here."

One tall, slender fellow came in, and he leaned over the table and said, "I would like to talk to you, but if I say something, they will take it out on my family." He was a Czech and Gallery understood. One Polish boy said the Nazis had killed his mother and his uncle and he was conscripted into the submarine service. . . . Gallery accepted that boy, and he wrote out a fake message that the boy had died and he was buried at sea. . . . His name was Ewald Felix, and he was turned over to the master-at-arms, who got him a pair of dungarees, a blue shirt, and a white hat so nobody would recognize him.

The crew on the *Guadalcanal* accepted him, and he was a nice kid, very cooperative. Every night I would come back from working in the boat and bring him up to my room. . . . He always put his head down, never looked at me. And to relax him I took out cigarettes and gave one to Benny [Coxswain Leon Bednarczyk], our interpreter, and one to Felix and told him, "Go ahead and light up." He answered that officers didn't give cigarettes to sailors in the German Navy. In response to my question as to why he didn't look me in the eye when I asked him questions, he said, "If I looked in an officer's face, they would slap me."

He would explain anything I didn't understand about the boat—how to bleed the torpedoes, getting air into the tanks so that I could blow ballast. . . . So I asked Gallery to let me take Felix over with me. He was hesitant. I said, "Don't worry about him because I question him every night to find out if I did things right!" Finally Gallery said okay. But they were scared that Felix would do something to the sub . . . but he was as loyal as any man in the U.S. Navy because he saw the freedom he had . . . and he asked our interpreter to ask the Captain if he could join the U.S. Navy. He would stay the rest of his life and never ask for any pay. . . . When he went aboard he found the line where the sub's fans were and started them, and we got circulation going throughout the boat. It cooled it off and it smelled better; then we worked to finish pumping out the control room, then the engine room and the after end of the boat until we came to full surface trim.

The salvage party in front of the conning tower of the *U-505.* Captain Gallery is at top center, with Commander Trosino to his right, and Lieutenant David to Gallery's left. The Polish crewman of the sub who helped Trosino is seated in the front row, third from the viewer's left. *NARA*

At 2:15 PM, Gallery began to maneuver the *Guadalcanal* to put her stern alongside the bow of the submarine, and within ten minutes, a 1-1/4-inch wire was made fast, and the sub was taken under tow. Some on the carrier endured several anxious moments as the *Guadalcanal*'s stern was at one point about fifty feet from the snout of the sub, with the torpedo tubes pointed directly at the ship. Probably most hands had the same thought about this time: "Suppose there was just one German left on the sub?" Fortunately, there was not!

At 7:16 PM, the Can Do boarding parties were brought back on board, together with hundreds more confidential documents. The task group squared away for the night, its prize flying a large set of U.S. colors, with a German naval flag below the victor's flag. The flags were flying from a boat hook planted in a voice tube on the sub's bridge.

With the U-boat dangerously close to sinking, the boarding party determines she must be towed to be kept afloat. Here a whaleboat delivers a lead towline to the sailors on the bow. *NARA*

While taking the sub in tow, Gallery was gravely concerned about whether the *Pillsbury* would remain afloat. He was also unsure whether he had enough fuel to make Casablanca. The *Flaherty* suddenly reported that she was investigating a disappearing radar blip. At the same time, the *Chatelain* radioed that she was starting a firing approach on a sound contact. Taking all of these things into consideration, Gallery decided to head for the nearest friendly port, which was Dakar. He signaled his intentions to Commander in Chief, U.S. Atlantic Fleet (CincLant), and headed for the port city in Senegal.

Boarding and salvage crew members gather on the bow of the U-boat to rig gasoline-powered pumps to remove water from the U-boat's interior. *NARA*

A few hours later he received a message from CincLant that fuel and a tug were on their way and that the task group was to make port at Casablanca. Washington intelligence agencies knew that Dakar was full of spies, and if the task group had gone there, news of the capture would quickly reach Germany. So at 7:35 PM, Gallery set course for the passage between Africa and the Canary Islands. The official time and position of the surrender and capture of the *U-505* were 1157 Zebra (Zebra = Greenwich mean time, the universal navigational time reference point), 21 degrees, 30 minutes north latitude, and 19 degrees, 20 minutes west longitude.

At midnight on June 4–5, the 1-1/4-inch wire towline broke. The sub's rudder was still jammed hard right, and she had been towing well out to the starboard quarter of the carrier. For the rest of the night, task group escorts patrolled around the sub while air patrols provided additional protection. This delay gave the *Pillsbury,* running on one screw and accompanied by the *Pope,* a chance to catch up to the task group.

At dawn on June 5, the *Guadalcanal* put her bow alongside the bow of the sub and passed her a 2-1/4-inch wire towline. The working party on the sub had been instructed to get the rudder amidships, and as soon as they reported that the rudder had been turned as ordered, the Can Do got under way again for Casablanca. While passing the towline, the sub seemed to be floating somewhat lower than she had been on the previous day.

Landing flaps lowered, a *Guadalcanal* Avenger makes its final approach to the carrier with the *U-505* in tow. *Special Collections & Archives Division, Nimitz Library, U.S. Naval Academy*

When the ship started moving, it became apparent that the *U-505*'s rudder was still hard right. The members of the boarding party thought they had moved it electronically from the control tower, but they had not gone all the way aft to the hand steering gear in the after torpedo compartment to check. The door to that compartment had not been opened because the party suspected that the main dog (the metal fitting used to close hatches and ports) had been booby-trapped. The boarding party also thought they might flood the boat if

they opened the door, because, during interrogation, prisoners had indicated that the after torpedo room was flooded.

Facing this situation, Gallery decided to put to use his three years of ordnance postgraduate study. He went over to the sub with a selected party to have a look at the "booby trap." He was convinced the sub had been abandoned so hastily and in such panic that no booby traps had been set. Inspection proved him right. The open fuse box cover, which was obstructing the main dog on the watertight door to the after compartment, had been jarred open accidentally.

So he closed the fuse box cover, opened the dog fitting, cracked the door to make sure the compartment was not flooded, and went aft and put the rudder amidships by hand.

Gallery's visit to the sub also convinced him that the pressure hull was intact from bow to stern.

On leaving the U-boat he noted, "My lads on the deck had been busy with a paint brush." In big red letters across the face of the conning tower they had emblazoned the name Can Do Junior. The U-505 was called Junior from that point on. Back aboard the carrier, Gallery received orders to take the sub to Bermuda if her condition supported it. He knew the pressure hull was sound, but there was a chance they could still lose her through leakage of the ballast tanks. He believed, however, that they could blow and pump her out if she started settling. Gallery also thought that if it were possible to get to Casablanca, it would be possible to make the twenty-five-hundred-mile run to Bermuda.

Oberleutnant Lange had been badly wounded in the face and both knees while on the bridge and had lost consciousness. When he came to, most of his men were on deck or jumping into the water. He tried to raise himself to crawl aft. From there he seems to have been blown farther over the side and into the

The *U-505*'s after torpedo room, as it looked when Captain Gallery entered it in order to turn the emergency steering control wheel at the rear of the compartment and thereby straighten the boat's rudder. The compartment is a shambles of debris partly attributable to the intense sledge-hammer blasts from the American depth-charge attack. Note the spare torpedo under the bunk. *Special Collections & Archives Division, Nimitz Library, U.S. Naval Academy*

German crewmen from the *U-505* here dress up in the dry clothes that the destroyer *Chatelain* has given them. *NARA*

water, perhaps by another explosion, at which point several of his men got him into a raft. Eventually, Lange and all the other prisoners were taken to the carrier.

Later, Captain Dan went to see the German officer in sickbay. Because of his wounds, Lange had not seen the U.S. sailors board his boat; he thought she had sunk. He would not believe the Can Do had her in tow until Gallery sent a party to the sub and retrieved a picture of his family from his cabin desk. This convinced him, and he said over and over, "I will be punished for this." Gallery tried to cheer him up by pointing out that Germany was losing the war and that there would soon be a new government. He kept shaking his head and saying, "No matter what happens, I will be punished."

Gallery believed Lange was the victim of circumstances. He had done exactly what dozens of other U-boat skippers did when they thought the end was at hand: he surfaced to give his crew a last chance to survive the war before scuttling his boat. However, Gallery received several letters from Lange after the war that indicated he was indeed experiencing "punishment"—being excluded from veteran U-boat organizations and ignored by other surviving U-boat skippers.

On the morning of June 7, the task group rendezvoused with the oiler *Kennebec* (AO-36), the *Abnaki* (a fleet tug that had been diverted from an eastbound convoy), and the destroyer escort *Durik* (DE-666). All this time the *Guadalcanal* had kept up continuous patrols night and day with the sub in tow, at times landing planes in the dark with barely fifteen knots of wind over the deck. Fueling of the task group began immediately, and the *Guadalcanal*'s 2-1/4-inch wire was passed to the *Abnaki* at 10:15 AM. When the ship stopped to pass the tow wire and the sub lost her headway, however, she settled to an alarming waterline. The boat was then riding with the end of the bow out of the water and the conning tower hatch almost awash. In

Captured *U-505* crewmen shower under saltwater hose alongside the deck of the *Guadalcanal*. *NARA*

fact, when the salvage parties had first got aboard and opened the hatch, every large swell that came along washed water down the hatch, so it became necessary to keep the hatch closed while personnel were below.

The salvage parties from the *Guadalcanal* and *Pillsbury,* under Commander Trosino and Lieutenant David, were again put aboard the sub while the *Abnaki* hauled the boat closer and kept moving ahead to keep the stern from sinking. Working feverishly, they rigged electric submersible pumps with leads from the *Abnaki,* and all possible loose gear was carried to the deck and transferred to motorboats. Meanwhile, the *Guadalcanal* rigged a bight (the middle part of a slack rope or line) of heavy wire with one end secured to the starboard overhang of the flight deck forward, the bight hanging in the water, and the other end going to the anchor windlass (the winch used to raise the ship's anchor). The ship was maneuvered into position so that, if those aboard the sub so signaled, she might move ahead and slip the bight under the stern of the sub, heave around on the anchor windlass until the line was taut, and thus cause the bight to act as a pontoon to hold up the sub's stern. This was to be the last desperate measure—and fortunately, it turned out to be unnecessary.

About this time, as bilges were pumped, tanks blown, and heavy weights removed, the stern of the sub began coming up. By 8:00 PM she was floating at the same level as she was when she was first boarded. The salvage party reported she was definitely seaworthy.

That afternoon, the seaplane tender USS *Humbolt* (AVP- 21) arrived from Casablanca with Commander C. G. Rucker, a qualified submarine commander and salvage expert. He conferred with Gallery and Trosino and confirmed that the actions being taken would make the U-boat seaworthy. With some further adjustment, by evening on June 8, 1944, she was at full surface trim. The *Jenks* was dispatched for Bermuda at maximum speed at 9:30 AM on June 9, with nine sacks and a box containing official mail, codebooks and related papers, and the Enigma machines.

Opposite: U-505 taken under tow by fleet tug USS *Abnaki. Special Collections & Archives Division, Nimitz Library, U.S. Naval Academy*

Right: Some of the *Guadalcanal*'s crew members look over the gear off-loaded from the German submarine to the carrier. *NARA*

Sonar Contact!

Excerpts from an interview with Ray Watts, sonarman on board the *Chatelain*.

It was just a routine morning like every other day, and suddenly, a few minutes after eleven, I picked this contact up, and it wasn't far away, either. It was about 060 degrees from the ship and six hundred to eight hundred yards away. The echo was sharp, very sharp. It was more of a metallic sound coming back, somewhat mushy.

We were on the top deck of the ship, where the officer of the deck and the captain were. Our sound hut was just in front of them, all enclosed, and we couldn't let any water get on the equipment. When we picked up the contact on the *U-505*, the first thing I did was to jump up and look out over the water. It startled me so to have such a sudden sharp contact. I thought maybe what happened was they had let one of our own ships cross the bow. Sometimes they won't tell you about it. I saw nothing. I went back to the sonar equipment and called through the voice tube to the officer of the deck, "Contact 060," and they called general quarters immediately. All gunners, depth charge, and hedgehog people went and manned their battle stations. We made a hedgehog attack first and didn't hit anything. The bomblets don't go off unless they hit something, so we made a depth charge run . . . and we crippled the *U-505*. . . .

They decided to surface immediately and get off their boat. We were closest to it and started shooting at it. We even shot a torpedo at it and missed. The carrier, of course, was taking off with some protective destroyer escorts across the water to get as far away as they could. Captain Gallery then ordered "Cease fire." . . . We wanted to get rid of the sub, but he had in mind to capture it. So everyone stopped firing. We didn't know at the time but found out later that its rudder was stuck. It could not maneuver except in a circle and it was coming toward us. We were sitting dead in the water at the time, and it looked like it was going to ram us. But the captain started the engines up and moved away.

Then the boarding parties started. Our ship had a whaleboat in the water, but the *Pillsbury* got there first, and they actually got on the ship and started taking things out of it. . . . During the firing on the U-boat, everybody except the guys in the air got the order to cease fire, and that's how the German got killed on the deck and the captain got his leg injured. The planes were diving on the sub, firing with their machine guns. . . . I saw some of the German crew being brought on board. They were made to strip off their clothes, and we gave them long underwear to put on since that was all the Red Cross gifts we had. . . . On our way back to Bermuda, whenever we sighted a ship on the horizon, one of our destroyers would intercept it and tell it to change course. Then we'd lay a smoke screen between our group and the ship so it couldn't see what we were towing. Actually, the destroyers took turns performing picket duty some ten miles from the carrier group.

Of course, the Allies already held Enigma machines and many of the other documents taken from the *U-505*. Yet the intelligence gained from taking the *U-505* remained significant. The capture of the most current German cipher keys, plus the grid plot code used by the German navy to identify positions, proved particularly valuable. They allowed the Allies to read German naval messages as quickly and completely as the Germans could. Arriving in Washington on June 12, only a week after D-Day, the *U-505* materials also freed crypt-analysis assets for use on German Army and Air Force messages. Ironically, the Germans had begun to direct their submariners to board disabled Allied warships and to capture codebooks and other sensitive material. On July 6, 1944, U-boat Command Headquarters sent the following message to all U-boats: "If there is a chance to board sinking escort vessels (destroyers or corvettes) or other warships, make every effort to get these documents out of the radio room or chart house. Otherwise do all you can to get them by other means, for instance from lifeboats. U-boats must take a certain amount of risk, boarding parties must be prepared for anything."

After an uneventful passage to Bermuda, Task Group 22.3 steamed into Port Royal Bay. Among the reception party was the head of the Tenth Fleet's Combat Intelligence Division, Commander Kenneth Alward Knowles, the man responsible for providing the U.S. Navy with its dynamic antisubmarine intelligence service. Knowles thought the U-boat should essentially vanish until after the war, and, to that end, she should receive a new name. Being an avid reader of Jules Verne sea adventures, he had suggested the *U-505* be renamed "Nemo" (Latin for "No one"). As a result, even before the boat reached Bermuda, she had officially been given this name, and the *U-505* was known as "Nemo" in the records of the U.S. Navy until victory in Europe was declared.

With his task group in friendly waters, Gallery was faced with the enormous task of keeping their accomplishment secret. If the Germans found out that one of their boats had been captured, along with coding machines, codebooks, etc., they surely would change their existing U-boat communication coding directives.

While en route to Bermuda, Gallery made sure that all hands (some three thousand Navy men) were briefed on the importance of keeping their achievement secret. Not even their families or closest friends were to be told of their successful mission. Impossible as it might seem, all of the men kept their word, and the fate of the *U-505* remained unknown to Germany until after the war. Perhaps more important, neither Hitler nor the German Navy ever believed that the Allies had broken their secret ULTRA communications system (special intelligence coded messages) and were reading their traffic on a daily basis.

At the same time Gallery demanded complete secrecy, he also laid down the law about souvenirs. "If anyone has picked up a souvenir, turn it in to the *Guadalcanal*'s exec's office tomorrow and no questions will be asked. But we will lower the boom on anyone found with souvenirs after tomorrow." The next day the exec's office looked like a warehouse. All ships had complied and transported to the Can Do souvenirs, including officers' pistols, flashlights, cameras, officers' and enlisted caps, medals, German cigarettes, magazines—anything connected with the German ship or her crewmen. Since Gallery knew the men treasured such items, everything was tagged with the names of the owners, and they were told that the Office of Naval Intelligence would return them at the end of the war. That was the last anyone saw of them, however. Gallery wrote, "After peace broke out, the Washington bureaucrats absconded with them." Gallery took great pride in his men. In his official action report he stated:

From the time that we sailed from Norfolk, the whole task group was determined that we would come back dragging a sub behind us . . . and they had what it took to do it. When remarkable luck was required, we had it. When perfect cooperation between aircraft and surface vessels was needed, the *Chatelain* produced it. When outstanding heroism was required, it was commonplace among the boarding parties. I believe every man in the task group would have volunteered for the boarding parties, and those who could not go were very envious of those who did. It is a great pleasure to report that all hands in the task group did their duty in an exemplary manner in keeping with the highest traditions of the U.S. Navy.

On the way back to Bermuda, Gallery did a bit of research into American naval history. He found that the incident of the *U-505* was the first time the U.S. Navy had captured an enemy vessel on the high seas since the War of 1812, when the USS *Peacock* had seized HMS *Nautilus*. Once they reached the harbor in Bermuda, the *U-505* (now USS *Nemo*) was camouflaged and hidden in Bermuda under heavy guard for the remainder of the war.

Meanwhile, the war against the U-boats continued, with the Allies increasingly achieving the upper hand. With the fall of France, Germany lost its U-boat bases

Members of the first party to board the *U-505* from the *Pillsbury* (left to right): Chester Mocarski, William Riendeau, George Jacobson, Zenon Lukosius, Gordon Hohne, Wayne Pickels Jr., Stanley Wdowiak, and Arthur Knispel. *MSI*

in that country, and advancing Russian armies denied their operation in the Baltic. Eventually, only Norway offered a safe haven for what remained of the U-Waffe. On April 30, 1945, with Allied armies fighting in the streets of Berlin, all hope was lost, and Hitler committed suicide. Admiral Karl Dönitz assumed leadership of the Third Reich that same day and began negotiating the surrender of German forces in the west. At the end of the war, 153 U-boats were transferred to the Allies in British or Allied ports, and 215 boats were scuttled or blown up by their crews.

Following the end of the war, the United States, Britain, France, and the Soviet Union divided the remaining

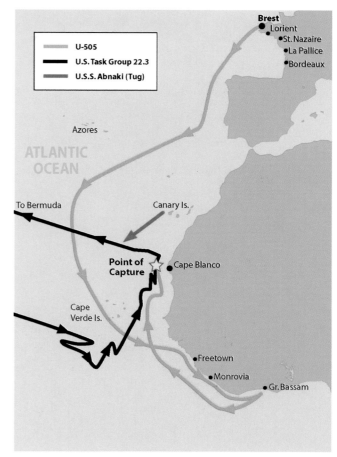

The Battle and the capture of the *U-505*. *Infinite Photo & Imaging*

Captain Gallery posing in front of the conning tower of the *U-505* after the sub has been pumped out and is on an even keel and en route to Bermuda. Note the faint letters "CAN DO JUNIOR" painted on the conning tower. *MSI*

intact U-boats among themselves to assess their capabilities. Per agreement, each was to take about a dozen boats of various classes. The Soviets, however, confiscated more than the twelve they were allowed; many U-boats were taken and transported from German shipyards to the Soviet Union as the Russian Army rolled through Germany. The Royal Navy took ten boats of various classes. In 1946 and 1947, five Type XXI boats were transferred to the Soviet Navy and recommissioned, serving until the mid-1950s. One of the boats taken by the United States, the Type XXI *U-3008*, was commissioned into the U.S. Navy. She became the genesis for the Navy's greater underwater propulsive power program ("Guppy").

In the end, the U-boat war had taken a heavy toll on both the Allies and their German adversaries. One hundred fifty-eight British Commonwealth and twenty-nine U.S. combatants, plus warships of other Allied nations, were lost during the battle. The Germans commissioned 1,171 U-boats during the war, but only 859 were deployed for operational patrols. Of this number, three-fourths—648 of them—were sunk or, in a few cases (like the *U-505*), captured at sea. In fact, just 321 U-boats had actually attacked and damaged or sank any Allied ships.

The weapon that came too late. Fortunately, the type XXI "Walter" U-boat, which could remain submerged indefinitely and travel at high speeds underwater, never got into the Battle of the Atlantic. A Type XXI is shown here after the war, this one having been commissioned into the U.S. Navy. *USNI*

Though winning the Battle of the Atlantic often is attributed to many factors—convoys, "small boy" surface escorts (destroyers, destroyer escorts, frigates, corvettes, etc.), a merchant fleet that consisted of hundreds of Liberty ships, innovative and highly productive shipbuilders, land-based aircraft, U.S. hunter-killer carrier escort groups, code breakers, brilliant scientists and technologists, radar, Huff Duff, new and effective weaponry, etc.—above all it was a battle fought by men.

In a salute to the victors, official U.S. Navy historian Admiral Samuel Eliot Morison in his series *History of United States Naval Operations in World War II* wrote, "To one and all, then, of the British, Canadian and the United States Navies, Air Forces and Merchant Marines, and to the gallant ships and squadrons of other Allied nations operating under their command, and to the scientists, the shipbuilders and builders of aircraft—this historian, who has followed them from the humiliating winter of 1941–1942 to the glorious summer of 1945, can only say—'Well done'; aye, magnificently done; and the free world is your debtor."

Awards for the Capture

Rear Admiral Albert C. Read, USN, Commander Fleet Air, Norfolk, is shown presenting awards to *Guadalcanal* pilots who participated in the capture of the *U-505*. Pictured facing the admiral (from left to right) are Lieutenant W. W. Roberts, and Lieutenant (junior grade) John Cadle Jr., both of whom were awarded the Distinguished Flying Cross; Lieutenant Norman D. Hodson, Commander of Composite Squadron Eight, who received the Bronze Star; and an unidentified officer. Admiral Read himself was noted for being the first pilot to complete a trans-Atlantic flight in a Navy seaplane, the NC-4, in May 1919. *NARA*

Awards for the Capture, *continued*

Medal of Honor. *MSI*

Navy Cross of Stanley Wdowiak,
donated by Margaret Wdowiak. *MSI*

Silver Star of Ernest J.
Beaver. *MSI*

Legion of Merit. *MSI*

Distinguished Flying Cross. *MSI*

For the capture of the *U-505*, the whole *Guadalcanal* task group was awarded the Presidential Unit Citation.

Lieutenant (junior grade) Albert L. David, who led the boarding party down into the submarine, was awarded the Medal of Honor. Captain Daniel V. Gallery was given the Distinguished Service Medal, while Commander Earl Trosino and Lieutenant D. E. Hampton were awarded the Legion of Merit. The latter two officers had played a large part in keeping the boat from sinking.

Crew members Stanley E. Wdowiak and Arthur W. Knispel had accompanied Lieutenant David on his first foray down into the boat, for which they were awarded the Navy Cross. The other members of the

Pillsbury boarding party—Zenon B. Lukosius, Gordon F. Hohne, Ernest Beaver, Chester A. Mocarski, William R. Riendeau, Phillip N. Trusheim, George W. Jacobson, and Wayne M. Pickels—won the Silver Star.

Ensign John W. Cadle Jr. and Lieutenant Wolffe W. Roberts, who piloted the two Wildcat fighters that attacked the *U-505*, were awarded the Distinguished Flying Cross.

Of course, none of these servicemen could tell what they had done to earn these prestigious awards until after the war. Once the capture was made public in May 1945, the citations that had read "for reasons which cannot be revealed at this time" were replaced with full citations detailing the actual accomplishments.

CHAPTER 7

Bringing the U-505 to Chicago

According to the memoirs of Wolfgang Schiller and Pharmacist's Mate Otto Dietz, the captured crew members from the *U-505* initially were turned over to the Commandant of the Naval Operating Base, Bermuda, and were housed in a fenced complex of large tents. Guard posts with manned machine guns protected the front and back of the camp. Each day, every prisoner was given a bucket filled with a half-liter of water. The water was for drinking and washing.

After several weeks, a destroyer took the prisoners of war (POWs) to Norfolk, Virginia, and from there they were sent by rail to a huge POW camp at Ruston, Louisiana. (The camp still exists today as a museum.) No one in Germany knew they were alive. German naval officials informed the families that the *U-505* had been sunk with the loss of all hands. At Ruston, the *U-505* crewmen were assigned a section of the camp, away from other prisoners, that easily could have held several thousand prisoners.

MSI

U-505 POWs were off-loaded at Bermuda, transported to Norfolk by destroyer, and then sent to a huge POW camp in Ruston, Louisiana. A group of *U-505* crewmen are shown in the cotton fields of Ruston. After VE Day the crew was split up and sent to camps in Texas, Mississippi, and New York. POW's return to Germany was often via Canada, England, and France. Some of the *U-505* crew did not reach home until late 1947. *MSI*

They were trucked away even from this camp on a Red Cross visit, so as not to give away the secret of the capture. The *U-505*'s skipper, Harald Lange, joined the crew four months later after recovering from a leg amputation, the result of the severe wounds he sustained in the attack.

When the war ended, the POWs were ordered to pick cotton and, eventually, were split up. Otto Dietz, for example, was sent to Camp Mexia, Texas, another "cotton" camp. Wolfgang Schiller was sent to Camp McCain in Mississippi and then to Camp Shanks in New York. Finally, in January 1946, the *U-505* POWs were sent by train to Long Beach, California, and put on board the troop transport *Ernie Pyle*. Lange had been allowed to write his wife and tell her of their ordeal and that the crewmen were on their way home. She spread the astonishing, joyous news to the other families. The crew landed at Liverpool, England; under heavy guard, they boarded a train that took them to Camp Sheffield, then to Camp Hartford Grange. They returned to Germany during 1946–47.

On May 16, 1945, nine days after the surrender of Germany, the story of the capture of the *U-505* was revealed to the American public. Manned by a U.S. Navy crew and sailing under her own power, the boat subsequently made a war bond subscription tour of Atlantic and Gulf of Mexico port cities. This was an impor-

On May 16, 1945, the story of the capture of the *U-505* was revealed to the American public. Manned by an American Navy crew and sailing under her own power, the boat subsequently made a war bond subscription tour for the seventh war loan of Atlantic and Gulf port cities. Here she is arriving off New York City. *MSI*

Freshly painted all black and very sharp in appearance, the *U-505* is shown with her American Navy crew during the 1945 war bond tour in Miami, November 1945. *MSI*

souvenirs—essentially everything not bolted down. Many other items had been taken from the boat before this.

When the United States, Britain, France, and Russia agreed to divide the intact operational U-boats at the end of the war, they had stipulated that the boats would be scrapped or sunk in deep water within two years. When the time came to carry out this agreement, Gallery, now a rear admiral, learned that the *U-505* was to be included. He pointed out that the *U-505* could not be included in the Four Power arrangement since that applied strictly to boats surrendered at the end of the war. Gallery strenuously argued that because the *U-505* had not surrendered but had been captured in battle on the high seas, she was therefore U.S. property, and the United States could keep her indefinitely. Since this case had no precedent, government bureaucrats could not produce a rationale to counter his argument. Gallery raised such a fuss, in fact, that the Navy Department finally agreed not to scuttle the boat. At the time, he had no plans

tant task, since the war still raged in the Pacific. The submarine stayed at each port she visited for about a week, and the curious waited in line for hours to tour the captured U-boat (the price for the tour was buying a war bond). In New York alone, millions of dollars were raised by this method. The boat was a great hit with the public.

After the Pacific war ended and the need for war bonds evaporated, the *U-505* was tied up in the Navy Yard at Portsmouth, New Hampshire, to await final disposition. As her bond tour crewmen departed the boat, they took away plates, gauges, and small pieces of equipment as

The *U-505* is put on display at the U.S. Naval Academy, Annapolis, Maryland, in October 1945, during the Academy's Centennial Exhibition. *NHC*

The War Bond Tour

Excerpts from an interview with former Navy submariners Jim Sisson and Joe Hill, who were part of the U.S. crew that sailed the *U-505* to U.S. ports as part of a war bond drive after the war.

Sisson: When the USS *Snapper* (SS-185) was decommissioned, I got a set of orders to report to the *U-505* and I picked it up in Jacksonville, Florida. We then made a bond tour from city to city, over to New Orleans, then back to Key West, Florida.

Hill: If you bought a war bond, you could go aboard the submarine, and there would be somebody to explain what a torpedo was and to give a tour

through the entire boat. Initially, we were snowed under with visitors. The boat was open for touring from 8:00 AM to 8:00 PM. We got a lot of questions about our subs compared to U-boats. U-boats were fine machines but gave little consideration to crew comfort. Our boats were bigger, and although cramped, we enjoyed more room and better accommodations.

Sission: We started from the sub base at New London and were programmed as to what to do and how to behave ourselves. We made our first stop at New York City and stayed there a month. They erected a little shelter or canopy on the forward deck and set up a table and sold war bonds. They were $18.75 for the smallest one, which could be redeemed for $25.00 after a certain time had expired. Next there were $37.50 and $50.00 bonds available up to $100.00.

We then went to Portland, Maine; Portsmouth, New Hampshire; down to New Bedford, Massachusetts; to Portsmouth, Virginia; and then to Jacksonville, Miami, and Key West, Florida. We visited the Gulf ports of Tampa, Pensacola, Mobile, and New Orleans. Following the visit to New Orleans, we were ordered back to Boston. The reason was that interest in war bond sales was dropping terrifically, and the Treasury and War

The *U-505* under way with an American crew during a war bond tour. *MSI*

for the *U-505*, but Gallery was not about to let the sub meet such an inglorious end after his men had performed so heroically off the coast of West Africa.

In his book *Twenty Million Tons under the Sea*, Gallery tells who first thought of moving the boat to Chicago.

After the reprieve on the scuttling order, my brother, Father John Ireland Gallery, had an idea about a possible use for the *U-505*. He was a naval reserve chaplain and had helped fight the Battle of the Atlantic with the Navy's Patrol Wing 7, which played a big part in the air offensive over the Bay of Biscay. Father John observed that there were monuments all over the country for land battles in every war that this country has fought, but naval memorials were few and far between. Father John asked himself, "Why not bring the *U-505* to Chicago and make it a memorial to the thousands of seamen who had lost their lives in the two great Battles of the Atlantic?" These

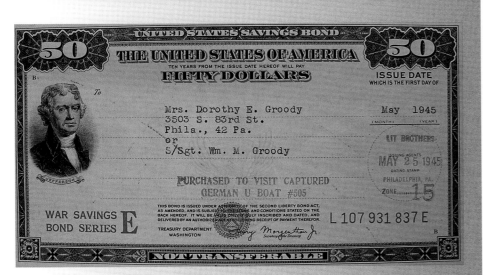

The price of visiting the *U-505* was purchasing a war bond. *MSI*

Departments didn't want us to spend any more money on it. New York and Miami were our best ports as far as the number of visitors who came aboard. We never did dive the *U-505*.

While we were in Miami, I had the thrill of a lifetime when ex-heavyweight boxing champions Gene Tunney and Jack Dempsey came on board. Gene Tunney was a full commander in the Navy; Jack Dempsey was a three-striper in the Coast Guard. And it was a real pleasure to meet these gentlemen. That visit was one of the memorable highlights of our tour.

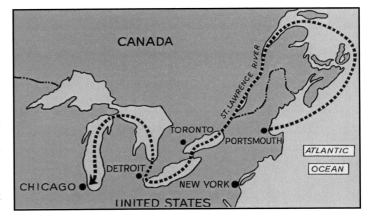

Admiral Dan Gallery, in his book *Twenty Million Tons under the Sea*, credits his brother Father John Ireland Gallery with presenting the idea of moving the boat to the Museum of Science and Industry in Chicago to Major Lenox Lohr (long-time president of the museum). His idea was met with great enthusiasm and Admiral Gallery became the prime mover in making it happen. Many obstacles stood in the way, notably towing the boat down the St. Lawrence River and across four of the five Great Lakes to Chicago, a distance of three thousand miles. *MSI/Infinite Photo & Imaging*

Now (in 1953) a derelict in appearance after years of neglect, the *U-505* is docked at the Navy Yard at Portsmouth, New Hampshire, awaiting final disposition. This is how the boat appeared to MSI staff members on an inspection visit. *MSI*

were two crucial battles in our history, and what could be a more appropriate monument to these battles than one of the very submarines around which the battles centered.

Of course, Father John's brother Dan thought it was a great idea.

One day while visiting the Museum of Science and Industry (MSI) near his Chicago parish, Father John mentioned this idea to Major Lenox Lohr (long-time president of the museum). The major lit up like a Christmas tree, pushed a button, and told his secretary to bring in the museum's "submarine file." In this file were letters going back twenty-four years, asking the Navy Department to give them an obsolete submarine for display. The major explained that when Julius Rosenwald endowed and established the museum in 1926, he specified he wanted it patterned after the Deutsches Museum in Munich, Germany, which is filled with modern exhibits featuring modern technology. The two principal attractions of that museum at the time were a full-scale model of a coal mine and an actual submarine that had been hauled out of the water and installed alongside the building.

The MSI, located five hundred yards from the shore of Lake Michigan, already had a coal mine exhibit, but it had been trying unsuccessfully for twenty-four years to get a submarine. Major Lohr immediately saw the possibilities in Father John's suggestion. Not only might a submarine now be available, but the *U-505* had a unique history. This venture was much more complicated than either Lohr or Father John imagined, however. The first steps included the museum gaining title to the U-boat, ensuring she was seaworthy, and towing her down the St. Lawrence River and across four of the five Great Lakes, a distance of three thousand miles!

Once she reached the shore of Lake Michigan adjacent to the museum, the U-boat would have to be hauled out of the water, moved across Lake Shore Drive (one of the busiest thoroughfares in the city), and then installed alongside the facility. Of course, the boat would require much restoration work to make her an authentic and presentable tourist attraction. In addition, a foundation would have to be built, and all the accompanying displays, explanations, photographs, and film would have to be prepared.

The major stumbling block, of course, was that the MSI had no funds to undertake such a staggering project. Nor was everybody enthusiastic about the idea. Local critics voiced their concern that most people wanted to forget the war, and that if the venture did materialize, "it will be just another cannon on the courthouse lawn." An editorial writer suggested that money donated for this "useless project" would better be sent to veteran's hospitals. During the next few years, however, some powerful figures in Chicago became avid supporters of the idea. Among them was Colonel Robert R. McCormick of the *Chicago Tribune*, who ensured that stories about the *U-505* and her value as a monument appeared frequently in his newspaper.

Of course, by any measure, the key individual in making the exhibit happen was Admiral Gallery himself. In 1952, he was assigned duty as Commander of the Naval Air Reserve in Glenview, Illinois, a suburb of Chicago. Thus, he found himself right in position to help push the project through. After his arrival, things began to move quickly. In 1953, Chicago Mayor Martin Kennelly appointed a committee to start the project rolling by raising funds. The *U-505* Committee, led by former Assistant Secretary of the Navy Ralph A. Bard, set a goal of $250,000 to be raised by its one hundred members making personal solicitations. For the next year and a half, the project became a citywide enterprise. Helping greatly in its eventual success was the unprecedented publicity given to it by the news media.

Eventually, $125,000 was raised and a similar amount obtained in free services from various corporations. A former head public relations officer for the U.S. Air Force came through with something quite unexpected. Gallery and Steve Leo had participated in lively conversations and traded barbs during a period of talk about service unification, but they had become good friends. When Gallery jokingly sent Leo a circular about their fund drive, he replied with a very supportive note and a check for $250.00. Gallery was floored.

Next, a businessman donated costly plaques for the sub, and the president of the Great Lakes Dredging and Dock Company agreed at no cost to lend Gallery and the committee its floating dry dock for six weeks to haul the *U-505* from the water onto the beach. It was the only floating dry dock in the Great Lakes. Tug companies offered to tow the boat partway to Chicago without charge, and eventually the Coast Guard would also offer its towing services free of charge.

The *U-505* left Portsmouth on May 14, 1954, in tow by the tug *Pauline L. Moran*. When the boat reached Lake Erie, the Coast Guard cutter *Arundel* assumed the towing duties. Earl Trosino, who had been responsible for keeping the boat afloat off Cape Blanco back in 1944, was on the bridge of the *Pauline L. Moran* as she transited the twenty-six locks of the St. Lawrence/Great Lakes Canal System (it was five years before the completion of the St. Lawrence Seaway project). Trosino had returned to his former job as chief engineer aboard a Sun Oil tanker, and now the company generously loaned him to the project for the duration of the cruise from Portsmouth to Chicago. Admiral Gallery and several members of the media would fly to Detroit to ride the *U-505* for the last leg of the voyage.

The *U-505* left Portsmouth on May 14, 1954, in tow and transited the twenty-six locks of the St. Lawrence/Great Lakes Canal System. Here she is shown entering one of the locks. *MSI*

Chance Encounter

Excerpts from an interview with M. Chapman, sonarman on board the USS *Chatelain* (DE-149).

I retired four or five years ago, and I was driving a school bus in Prince George's County in Maryland. Besides taking the kids to school and bringing them home, we went on field trips.

One day we took a field trip to the Owens Science Center, which was on the curriculum. I went into the center and talked to a woman who was teaching them. Her name was Brill, and she was German. I asked if she could turn the children loose about fifteen minutes early, since I had to do a video interview at my home. She asked me about the subject I was to discuss and I said, "The capture of the *U-505*, a German submarine." Her expression changed, and I asked her what was the matter. She said, "The captain on the submarine was a personal friend of ours." I said, "Really?" I asked her his name and she said, "Captain Lange." I said, "Did anybody get hurt?" She said, "Yes, the Captain lost his leg." And she went on to tell me that after the war, he was given a job on the docks in Germany supervising the unloading of food from the ships. And she said, "Believe me, without him, we wouldn't have had any fresh vegetables or fruit, because he saw to it that our family got a good share." I thought that experience was one in a million.... What a small world!

On June 26, 1954, the *U-505* arrived at Chicago to a huge waterfront reception. Several hundred yachts escorted the boat, while fireboats saluted her with a cascade of waterspouts, and the mayor, surrounded by a massive crowd, met the party at the Michigan Avenue bridge.

Maneuvering a submarine overland is a unique engineering accomplishment. When the problem of moving the *U-505* from the waters of Lake Michigan to a dry land permanent berth at the east side of the museum building was first discussed, many different routes and methods were proposed. It

Upon her arrival off Chicago, the boat is met with a huge waterfront reception. Here she is shown under a drawn bridge on the Chicago River. The Navy Pier can be seen in the background. *MSI*

The *U-505* is placed in American Ship Building Company dry dock where the thirty thousand gallons of fuel and lubricating oil remaining in her tanks and an additional 80 tons of pig iron ballast from the keel were removed, reducing her weight to approximately 670 tons. *NARA*

The boat was then placed on a floating dry dock, where she was mounted on a specially constructed steel carriage that would ride on rollers and rails. A special pier was built, jutting 50 feet out into the lake from the shoreline adjacent to the museum, and a 325-foot channel was dredged to accommodate the dry dock and its submarine cargo. The floating dry dock and its cargo are shown approaching the beach. *ITEC*

was not so much a question of how it could be done as of determining which method was the most practical and economical.

At this stage, retired Chicago engineer Seth M. Gooder, who had spent some forty years in the business of moving huge buildings and a variety of odd-shaped structures, suggested that the *U-505* be moved on rollers, as you would move a house. It was true that the *U-505*, weighing around 900 tons at 252 feet long, 22 feet at her widest point, and standing about three stories high, presented a rather unusual kind of house. Accordingly, under his guidance the *U-505*'s trip—an overland journey of roughly 800 feet—was planned.

When the *U-505* arrived in Chicago, she was placed in a standard dry dock to prepare her for the overland haul. After removing some thirty thousand gallons of fuel and lubricating oil that remained in her tanks, and an additional 80 tons of pig iron ballast from the keel, her weight was reduced to approximately 670 tons.

The next step was to place her on the floating dry dock, where she was mounted on a specially constructed steel carriage that would ride on steel rollers and rails. The carriage consisted of two large "H" beams, 135 feet long, placed parallel with the boat's length; twenty-one transverse beams, each 14 feet long, were used to strengthen the carriage. All intersections of the carriage were welded and bolted for additional strength.

Timbering provided maximum contact between this carriage and the curved shape of the *U-505*'s hull, with the last few inches shaped by a concrete grout. In this way, the weight of the submarine was evenly distributed on the steel carriage, which would ride on the rollers.

While this was being done, others prepared the beaching site at a point directly east of the museum. A special pier jutting 50 feet out into the lake from the shoreline was built and was secured firmly. Then a 325-foot channel, 9 feet below the waterline, was dredged to accommodate the floating

Bathers at the beach around the *U-505* as she awaits her overnight move across the busy thoroughfare, Lake Shore Drive. *MSI*

dry dock and its submarine cargo. Four steel rails were then laid on heavy timber cribbing that extended from the edge of Lake Shore Drive to the end of the pier to receive the *U-505* on the first leg of her overland trip.

Despite the date's superstitious overtones, on Friday, August 13, the operation began. A couple of tugs gently nudged the dry dock into position. When all was secured, the dry dock was sunk until the *U-505*, resting on her carriage—which in turn rested on rollers and track—leveled up with the track waiting for her on shore.

The critical problem as the *U-505* was pulled ashore was to compensate for the weight leaving the dry dock as the submarine moved off of it by filling the tanks of the dry dock with an equal weight of water. This was calculated at twenty-seven tons of water for every four feet of the sub's progress. Many weeks of calculations had helped prepare for this move-

A crowd watches as the U-boat is pulled onto the beach. *MSI*

ment, but few of the fifteen thousand people who had gathered that night to watch the *U-505* come ashore were aware of the factors that had to be considered in accomplishing this critical part of the move.

The submarine was pulled about a foot at a time by a power winch and four lengths of wire cable. Once safely ashore, the *U-505* had to be raised four feet, four inches, to bring her to the proper level for crossing Chicago's busiest highway—the "outer drive." This "raising" was accomplished by using forty-two mechanical jacks.

On Friday night, September 3, the *U-505* was ready to cross the drive. Traffic stopped at 7:00 PM, and the huge monster began the crossing. At midnight, she was halfway across, and by 4:15 the following morning, she had cleared the roadway. Gallery's sense of humor was evident in the signs he had had prepared and posted

Admiral Gallery poses with his son, Daniel V. Gallery III (at left, middle), and chief project engineer Seth Gooder (far left) as the *U-505* crosses Chicago's Lake Shore Drive during the evening hours of September 2, 1954, en route to her new home at the museum. *MSI*

The *U-505* approaching the museum building stern first. *NARA*

The submarine finally in place on the eastern side of the museum, resting on reinforced concrete cradles. *MSI*

The *U-505* was formally dedicated on September 25, 1964, as a memorial to the fifty-five thousand Americans who perished at sea during the two world wars. The colorful ceremony opened with a seventeen-gun salute, as Fleet Admiral William F. Halsey, a famous naval commander of World War II, was piped aboard to deliver the dedication address. *MSI*

When the submarine was finally in place on the eastern side of the museum, she was suspended several feet over her permanent foundation; the next step was to lower her into place by reverse jacking.

The foundation consisted of three (sixteen-by-eighteen-foot) reinforced concrete cradles. The unique feature of these cradles was that only one, the center cradle, was attached to

on Lakeshore Drive; they read "Submarine Crossing" (obviously a new kind of wildlife).

The transit complete, the U-boat was then pulled in a diagonal approach (moving stern first) close to the museum building through a series of similar operations. To set the boat in her permanent position with the bow pointing north, it now was necessary to swing the hull through a 67-degree arc. This was accomplished by establishing a pivot point at the intersection of the centerline of the submarine with the centerline of the permanent foundation. Tracks again were laid on cribbing arcs (actually short tangents), and the pulling was done from a right angle off the bow.

U-505 dedication ceremony with a blimp overhead. *MSI*

the submarine's keel. On this rested a third of the *U-505*'s weight. The other cradles, one at each end, each bore a third of the weight, but this weight was distributed across twenty pairs of eight-inch steel rollers, which in turn rested on a track set in the cradles.

Thus, two-thirds of the *U-505*'s weight now rested on wheels, a strange concept for a submarine. This arrangement would allow for the expansion and contraction of the hull that would result from temperature changes between summer and winter. A temperature differential of 150 degrees or a maximum

movement of two and a half inches each year was factored in to compensate for contraction and expansion of the boat's steel hull.

Stabilizing concrete arms were built along the sides of each cradle to prevent any possible sideways shift of the submarine. A sliding contact on each of these arms permitted movement.

In the last step of dry berthing the *U-505,* the steel undercarriage on which she completed the overland trip was removed. Thus, the civil engineer contributed a new chapter in the history of transportation—"How to Move a Submarine over Land."

The *U-505* was formally dedicated on September 25, 1954, as a memorial to the fifty-five thousand Americans who perished in the Battle of the Atlantic during the two world wars. The colorful ceremony opened with a seventeen-gun salute, as Fleet Admiral William F. Halsey, a famous naval commander of World War II, was piped aboard to deliver the dedication address.

Halsey was introduced by Arthur Godfrey, radio and television star and a reserve Navy lieutenant commander, who acted as master of ceremonies. Bishop Weldon of Springfield, Massachusetts, chaplain of the *Guadalcanal* when the *U-505* was captured, gave the invocation.

"The *U-505*," said Halsey, "will always serve as a reminder of a . . . way of life

Following Admiral Halsey's address, a dedication plaque was unveiled by Earl Trosino which paid tribute to the capture of the *U-505,* in part stating that "THIS PRIZE OF WAR IS DEDICATED TO THE MEMORY OF THE AMERICAN SEAMEN WHO WENT DOWN TO UNMARKED OCEAN GRAVES HELPING TO WIN VICTORY AT SEA." *MSI*

that puts might over right and makes its citizens slaves of the state. As a permanent exhibit at the museum, it will always remind the world that Americans pray for peace and hate to fight, but we believe in our way of life and are willing and capable of defending ourselves against any aggressors."

About one hundred members of the task group were on hand for the ceremony, including Captain Earl Trosino and all nine surviving members of the *Pillsbury*'s original boarding party. About forty thousand Chicagoans gathered under the trees in Jackson Park to witness the rites.

The evening before, Secretary of the Navy Charles S. Thomas had presented the Navy's highest civilian award, a gold medal for distinguished service, to Robert Crown and Carl Stockholm, cochairmen of the *U-505* Committee; to Ralph Bard, the committee's honorary chairman; to Seth Gooder, the engineer who directed the beaching and overland move of the *U-505*; to William V. Kahler of the *U-505* Committee; and to Lenox R. Lohr, president of the museum.

In one of his books, Admiral Gallery would later point out the irony involved in the Secretary of the Navy's appearance. Despite Gallery's many attempts to convince Navy officials about the huge publicity that the submarine exhibit would afford it, the Navy offered little help in making the submarine an exhibit in Chicago. Secretary Thomas, however, had a personal reason to be present: his own son Hayward had been an engineering officer on the *Guadalcanal*.

The *U-505* opened as an exhibit shortly thereafter, and she quickly became the most popular attraction at the museum.

Reunions

U-505 dedication reunions have been held at the Museum of Science and Industry (MSI) in 1954 (dedication event), 1964 (twentieth anniversary dinner), 1974 (thirtieth anniversary dinner), 1979 (rededication event), 1982 (task group/*U-505* crew reunion), 1994 (fiftieth anniversary dinner), and 2004 (sixtieth anniversary dinner). Captain Lange, at age sixty, came to the museum in 1964 to attend ceremonies commemorating the twentieth anniversary of the capture of the *U-505*. He and Admiral Gallery spent several hours on the *U-505*. While on deck, Lange pointed out holes in the conning tower that were made by shells fired by the sub's attackers. Those holes remain in the sub today.

The highlight of the twentieth anniversary was a dinner at the museum given by the Chicago Commandery of the Naval Order of the United States, headed by Maurice L. Horner. Speaking before the dinner, Captain Lange told of the sea conflict and expressed his belief that

The twentieth anniversary celebration commemorating the capture of the *U-505* (1964), held at the Museum of Science and Industry. Rear Admiral Gallery is shown returning to former *U-505* captain Harald Lange his Zeiss 8 x 60 binoculars. *MSI*

Reunions, *continued*

"radar turned the tide of battle against Germany." He explained, "A submarine is a great weapon when it can be used to attack by surprise, but a weak weapon when its whereabouts are known—and your American radar kept our submarines hiding."

At the close of the evening's festivities, Admiral Gallery returned Captain Lange's binoculars, which he had taken when the sub was captured. Lange's binoculars stayed in the family, and when he died in 1967, his wife donated them to the E-boat (motor torpedo boats) archives in Germany, where they are on display today. They are the only set of *U-505* binoculars not in the MSI collection.

In 1979, during rededication ceremonies marking the thirtieth anniversary of the capture of the *U-505,* Assistant Secretary of the Navy George A. Peapples announced that the Navy would name one of its new guided-missile frigates *Gallery* after the late Rear Admirals Daniel and Philip Gallery. Recognizing the Gallery brothers, including Rear Admiral William O. Gallery and former Navy chaplain Reverend John I. Gallery, both of whom attended the ceremonies, Peapples said, "All of them have demonstrated uncommon leadership, resourcefulness, and dedication, and it is only fitting that we recognize the contributions they have made to our country with one of the highest honors the Navy can offer. Their name will offer an outstanding example for the ship to follow, will lend inspiration to her crew, and [will] set a high standard for them to meet in the years ahead."

The event was also a reunion for fifteen members of the task group that captured the sub, some of whom traveled across the country to attend the ceremonies. Among the many dignitaries who attended was Lieutenant Commander Philip D. Gallery, son of Rear Admiral and Mrs. Philip D. Gallery.

The twenty-fifth anniversary of the 1954 dedication, September 25, 1979. *MSI*

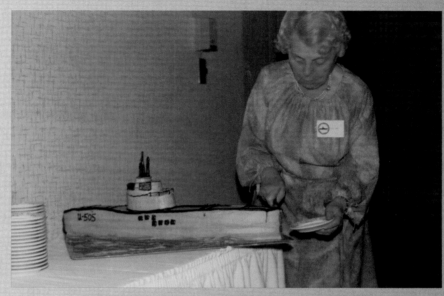

Group photo of the 1982 reunion. American task group members attending the reunion are shown on the left; German crewmen on the right. This was the first time the Germans had seen their boat since the war. *MSI*

Frau Lange, the widow of Oberleutnant zur See Lange, is shown cutting the *U-505* cake at the 1982 reunion. *MSI*

During a September 1982 task group/*U-505* crew reunion, eleven former crew members of the *U-505* met with forty-five former members of the USS *Guadalcanal* task group for the first time since the war. Although this was the third reunion for the German group, it was the first reunion planned to be at their boat. Captain Lange's widow, Karla, and twelve members of the crewmen's families were part of the German group, which totaled twenty-four people.

One of the former German crewmen explained what it was like to be in the *U-505* during the attack. "The lights went out and everything, including the steering, was out of control. We went deeper and deeper. 'Anblasen!' ['Blow negative!'] cried the commander, and thank goodness, the air pipes were still in order, and we got to the surface, where the planes now came over us like a pack of dogs. . . . After two hours of swimming I got picked up

Reunions, *continued*

by a destroyer where I got new clothes, coffee, and my first cigarette and, I like to emphasize, very fair treatment, for which I am extremely grateful."

When James Biggin and James G. Sanders, former flight deck officers on the *Guadalcanal,* heard that the German crewmen were coming to Chicago, they arranged for the American veterans to join them at the MSI. The wartime adversaries returned as "peacetime friends with memories of the past and hopes for the future," stated museum President and Director Victor J. Danilov in a welcome address at the museum.

"It was a thrilling event," said Hans Goebeler, former machinist's mate in the *U-505,* who organized the German visit. It was also a nostalgic moment for the crewmen when they were united at the boat. "We had some very good times together, but also spent the worst hours of our lives on board, with weeks of boredom followed by moments of sheer terror!"

During the reunion, the U.S. and German veterans attended a memorial and wreath-laying ceremony at the Daley Civic Plaza in downtown Chicago.

The USS *Guadalcanal* Task Group 22.3 Association has held annual reunions, with few exceptions, since 1954. Destroyer escorts *Pope, Jenks, Flaherty, Pillsbury,* and *Chatelain* have held reunions over the years as well.

The *UC-97* and the *Eastland*

The *U-505* was not the first U-boat to reach Lake Michigan waters. A log entry of the gunboat USS *Wilmette,* dated June 7, 1921, records the sinking of the last remaining World War I German U-boat in accordance with the provisions of the Treaty of Versailles. That the demise of the submarine should have occurred some three years after the armistice and in Lake Michigan is a story formerly known only by a few maritime associations and naval history buffs.

The *UC-97,* a minelaying submarine, was launched in Hamburg, Germany, on March 17, 1918. She was not commissioned in the German Imperial Navy because she was not ready for sea prior to the signing of the armistice on November 11. The boat subsequently was interned at Harwich, England, a destroyer and submarine base on the English Channel.

Because Germany had been the major submarine builder in the world during the war, the victorious Allied nations were eager to get their hands on the surrendered boats to study their construction and equipment technology. The United States had financed its war effort through the sale of Treasury Department Liberty Bonds, and since a sizable debt remained after the war, the country needed innovative ideas to promote the sale of new bonds. The exhibition of surrendered German U-boats in U.S. coastal and inland ports appeared to hold much promise, and in early 1919, six U-boats were allocated to the United States. In addition to the *UC-97*, the *U-117*, the *U-140*, the *U-164*, the *U-111*, and the *UB-88* were selected for delivery to the United States.

Twelve officers and 120 enlisted men were sent to England to bring the boats across the Atlantic in March 1919. Given the name Ex-German Submarine Expeditionary Force, four of the boats, including the *UC-97*, departed England in early April. After brief stops in the Azores and Bermuda, the expeditionary force arrived in New York to be greeted by a throng of tourists, reporters, and Navy and civilian technicians.

Later, each boat received her itinerary for the Liberty Bond Campaign. The *UC-97*, under the command of Lieutenant Commander Charles A. Lockwood Jr., U.S. Navy, who later in World War II was to gain fame as Commander, Submarines Pacific Fleet, was assigned to the Great Lakes region.

On reaching the Great Lakes, the U-boat began a series of port calls at lakes Ontario, Erie, Huron, and Michigan. Wear on the engines finally cut short the tour, and Commander Lockwood brought the boat to the Navy pier in Chicago by late August. A few of the crew who were "duration-of-the-war" men were paid off. The remainder were ordered to Lockwood's new command, the *R-25* (submarine number 102), under construction in Bridgeport, Connecticut. The *UC-97* was turned over to the Commandant of the Ninth Naval District.

The submarine later was moved and tied up and opened to tourists at the foot of Monroe Street on Chicago's lakefront at Grant Park. .

The *UC-97* remained on display for the next few years until a clause in the armistice treaty was recalled which stated that all German combat vessels held by Allied forces were to be "destroyed before July 1st, 1921." Franklin D. Roosevelt, then-Acting Secretary of the Navy, directed Captain Edward A. Evers of the *Wilmette* and Captain Daniel W. Wurtsbaugh, Commandant at Great Lakes, to arrange for the destruction of the boat.

During the first week of June 1921, all ships of the Great Lakes flotilla put to sea for maneuvers. Some two hundred Midwest reservists stood by to take part in the historic sinking. The USS *Hawk* (IX-14) sailed from Milwaukee, Wisconsin, to tow the *UC-97* into Lake Michigan, where she would be a target for Naval Reserve gunners on board the *Wilmette*. Before

The *UC-97* and the *Eastland, continued*

World War I U-boat *UC-97* entering New York harbor destined for the Great Lakes and a Liberty Bond tour, 1919. One of several U-boats allocated to the United States after the war, the U-boat eventually became inoperable and was docked at Navy Pier in Chicago. In accordance with the Treaty of Versailles the *UC-97* was sunk in Lake Michigan on June 7, 1921, by the U.S. gunboat USS *Wilmette*. The *Wilmette* was the former excursion ship *Eastland*, which met disaster when it capsized in the Chicago River, causing the deaths of over eight hundred Western Electric picnickers. *NHC*

the U-boat was taken under tow by the *Hawk*, all of her armament, propulsion, and navigational gear was removed.

At 8:17 AM on June 7, the *Wilmette* weighed anchor in Lake Michigan. The weather was clear and the lake waters calm. About two hours later, after picking up the *Hawk* with the *UC-97* in tow, the *Wilmette* stopped dead in the water some twenty miles offshore. At 11:45 AM, the gunboat commenced firing her four-inch battery at the abandoned U-boat. Gunner's Mate J. O. Sabin of Muscatine, Iowa, fired the first shot. The man whose "hit" sent the sub to her final resting place was Gunner's Mate A. H. Anderson, who fired the first U.S. torpedo at a German submarine during the war.

The civilians on board who watched the sinking gave each of the gun crews of the *Wilmette* a purse of $100. It took eighteen rounds and fifteen minutes to send the U-boat to the bottom. This was the first time a U.S. naval gun had fired an explosive shell on any of the Great Lakes since Commodore Oliver Hazard Perry defeated the British on Lake Erie in September 1813.

In the years following the historic sinking of the *UC-97*, the incident was forgotten. Indeed, when naval historian David A. Myers of Waukegan,

Illinois, began to research the boat in 1960, few people believed that such a U-boat had ever visited Chicago. Myers persevered, however, and after researching the logs of the *Wilmette* and other ships, he was able to approximate the site of the sinking. Beginning in the 1970s, private salvage vessels and naval air antisubmarine warfare and surface reserve units cooperated with the Great Lakes Navy Association and the Great Lakes Naval and Maritime Museum in an attempt to pinpoint the location of the wreck. The sunken vessel finally was located approximately twenty miles north of Chicago off the lakeshore town of Wilmette. She will remain in her watery grave, however, until funding (approximately $1 million) can be procured to raise her.

A final footnote to the incident is the history of the gunboat *Wilmette*, originally the passenger steamer *Eastland*. On the morning of July 24, 1915, the *Eastland* was on the Chicago River boarding more than two thousand Western Electric employees en route to Michigan City, Indiana, for a day of picnicking. Early arrivals crammed on the boat, and she soon became vastly overloaded. As more passengers boarded, exceeding the boat's maximum capacity, the ship became top heavy and began to tilt from side to side. Mingling, dancing, and enjoying themselves, few of the passengers seemed concerned as the boat developed a substantial list. They playfully shouted as the ship became increasingly unstable.

Unable to trim the boat, and sensing catastrophe, the engineering crew abandoned their stations below decks as the boat listed to port 33 degrees. The passengers were ordered to move to the starboard rail, but this became impossible because of the list and the moisture on the decks. Still, many thought the ship would right herself, and they remained on board. Finally, as water began to flow into the ship, the *Eastland* rolled on her side and capsized. Eight hundred and forty-four passengers drowned in the tragedy; in many cases, entire families were lost.

Remarkably, one of the survivors (an engineer) also had survived the sinking of the *Titanic* after she struck an iceberg while making her maiden voyage from Southampton, England, to New York City three years earlier.

The *Eastland* was eventually raised and sold to the U.S. Navy, which converted her to a Naval Reserve Training ship and renamed her the *Wilmette*.

CHAPTER 8

Restoration—A Continuing Task

Prior to the *U-505*'s departure from Portsmouth, personnel from the Museum of Science and Industry (MSI) visited the boat a few times to ascertain her complexity and condition, to plan her water transit to the museum, and to determine just how the boat could be made into an exhibit. The engineers were also to estimate how much gear would have to be moved or removed to clear a pathway through the boat for touring visitors.

They decided to put holes in the port side but could not determine where the visitors should enter or exit. Should they enter the boat through the electric motor room, and exit through the petty officers' compartment, or should they come in at the rear torpedo room and exit through the forward torpedo room? The engineers selected the former plan. The whole port side of the petty officers' compartment is presently missing its bunks to accommodate guided tours of the boat. Additionally, the converted petty officers' compartment is presently missing its bunks to accommodate guided tours of the boat. Additionally, the converted petty officers' compartment provided a large space for visitors and their guide to further discuss the internal features of the boat before they left the boat. The floors in this compartment were lowered to allow visitors to exit the boat at the proper height to match the museum's floor plan. In anticipation of high numbers of visitors coming to the boat, the hatches to and from the control room were also cut out and enlarged so that visitors would have not have to climb through them. This would allow more people to experience the boat without slowing down the tours.

As we have seen, the boat had been threatened with scrapping at many points in her early postwar life. It was because of Admiral Dan Gallery and John F. Floberg, Assistant Secretary of the Navy for Air, that she was saved. In the meantime, however, pieces had come out, radio and sound gear and periscopes had been removed, and spare parts had been sent to other navies that were using surrendered German subs. The French Navy had off-loaded much of the *U-505*'s gear, including spare parts, because it needed an array of items to operate its confiscated boats.

When the exhibit opened in 1954, visitors touring the *U-505* entered the boat through a portside entry into the electric motor room. A tour guide walked them forward through the various compartments until they reached the petty officers' and chiefs' quarters (shown here) where they left the boat through a port exit. Watertight hatches throughout the interior passageway were removed by the museum to enable visitor access. In the new exhibit, visitors tour the boat from the bow aft to the stern. *MSI*

The bunk frames in the berthing spaces had all been removed and were scattered about in the forward and aft compartments. The mattresses themselves were gone. In fact, just after the boat was captured, the U.S. crew got rid of the German horsehair-stuffed mattresses because they found them uncomfortable. They were replaced by Navy-issue mattresses, which also disappeared when the boat went into storage. Gingham sheets matching the original ones were eventually put back in the boat. It has been the museum's goal all along to present the *U-505* the way she was when the crew lived aboard and operated her.

The heavy batteries (weighing some eighty tons) that were housed beneath the deck plates had been removed to reduce the weight of the boat when she was

towed. The boat's spaces were cluttered with various pieces of equipment, including the main ventilator motors from the diesel engine compartment, which were discovered in the battery well under the officers' quarters. The entire radio and sound rooms had been dismantled. In addition, safes that had held the boat's secret codebooks were missing from the radio room, captain's bunk, and officers' room.

The *U-505*'s antiaircraft deck guns had been removed for test and evaluation after the boat arrived in Bermuda. Just when they were returned to the boat is unknown. Except for one of the barrels, all deck guns are original to the *U-505*. The substitute barrel is from the *U-858* (Type IXC/40), which was the first U-boat to surrender to the U.S. Navy at the end of the war. Coincidentally,

her commander, Kapitänleutnant Thilo Bode, had served as 1st Watch Officer on board the *U-505* in 1942.

In order to present as complete a boat as possible, the museum requested that the Navy return any of the *U-505*'s original equipment that could be found or to replace what was missing with similar parts from other confiscated boats. The museum got a lucky break in this regard from a man named Carl T. Milner, who had worked at the Naval Undersea Sound Laboratory at the Portsmouth Naval Base. While the *U-505* had languished at Portsmouth, all her radio and sound gear had been thrown into dumpsters on the base. Milner, whose hobbies included anything electronic, recovered the gear and stored it in his basement. He toured the boat following her opening exhibit, and after his visit, he contacted museum personnel and asked if they were interested in the gear in his basement. Needless to say, the museum was most interested. Milner subsequently sent everything he had at his own expense, and the gear was reinstalled in the boat. He didn't have everything that was missing—some was *U-505* gear and other items were from other boats that operated later in the war—so the *U-505* gear was distributed between the radio and sound rooms. Using classified wartime U-boat documents released in the 1990s, the museum was able to identify what was missing. Hopefully, one day it will be able to recover those items and display the rooms in their original state.

Americans removed and tested the sub's antiaircraft guns in Bermuda but eventually returned them to the sub. The Germans had installed these weapons when the Allied air threat became severe. *MSI*

When the *U-505* arrived at the museum, restoration began immediately. Workmen repainted the boat inside and out, and worked for years attempting to present the boat the way she was when her German crew was aboard and operating her. *MSI*

When the *U-505* arrived in Chicago, restoration started immediately. The first pressing task was repainting. Her interior still had a lot of its original paint; it had simply been painted over several times. Once the boat was in place, U.S. painters went through the interior and repainted everything, using a color the U.S. Navy was accustomed to seeing—bright white. In reality, the Germans used what they called *elfenbein,* or ivory, for the basic interior compartment color; it is noticeably more yellow than U.S. Navy white.

In order to present the interior of the boat in its original color for the new exhibit, the museum has turned to sophisticated techniques. Using rare World War II color and black-and-white photos, color motion picture film, and even a World War II Kriegsmarine warship painting manual that was located in a German archive, museum personnel, led by *U-505* Curator Keith Gill, were able to document what original colors had been used in U-boats. Applying archaeological techniques, museum restoration personnel set up a 40x stereo micro-

Having discovered German painting regulation manuals dating from 1940, *U-505* Curator Keith Gill (shown here) worked to restore original interior colors of the U-boat. *Photo courtesy of The Sherwin-Williams Company*

Thirteen color shades were documented inside the *U-505,* in part because valve handles with differing functions had originally been color coded. Sherwin-Williams experts on the McCrone Institute staff helped the museum match the wartime paint of the sub. *Photo courtesy of The Sherwin-Williams Company*

scope in the control room of the boat and looked at paint layers of nearly five hundred paint chips from every valve handle, machine, wall surface, pipe, and every other piece of equipment in the boat to try to document the original colors present when the *U-505* was captured.

In all, thirteen different colors were documented in the boat, and there may be a few more. The closest match of the color sought was found in the German paint system standard RAL, which has been in existence since 1926. In many cases, the names of the colors or color codes still were the same. With the new RAL color chips, the museum then worked with Sherwin-Williams Company representatives to find a custom match in a latex paint system. Except for the diesel engine surfaces, the entire interior was then painted using latex enamels rather than oil-based paints. This allows the restoration team to reverse their painting process should they ever want to reveal the original paint below, a standard practice in artifact conservation. Latex also allows for touch-up work to the interior at any time without unpleasant odors of oil-based paint, and this can be done quickly after hours if needed.

Interestingly, the Germans used a lot of phosphorescent paint that glows in the dark for a period of time after being exposed to light. This was especially critical in a submarine if all the lights went out, for the glow of the paint allowed the crew to continue their work in emergency situations. All of the *U-505*'s important gauge faces have this paint, as do all hatches, ladder rungs, and the main overhead air ventilation pipes. During a microscopic analysis, these lay-ers were readily apparent. While museum personnel were doing research at the German military archives, they found a manual on the use of phosphorescent paints. To restore this effect in the boat, the German manual instructed the painter to first brush on a flat white primer and then to add a layer of phosphorescent paint over this. The white served as a very effective reflector. Now when the boat's lights are turned off, all of these surfaces glow once again, as they did during the war.

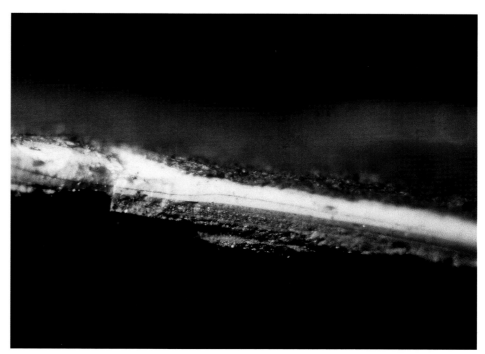

Examination of microscopic paint chips, such as this one from a valve handle inside the submarine, revealed several color changes over the years. *Photo courtesy of The Sherwin-Williams Company*

The other interesting part about the paint restoration concerns the exterior of the boat. During the *U-505*'s tow to Chicago, project planners decided she looked pretty bad and needed to be dressed up for her arrival ceremonies. Two house painters were sent from Chicago to Cleveland, where they met the boat in early June 1954. They proceeded to paint her black so she might look good when she finally got to Chicago. U.S. submarines had been painted black in the early-to-mid 1920s, and this standard was continued into the 1930s. The practice was resumed in the early 1950s, when U-boats were painted a mud gray on the top and a very dark gray on the bottom, making them almost look black. Some evidence in the *U-505*

Before being put on display in 1954 the exterior of the submarine had been sandblasted and then repainted. Over the years she has been repainted numerous times but always with the wrong colors. Here painters are shown giving the U-boat a coat before she was first opened up for tours. *MSI*

Here former museum president Lenox Lohr, whose vision made the *U-505* one of the most famous exhibits in the country, is shown with Axel Loewe, the first commanding officer of the *U-505*, touring the U-boat. Loewe joined the German Federal Navy following the war and is shown here wearing the rank of Kapitän zur See. *MSI*

photographs suggests a waterline was painted down the middle, which was a practice used earlier in the war; supposedly it was stopped as the war went on.

When the boat arrived in Chicago, she did look good above the waterline. But then, of course, when she was pulled out of the water, the whole bottom was rusty. The boat was scraped, sandblasted, and repainted for the opening ceremony at the museum in September 1954. Since then, she has been sandblasted and repainted three times, but always using the wrong colors: the typical U.S. Navy battleship gray on top and black on the bottom. Eventually, the original exterior paint color of the boat was matched as the interior colors had been, and the exterior was repainted using the proper wartime colors.

Shortly after the boat went on display in 1954, a decision was made to get the boat back into working condition as much as possible. Lenox Lohr was an engineer at heart and actually an engineer in true life. He felt that whatever was

The boat's diesel engines were made in 1940 by the Maschinenfabrik Augsburg-Nürnberg A.G. (M.A.N.) Company. After the war, this German company helped the museum get the engines operating again. General Motors engineers also assisted in 1954 and 1994, and other corporations joined the task of restoring the boat. For example, Illinois Bell helped get the boat's telephone system working. *MSI*

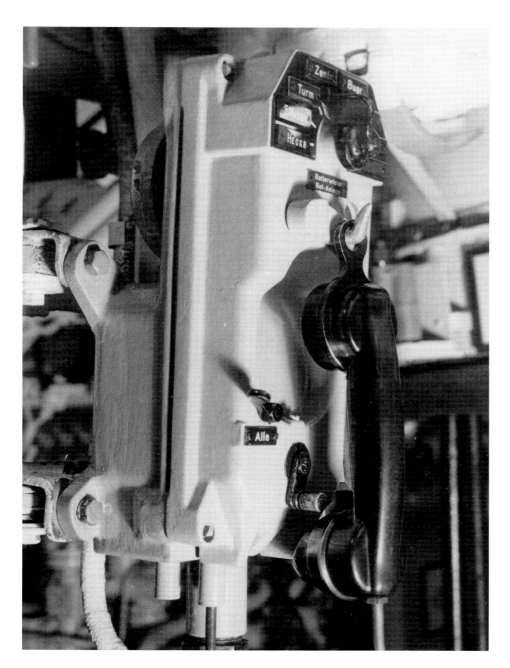

on display in the museum should be operational for visitors to appreciate. That philosophy extended to the *U-505*. People should hear, see, and smell the boat, as opposed to just looking at her from a distance.

The diesel engines were probably the biggest success story in the restoration of the boat. The Maschinenfabrik Augsburg-Nürnberg A.G. (M.A.N.) company in Germany made them in 1940, and they complied with the museum's request to provide technical support and information to get the engines running. The company was able to locate eighteen fuel-injection needle valves, cooling water thermometers, and assorted parts, and they donated them to the project. Engineers from

Palace to Museum

The World Columbian Exposition of 1893, planned to celebrate the four-hundredth anniversary of Christopher Columbus's voyages to the New World, was a cultural event unequalled in U.S. history at the time. Fourteen "great" buildings and hundreds of smaller buildings were constructed on 633 acres of Jackson Park along the south shore of Chicago's Lake Michigan. From May 1 to October 31, 1893, approximately twenty-seven million people from all parts of the country visited the fair. Some sixty-five thousand exhibits filled the exhibit halls.

In addition to Chicago, the cities of St. Louis, New York, and Washington had also petitioned to host the event. The U.S. House of Representatives gave Chicago the nod in 1890, and the following year, forty thousand skilled workers were hired to construct the fair. Along with the exhibit pavilions, workers built waterways fed by Lake Michigan to transport visitors by electric boat to exhibit buildings. An elevated railway provided additional transportation. The fourteen great halls built in the Beaux Arts style were all the same height and covered with the same hard white plaster covering. The result was a brilliant-looking set of buildings that became known as "White City."

On May 1, 1893, President Grover Cleveland officially opened the fair, surrounded by thousands of visitors.

All of the exposition buildings were temporary structures, to be torn down at the close of the fair. The Palace of Fine Arts was saved from the wrecking ball because it had a brick substructure. From 1893 to 1920, the building was occupied by the Field Museum of Natural History, which had been built to permanently house the biological and anthropological exhibits from the Columbian Exposition. In 1921, however, the Field Museum moved to Grant Park. The old palace structure that was left behind began to crumble, and there was talk of razing it.

At this point, a group of wealthy business leaders in Chicago, headed by Julius Rosenwald, president of Sears, Roebuck & Company, stepped in. They were determined to save the building, even if it meant rebuilding it stone by stone. Rosenwald envisioned converting the structure into a museum dedicated to science and industry. He had been inspired and impressed, while traveling in Germany with his family in 1916, by the Deutsches Museum in Munich, which was devoted to recording Europe's industrial progress.

Back in the United States, Rosenwald found that other cities—Washington and Pittsburgh included—had similar plans for such a museum. He grabbed the initiative, first by offering $1 million to the project in 1926, and then by giving another $3 million to establish the museum in Chicago. Supported by the Commercial Club of Chicago, whose membership included the city's industrial and business elite, an organizing committee was formed. Rosenwald subsequently announced that the museum site would be the old Palace of Fine Arts.

Rosenwald's concept of a Museum of Science and Industry differed from what he had seen in Europe, where museums dwelled on history. His museum would focus on contemporary technology and American inventive genius. Through this emphasis, he hoped to educate the American public about existing technologies they used in everyday life and to stimulate their thinking as to what the future might hold for "the greatest industrial nation in the world."

A search committee was formed to hire the museum's first director, and the science editor of the *New York Times*, Waldemar Kaempffert, was selected. Upon his arrival in Chicago in 1928, Kaempffert set about hiring a competent staff of scholars and practitioners to plan and design a wide array of exhibits. Restoration of the exterior of the building began, piece by piece, using Bedford limestone quarried and cut in Indiana. Progress was slow and the project's board of trustees became frustrated, factors which led to Kaempffert's resignation in 1931. Other directors followed, including Otto Kreusser (former chief engineer of the General Motors Testing Ground in Michigan), astronomer Dr. Philip Fox, and long-time creative innovator Major Lenox R. Lohr (former president of the National Broadcasting System), who established a number of the "long-lived" icons (grand exhibits) of the museum.

The Museum of Science and Industry was opened to the public on March 1, 1933. Its exterior looked much the same as it did in 1893, but in place of the original plaster, now there was limestone. Although several of the exhibit halls were empty initially, over the years they have been filled with new and more sophisticated technology equipment; new discoveries in science, communications, and human anatomy; classic train and automobile displays; a coal mine; an Omnimax theater; and developments in defense, including the air and space competition of the Cold War, and technology at sea. The technology at sea section centers on the unique *U-505* exhibit.

This "palace" would become a famous museum. *Library of Congress*

General Motors' Electromotive Division (located in LaGrange, Illinois) worked for several months to put the diesels into operating condition. (They had to work during the night because during the day, the boat was crowded with visitors.)

By 1956, the engines were running, and remained operational until 1968. In the 1990s, a new team from M.A.N. and the GM Electromotive Division was assembled to return the starboard engine to operation. It was started officially for the fiftieth anniversary and for five other ceremonies, including the CTG 22.3 veterans' reunion in 1994.

The museum received valuable assistance from other corporations, as well. For example, Illinois Bell helped get the boat's telephone system working. The lighting system had to be reenergized and put back into working order. The diving alarms had to be restored so they would ring as people toured the boat. The sights and sounds of these operational devices helped to make the environment more realistic.

When the story broke that the museum was getting the submarine, and that she was on her way, former German U-boat crewmen who had emigrated from Germany started volunteering their knowledge to the museum. Over time, several former submariners would visit the museum and lend a hand. Their assistance was invaluable.

When these men made themselves known, Lohr made sure they were treated well. They were taken to dinner and put up in nearby hotels (if they did not live in the Chicago area) so they could spend extra time at the museum. All labels that identified equipment in the boat had to be replaced because many of them had been taken as souvenirs at various times. When the boat arrived, much of the equipment could not be identified. The visiting U-boat crewmen helped to decipher what the equipment was and where it belonged in the boat. A label-making machine was purchased so that the hundreds of necessary labels (now in English) could be engraved to put on the equipment.

The *U-505* curator staff is often asked how the U.S. sailors knew how to operate the boat during her evaluation trials in Bermuda and her war bond drive along the East Coast in 1945. When the war officially ended, the United States, Britain, the Soviet Union, and France each took a number of U-boats of various models. The U.S. Navy wanted to evaluate and operate theirs as soon as possible. They looked to the manuals and publications that were on board the *U-505* when she was captured. The Navy picked the most important ones—from an intelligence point of view for at-sea trials—and had them translated immediately. At base, however, a sub is a sub: air is for diving, surfacing, and starting the diesels, and fuel and lube oil are for the engines. It helped that the *U-505* engines were standard types. Still, it must have been fascinating for the U.S. test crew that took her out on the first of several dives in Bermuda.

The boat had two Enigma machines when she was captured, which the National Security Agency (NSA) retained, along with other devices. They finally were declassified in the mid-to-late 1990s, and their related records were sent to the National Archives. The museum was notified of this action.

In 1993 the *U-505* exhibit underwent restoration for the fiftieth anniversary of the capture. The exhibit itself had not been changed since 1954, and it was decided to freshen the boat up with new carpeting and a new coat of paint. New artifacts were also put on display to liven up the exhibit. In this regard, Curator Gill made a trip to the National Archives in Washington, D.C., to copy information and to find material for this exhibit. Part of his trip included picking up an Enigma machine on loan from the NSA's National Cryptological Museum at Fort Meade in Maryland. While touring the NSA museum he saw the Enigma machines the agency had in storage and found that they had a dozen or so machines of various types: Wehrmacht (army), Luftwaffe (air force), and Kriegsmarine (navy). On a display table in one room, they had two machines in good condition. Both had a printing device attached, something Gill had not been aware of before. As he and the NSA curators were talking about the machines, his eye caught the serial number stamped on one of the machines. He didn't know why the serial number stuck with him, but it did.

He returned to Chicago with a plain four-rotor machine (the one with no noticeable serial number on it), with no printer, and a suitcase-load of photocopied material from the National Archives. As he was going through the paperwork in more detail, he came on a list of publications that had been taken from the *U-505*. It inventoried every book, map, and document and broke them into subgroups. The section on communications listed both Enigma machines that were on the boat, including their serial numbers. Each machine was documented as having had its own box of rotors, and one happened to have a printing device with it. Gill took note of that, looked at the serial number, and was almost positive it was the very same machine he had seen at the NSA museum.

When the loan came up for renewal in 1996, Gill made another trip to Washington and once again visited the NSA museum. When they told him they wanted the machine on loan returned, he asked if the MSI could have the other machine he had been shown. He informed them that, according to National Archives records, that machine was actually one of the two *U-505* Enigma machines. Having read the paperwork in support of that claim, NSA loaned the machine to the MSI, where it has been placed in a secure area equipped with extra alarms. The NSA has been very supportive of the exhibit, and a label placed next to the machine properly credits the National Cryptological Museum for the loan.

The periscopes present on the boat when she was opened to the public in 1954 were not actually the *U-505*'s periscopes. When the museum received the boat, the original periscopes were missing. Because museum officials felt the periscopes would be a major attraction, they asked the Navy to look into the matter. The Navy immediately began searching through files to determine their whereabouts. Initially, the Navy concluded that the scopes had been removed from the boat and sent to Bausch and Lomb, or another company, for testing and evaluation. The Navy never expected such equipment to be returned because it was often tested to the point of destruction or just scrapped on site after the testing was completed. The test information had become more important than the equipment.

There was also some indication that the *U-505* periscopes might have been sent to another country to keep one of the former German submarines operating.

But no direct proof ever surfaced; the paper trail left some doubt about their disposition. Nevertheless, the Navy notified museum officials in 1956 that it had found a periscope from the *U-505* and was arranging to ship it immediately. The truck arrived with a steel periscope case, but when the case was off-loaded and opened, it was empty. Apparently, at one time the case had carried one of the U-boat's periscopes, because the serial identification noted on it matched the official records. All hope was lost at that point, and the museum just made do with two replicas: one a stainless steel tube made to look like a scope in the up position, and the other a British periscope.

The search for the scopes continued, however, and in the early 1990s, some U-boat periscopes were found to be on display in Germany. The technical director of the movie *Das Boot* was contacted, and he told MSI personnel that he had located one of the scopes, but it was the property of the film studio and was on display on the movie set. He offered to search for the other scope and later informed the museum that a friend of his in Finland had bought a scope. He was going to put it into a restaurant, but the deal fell through. The periscope was for sale for $30,000. MSI staff thought the selling price was too high, especially since there was no indication that it was even the correct model for the *U-505*.

In the mid-1990s the museum got a call from a man in charge of a National Park Service project concerning a historic site at Point Loma, California, the Navy's old Arctic Submarine Laboratory. It was a Cold War–era research and test facility used for testing the effects of a submarine sail (which contained the sub's bridge and conning tower) as it punched through ice. The laboratory was constructed over a gigantic pit that was filled with water and frozen three or four feet thick at the surface. The sail of a submarine would then be punched through the ice with a hydraulic ram and the results recorded. A German periscope at the facility was used to look underwater and observe what was happening while a test was conducted.

Those working at the facility talked with several people and determined that the scope was most likely from the *U-505*. The museum, though excited about

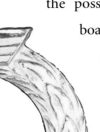

the possibility of finding the boat's periscope, contended that many surrendered German subs had been distributed at the end of the war and that the scope could have come from any one of those boats. But the caller responded that from the start, some of the "older guys" who had been involved in the project were certain that the scope had come from Portsmouth and was from the *U-505*. They remembered how it had been easier to get a German periscope than an old U.S. Navy scope, but even so, they had had to exercise "creative acquisition" in order to procure it for their tests.

Soon the ball started rolling to secure the periscope for the MSI's exhibit, but it took several years for that to happen because the site of the laboratory had been declared a National Historic Landmark. It had been a hidden gun emplacement adjacent to the harbor in San Diego dating to before World War I. The gun pit itself was determined to be of a historic nature, worthy of saving, but everything else associated with it was not, including the Arctic Submarine Laboratory. A very long delay ensued, during which officials tried to figure out how to remove the periscope. After careful study, they determined that the only

method that would work was to lower the periscope into the hole that was dug for it, to cover it, and then to destroy the building around it. This is exactly what they did. Once they started the process, however, lead paint, asbestos, and dangerous chemicals were released and caused major problems. The process ended up being very frustrating for everyone involved.

Eventually, the periscope was freed, and its discovery made big headlines across the country. The Naval Historical Center (NHC) in Washington, D.C., immediately accepted the paperwork for transfer of the periscope from Commander, Navy Region Southwest. And from there the periscope was accessioned and catalogued into the Navy's central artifact database in Washington. Finally, the NHC facilitated the legal and logistical issues associated with the loan of the scope from the Navy to the museum, and the long-lost periscope finally returned home to the *U-505*.

Several German medals and badges were discovered in the living spaces of the submarine, and others were donated later. Many are on display at the museum. Here we see (*left to right*) (a) the Iron Cross 2nd class with ribbon; (b) a Hitler Youth Rally badge; (c) a Minesweeping, Subchasing and Security Units badge; (d) a Submarine War badge; and (e) a Wound Badge. a, b, *and* d *on loan from Wolfhart Hauser;* c *and* e *MSI*

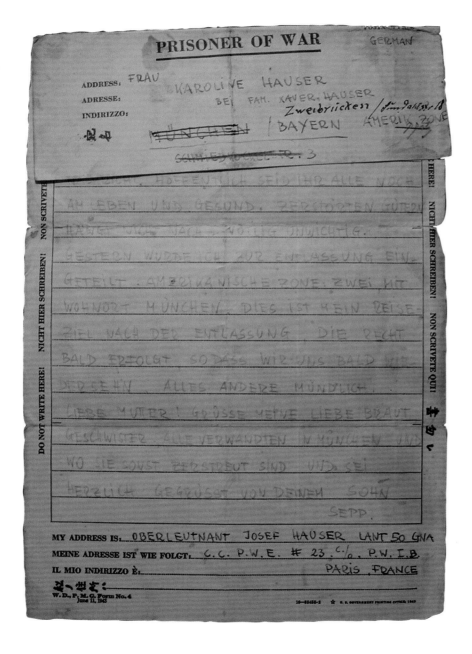

Upon its arrival at the museum, it was found to be the *U-505*'s navigation periscope and in good condition. It is now on exhibit next to the boat.

At the time the boat was opened for visitors in 1954, the U.S. Navy sent a small batch of artifacts to the MSI on a long-term-loan basis. Likewise, Admiral Gallery had a number of souvenirs that he made sure were turned over to the museum. Included among them were: a scrapbook; a German Navy flag; a small

Included in the exhibit is a letter that *U-505* crewman Oberleutnant Josef Hauser wrote to his mother from a POW camp in France just before his release to return home following his internment. Translated, the message reads:

German
PRISONER OF WAR
Address: Mrs. Karoline Hauser
At FAM. Xaver Hauser
Zweibruecken / Lundahlstrasse 18
Bavaria   American Zone
Message: After two years, I am again on the coast of Western Europe. I am healthy, and am returning soon. I have had no news from you, (my) finacée and siblings since my last journey. Hopefully you all are still alive and well. Don't shed any tears over property that has been destroyed. Yesterday I got the order for my release. American zone: two, residency Munich. This is my destination after my release, which is supposed to happen quickly; so we can meet again soon. About everything else we'll talk!

Dear Mother! Give my greetings to my lovely bride, my siblings and all relatives in Munich and wherever they may be scattered.
Best regards from your son Sepp.
My address is: First Lieutenant Josef Hauser LANT 50 GNA
C.C.P.W.E. #23. c.o. P.W.I.B.
Paris, France
MSI/The Hauser Collection

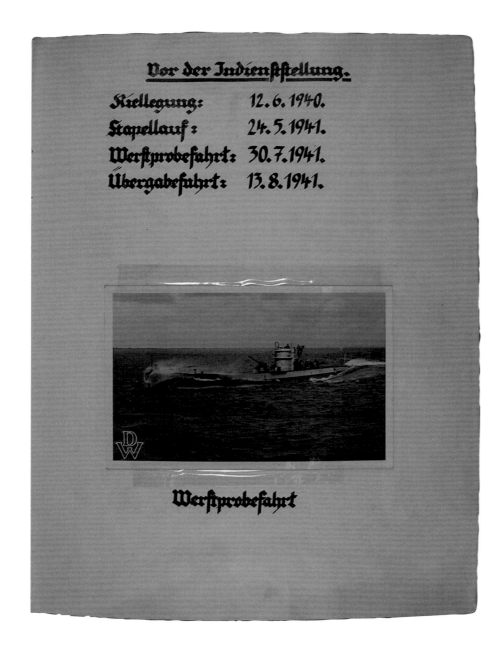

Vor der Indienstellung.

Kiellegung:	12. 6. 1940.
Stapellauf:	24. 5. 1941.
Werftprobefahrt:	30. 7. 1941.
Übergabefahrt:	13. 8. 1941.

Werftprobefahrt

Several Zeiss binoculars were found on the U-boat and are now in the museum's collection donated by boarding party members. *MSI*

collection of medals, pins, and photographs that were taken out of some of the living spaces; newspaper articles the German crewmen had saved; an Iron Cross 1st Class medal; and a pair of binoculars that belonged to Oberleutnant zur See Harald Lange (Gallery returned them to Lange at a 1964 reunion). A lifeboat from the sub and a set of leather clothing are also in the museum's collection, and from time to time, Navy veterans give more artifacts to the museum for the *U-505* exhibit.

Admiral Gallery donated to the museum an informal "cruise book" found on the sub, which included the page shown here having to do with putting the sub in service. It indicates that the keel was laid on June 6, 1940, the boat was launched on May 24, 1941, the shipyard test cruise took place on July 30, and the cruise in which the boat was handed over to the *U-505* crew took place on August 13. Note the 10.5 cm deck gun in the photo. *USNI*

American crewmen discovered many cartons of German cigarettes on the *U-505* when they captured the boat. Admiral Gallery distributed them throughout his task group. *MSI*

Through the years, the museum has attempted to locate families of former Task Group 22.3 crew members with the hope of recovering additional artifacts. This endeavor has yielded several binoculars and a piece of a German uniform insignia. German cigarettes have been the most common item returned because cartons of the German cigarettes were found on board the U-boat, and those were one souvenir Admiral Gallery felt he could share with all hands. The museum collection also includes a fountain pen from the captain's compart-

ment. Previously undiscovered artifacts that were found on board the sub include a canteen, a breathing filter for scrubbing carbon dioxide, and some tools lost in the periscope well or under torpedo tubes.

Don Carter was a signalman with the second boarding party from the *Guadalcanal.* He was interested mostly in flags and signal pistols as his souvenirs. Finding several flags on board the boat, he grabbed one. Word spread that Captain Gallery wanted a German flag to put on the *U-505* periscope under the biggest American flag the crew could find so they could make a grand entrance into Bermuda. Nobody knew where the German flag was. They all figured Don Carter probably had it, so Gallery sent for him and Carter coughed it up. Not wanting Carter to go away empty-handed, Gallery traded a flare pistol for the flag. Carter donated the pistol to the MSI in the early 1990s.

Fortunately, Dan Gallery had kept one of the commander-size ensigns and donated it to the museum in 1953. The flag that Dan Carter took was the one used at sea and therefore battle worn. Gallery presented that ensign to Admiral Jonas Ingram, Commander in Chief, Atlantic, in 1944. He, in turn, gave it to the

A crewman's identification disc found on the submarine. *MSI*

This belt buckle reading "God with us" and featuring the swastika was found on the *U-505. MSI*

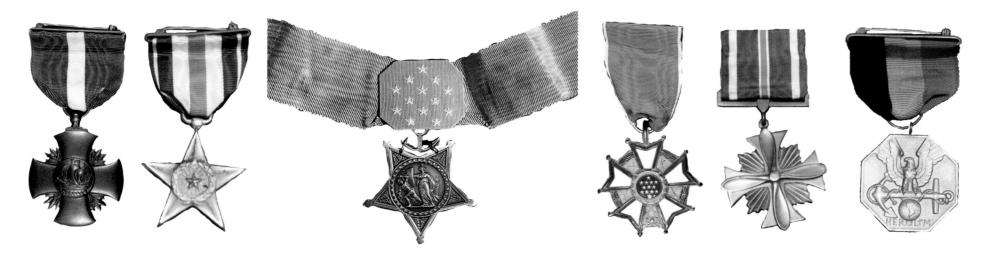

The museum exhibit displays numerous medals and ribbons that were earned by members of the American task group responsible for the sub's capture, several of them donated and others loaned by crew members or their families. Shown here from left to right are the Navy Cross (donated by Mrs. S. Wdowiak); Silver Star (donated by Mrs. Anne Mocarski); Medal of Honor; Legion of Merit (on loan from Mr. D. E. Hampton); Distinguished Flying Cross (donated by Mr. J. Cadle Jr.); Navy-Marine Corps Medal (on loan from Mrs. Darlene Bednarczyk); and below, top to bottom, Navy Commendation Ribbon (on loan from Mr. Don Carter); and the Presidential Unit Citation Ribbon (on loan from the Riendeau famliy), which was awarded to Task Group 22.3 and all its members. *MSI*

U.S. Naval Academy where, according to tradition, it now resides in Memorial Hall with other captured enemy ensigns from the earliest days of our Navy.

Most fortunately, the MSI has received the following individual awards from those who participated in the capture and/or their families: a Navy Cross medal, five of nine Silver Star medals, a Legion of Merit medal, two Distinguished Flying Cross medals, and a Navy-Marine Corps medal. All are now on display.

When holes were cut inside the boat to allow visitors access in and out, the steel was cut into small tablets that were sold in the gift shop as souvenirs. About three to four hundred feet of anchor chain were also cut, a link at a time, and sold in the gift shop. Machinists ground off the edge of the link, stamped *U-505* on it, and put it on a nicely cut wooden board for home display. Those were sold up until the 1980s. The museum has only about six feet of chain left.

One of the most official souvenirs of any surrender is the sidearm of an officer. It has been generally assumed that a German officer had a Luger or a P-38 sidearm issued to him. National Archives' records identify those carried on the *U-505* boat as HsC Mausers. They were very small .32-caliber pistols, easy to conceal and carry and easy to stow away in a locker

on the boat. The museum has pursued tracking down the five or six pistols that were on the boat; three have been located thus far, but their owners have elected to keep them in their possession.

Every time the museum has a reunion or a well-publicized event, veterans of the capture or their families return souvenirs. When the fiftieth anniversary ceremony of the capture took place in 1994, five hundred American veterans attended. One of them came with a fleece-lined leather jacket originally worn by the doctor on the U-boat. When he came aboard the U.S. ship that rescued him, he was issued dry clothes. The American crewman ended up with the German's old jacket, and he squirreled it away. It took two more patrols before he had the courage to smuggle it off the ship. After allowing his children to wear it as a Halloween costume in the 1970s, the Navy man finally donated it to the museum. For a long time, this was the only piece of uniform in the MSI's *U-505* collection. Since then, however, a pair of leather pants and a pair of shorts (tropical) have been added.

The search for *U-505* artifacts continues to this day.

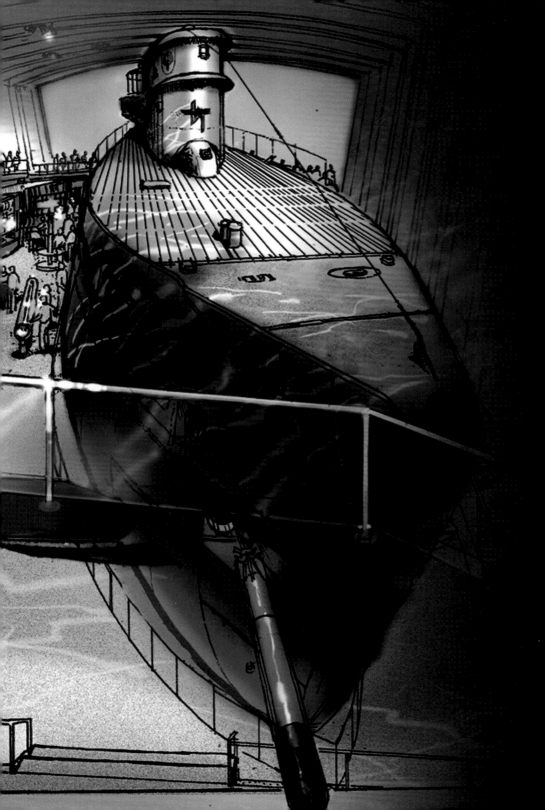

CHAPTER 9

The New U-505 *Experience*

Since her Chicago dedication in 1954 as a memorial to the fifty-five thousand Americans lost at sea during the two world wars, the *U-505* has been a premiere exhibit for the Museum of Science and Industry (MSI). As one of the leading cultural attractions in the region, the museum hosts more than two million visitors a year, many of whom are fascinated to see a unique piece of wartime maritime history. Consequently, more than twenty-four million people have boarded the submarine to date. The *U-505* has created indelible memories for generations of children, and she has become for veterans a triumphant reminder of a hard-won peace.

Designated a National Historic Landmark in 1989, the submarine symbolizes what is best about the MSI: authentic encounters that cannot be duplicated anywhere else in the world, bringing science and technology to life. From the beginning, visitors

MSI

The *U-505* rests alongside the east facade of the Museum of Science and Industry before moving to her permanent underground site at the northeast corner of the museum. *MSI*

were simply intrigued by the experience of being inside a submarine. Nevertheless, many of the children and adults who first visited the *U-505* after World War II understood the compelling context of the artifact. More recent visitors, though, have often had less understanding of the U-boat's technological or historical importance.

In addition, the boat had been deteriorating at an alarming pace from long exposure to the elements. Analysis done in 2001 revealed that the hull metal had in some places

Shown with Museum President Lenox Lohr and Admiral Gallery, young Arthur Ley Jr. of Torrance, California, is honored as the four millionth visitor to tour the *U-505*. By the time of its move underground in 2004, more than twenty-four million people had visited the submarine. *MSI*

eroded to as little as one-fourth its original thickness. The *U-505*'s structural integrity was in jeopardy, and if not moved inside to a temperature-controlled environment, the submarine could be lost forever. The critical time had arrived for the museum to fully protect one of the nation's technological and historical treasures. At the same time, creation of "The *U-505* Experience" could take advantage of the many advances in museum capabilities and immerse visitors in an exhibit experience to tell anew a gripping story of a complex machine and courageous men.

Preserving and introducing the *U-505* in a new and dramatic fashion was a matter of responsible stewardship, the kind expected from any custodian of a priceless and irreplaceable artifact. To create a safe harbor to protect the U-boat from the weather and to provide an enhanced experience that would allow visitors to encounter the submarine from every angle required a significant financial investment. The museum launched a campaign that raised more than $29 million from public and private sources. Federal, state, and local governments contributed 52 percent of the total. Led by the museum's board of trustees, more than forty-three hundred individual donors have committed gifts making up another 24 percent; foundations added 22 percent and corporations 2 percent. The relocation and preservation project began in 1997 and was completed in 2005, in time for the sixty-first anniversary of the sub's capture.

Moving the Boat

The *U-505* had to be moved, slowly and carefully, by a circuitous route around the east end of the museum to a new underground home below the northeast corner of the museum's front lawn.

Lohan Caprile Goettsch Architects of Chicago designed the climate-controlled

Standing outside of the Museum of Science and Industry and adjacent to Lake Michigan for fifty years, the *U-505* has suffered greatly from the extremes of weather. Erosion of the ship's hull, as shown in this photo, came to threaten the integrity of the submarine. *MSI*

underground exhibit space especially for the *U-505*. Working with W. E. O'Neil Construction, the museum broke ground in February 2003. The exhibit space is thirty-five thousand square feet and extends forty-two feet below ground.

Patrons enter the exhibit experience through an underground passageway that connects it to the museum's east pavilion, where a dramatic new display enables visitors to view the entire boat from a few yards away, as well as to see many associated artifacts and displays that explain the sub's operation and capture. The large and carefully designed space also makes it possible to introduce visitors to the submarine in a full historical context. Following a vivid presentation on World War II and the Battle of the Atlantic, they are—by means of compelling storytelling, combined with state-of-the art audio and visual

techniques—transported back in time to the dramatic events of June 4, 1944. Visitors walk around the sub on a fully handicapped-accessible ramp descending to the football-field-sized exhibit floor.

Before the museum could relocate the U-boat, it had to determine how the move would affect the fragile treasure. Structural engineers used finite element analysis computer models to simulate the relocation, testing different configurations for the cradles that would support the boat during the move. They discovered it would take six cradles, plus special reinforcement, to safely guide the *U-505* to her new site.

Investigators crawled through tight openings to get into the spaces between the submarine's exterior hull and interior pressure hull to identify places that needed to be strengthened. Brackets, stringers, and ribs were remanufactured using original construction drawings recovered from Germany and the patterns from badly corroded parts. Then, ballast tank by ballast tank,

Plans were made to move the *U-505* out of her original location alongside the museum and back it down Science Drive. Then it was to travel bow first past the Space Center and East Pavilion before turning north and being lowered into its new home. Lake Michigan is at the bottom of this diagram. *MSI*

workers installed the reinforcements, focusing on jacking points and cradle locations. It took nearly two years to ensure that the *U-505* was capable of withstanding the one-thousand-foot relocation. A structural repair team led by Toledo Ship Repair did a remarkable job in keeping true to the original method of construction in making their repairs.

Moving the submarine required precision work by a team experienced in the relocation of large maritime and industrial items. NORSAR, which specializes in such work, was hired to accomplish the task. First, NORSAR created six specially designed and engineered lifting cradles to place under the sub for jacking the boat up. These lifting cradles were intended to lift the boat primarily by the keel without putting any stress on the outer hull of the boat. Unlike many more ordinary moves of heavy objects, no cranes or lifting straps were used at all. Then the boat was jacked straight into the air to about six feet off the ground so dollies could be

installed. Eighteen sets of dollies with eight tires apiece (each tire capable of carrying twelve hundred pounds per square inch) were positioned under the boat. The dollies were designed with individually adjustable hydraulic rams for maneuvering over uneven surfaces, and were individually controllable for easy steering. The museum cleared the submarine's path, planking over curbs and clearing such other obstructions as signs and fences. The boat was to be liter-ally driven around the museum by these hydraulically motorized dollies—a far cry from the very labor-intensive effort required to move the boat in 1954!

The *U-505* backs away from her fifty-year home alongside the museum's east facade. Visible below the vessel's stern are the two rud-ders and one of the sub's two propellers. Also visible in this photo, if one looks closely, are two covered hatches that the museum cut into the port side for easy access. *MSI*

On April 8, 2004, the U-boat began her journey after a cham-pagne christening. Guests on a viewing platform draped with cer-emonial bunting included Chicago Mayor Richard M. Daley and four World War II veterans who had participated in the capture of the boat in 1944. A Navy brass band filled the clear blue skies with familiar tunes, and the festive mood of the crowd harkened to for-

Still backing, the *U-505* rides its cradles, dollies, and many tires over temporary decking toward Lake Michigan, visible at the top left of the photo. From this point of view, one notes the lifeline ringing the wooden deck and the boat's two bow planes. The lifeline was put on by the *MSI* staff and is not original. It has been removed. *MSI*

The sub continues around the northeast portion of the museum, now traveling bow first and with Chicago's Lake Shore Drive on the sub's right. A workman standing on a platform suspended along the port side of the vessel operates the hydraulic pump that keeps pressure on the hydraulic jacks and also propels the sub along its short journey. On the sub, note the ports of the stern torpedo tubes (one closed, one open), and below them the rudders, stern planes, and propellers. *MSI*

mer times, when U-boats departed on their maiden voyages.

As Kurt Haunfelner, the museum's vice president of exhibits and collections, remarked, "We are taking extraordinary efforts to restore and conserve the submarine and make it part of a brand-new visitor experience that will give visitors compelling insight into the Battle of the Atlantic, the significance of the *U-505*'s capture, and the heroism displayed by Captain Dan Gallery and the men of Task Group 22.3."

Over the next five days, the NORSAR team guided the *U-505* a thousand

Opposite: The *U-505* approaches its new home at the northeast corner of the Museum. *MSI*

feet around the end of the museum into position over her new home—a seventy-five-by-three-hundred foot, forty-two-foot deep submarine showcase. The boat was jacked up and placed on Teflon pads to help minimize friction as she was pushed across the span of the new exhibition hall on four enormous steel bridge beams. Powerful jacks attached to eight cribbing towers anchored to the floor of the pen rose to accept the *U-505*'s weight as she made her two-day, four-story descent to the floor below.

Creation of the *U-505* Experience had begun.

The *U-505* is lowered into the new exhibit hall with the aid of powerful jacks attached to eight cribbing towers anchored to the exhibit floor. On one side of the sub's bow can be seen the recess for the boat's anchor (the anchor was taken off for the move); the port for the starboard bow torpedo tube; and the starboard bow plane, projecting to the side. It was one of these projecting bow planes that holed the escort *Pillsbury* during the capture. *MSI*

Visitors entering the exhibit are confronted with images of the world at war and Hitler's Blitzkrieg, which over-ran much of Europe. *NARA*

The New Exhibit

The *U-505* enters the twenty-first century thoroughly refurbished and completely protected in an enclosed climate-controlled space. She is now one of the best-preserved warships in the world. Preservation, though, is not the end, but the means. World War II is as distant from today as the time of President Cleveland and Queen Victoria was from the day the *U-505* last cruised the high seas. The $35 million spent on preserving and sprucing up this valuable prize brought home by Dan Gallery and the men of TG 22.3 also prepares the U-boat for a renewed purpose and mission: to give accurate and vivid testimony to the people and events of the struggle in which the *U-505* played a dramatic role. Museum president David Mosena noted that the new exhibit is a richer experience that puts the Atlantic sea battles of World War II in a larger context. He commented, "Our view is the long view. This creates a legacy that will live far beyond our generation."

Visitors to the exhibit enter the world at war. Large screens show Hitler's Blitzkrieg overrunning much of Europe. Germany, Italy, and Japan join together as the Axis powers. England's back is to the wall. Then, in

On December 7, 1941, Japan attacked the American fleet at Pearl Harbor. Sights and sounds of the exhibit make clear that America had now joined the Allies in the war. *NARA*

The exhibit moves imaginatively to the Battle of the Atlantic, during which German U-boats attempted to inhibit Allied ships from carrying materials and men from the United States to Europe, even taking the war to America's East Coast. Here, the SS *Byron T. Benson* is shown burning after being torpedoed near Cape Hatteras, North Carolina, on April 5, 1943. *NARA*

December 1941, Japan attacks the American fleet at Pearl Harbor. Sights and sounds make clear that America is at war, fighting to defend our way of life. The following month, German U-boats begin a devastating attack on shipping along the East Coast in "Operation Drumbeat." In the Battle of the Atlantic, German U-boats attempt to cut the life-line carrying material and men from the United States to the other side of the Atlantic.

One answer to this challenge was the U.S. Navy's hunter-killer groups. One such group was Dan Gallery's Task Group 22.3, with a small aircraft carrier (the USS *Guadalcanal*), her aircraft, and five escort destroyers. Visitors will hear Gallery's words to his men, with the motto they adopted: "Can Do."

Descending stairs through the sounds of 1944, visitors enter F-21, the U.S. Navy's top secret Naval Intelligence Center. Into this center comes information from High Frequency Direction Finding stations and from decrypted German message traffic. Women Accepted for Volunteer Emergency Service (WAVES) can be seen using this information to plot the path of the

U-505 on a huge chart of the Atlantic. From here messages tell the hunter-killer groups where to look.

Next we board the bridge of Gallery's flagship, the carrier USS *Guadalcanal*. It is a quiet Sunday morning, June 4, 1944, when suddenly the destroyer escort *Chatelain* detects the *U-505*. We overhear the radio chatter between the ships, as

Navy women shown in a portrayal of a top secret Naval Intelligence Center. The Center radioed information about the general location of the *U-505* to Gallery's task group. This information had been obtained by the use of high-frequency radio intercepts and decrypted German naval messages. *MSI*

well as the orders of the carrier's Officer of the Deck as the task group swings into pursuit. Hedgehogs and depth charges splash into the sea to explode below. The wounded submarine surfaces under fire from ships and aircraft. For the first time since the War of 1812, a U.S. naval officer orders "Away all boarding parties!" American sailors in small boats speed in to capture the still-moving U-boat while German sailors hastily abandon ship.

Leaving the ship's bridge, visitors suddenly meet the *U-505*, bow-on and only a few feet away. We might be floating in the Atlantic that day in 1944! From there, a ramp leads around and past the submarine, descending to the floor near the stern. The context of global struggle that gives meaning to the preservation of the *U-505* has been established. Now in our walk down the display ramp to the large exhibit space below, we can learn

After learning the details of the capture, visitors meet the *U-505*. From here they walk down a long ramp that parallels the submarine as they proceed to the exhibit floor. *MSI*

On the exhibit floor, through an interactive display, visitors can learn how the German crewmen used their periscope to lock onto a target and sink a surface ship. *MSI*

the details of this deadly artifact of war and the heroism that ultimately brought her here.

Visitors of various ages will have different questions: What did the boarding parties have to do? What were the risks? How hard and how dangerous was it to keep the sinking sub afloat? What happened to the German prisoners of war? How does a submarine go up and down? What does it feel like to lie in a submariner's berth? What happened to the *U-505* before the boat came to Chicago? All these questions and more are answered by video displays, artifacts, and interactive exhibits surrounding the *U-505*. The oral histories of the boarding party members and U.S. task group veterans describe their actions in attacking and boarding the sub, removing important materials, and keeping the boat afloat.

Adjacent to the submarine is an advanced T5 acoustic torpedo of the type taken from the *U-505*, with a display showing the inner workings and how the torpedo is locked onto its target. There, too, is one of the *U-505*'s actual periscopes as well as an interactive mock-up conning tower showing how a periscope works. Also, in a stylized version of the dive control station aboard the *U-505*, visitors can take the seats of the submarine planesmen and operate the wheels that control the bow and stern dive planes. As this "crew" dives the sub, the control room tilts on a motion base to mimic the dive angle.

Displayed nearby is one of the famous Enigma encryption machines. It is one of two found aboard the *U-505*, an unusual advanced model with an attached printing device. Recovery of the machine plus the actual Enigma code keys, as well as a coded grid chart of the Atlantic and other cryptographic material, made the submarine's capture particularly valuable. Visitors can send and receive coded messages between interactive computer-simulated Enigma stations.

In another interactive exhibit, visitors can take the seats of the submarine planesmen, turn the wheels, and try to dive the boat. The control room tilts to mimic the dive angle chosen. *MSI*

Of course, the submarine herself is the most interesting display of all. Painted on the conning tower are the seashell emblem of the U-boat's last captain and the insignia of its unit, the 2nd U-Flotilla. *MSI*

Perhaps the highlight of the whole exhibit is the tour of the *U-505*. How could fifty-nine men live, eat, and work for months and then fight, suffer attacks, and even die in such a constricted space? These photographs of the boat's interior do not adequately convey the size of the submarine; you must experience the tour for yourself. The captain's and navigator's tracking chart table in the central control room is shown here. *MSI*

Then there is the submarine herself—252 feet long. Descending the display ramp only a few yards from the hull, visitors pass the bow planes, the conning tower, and the deck guns. The conning tower sports the stylized seashell emblem of Oberleutnant zur See Harald Lange, the U-boat's last captain, but it also bears the shell holes made the day of the capture. Reaching the floor of the exhibit hall, visitors then encounter the story of the men who kept the submarine afloat in the dangerous minutes and hours following the boarding, and who ensured a safe arrival at the haven of Bermuda. Coming around the stern, we pass within arm's reach of the two great propellers, the aft dive planes, and the rudders, and we gaze into one of the four stern torpedo tubes. The torpedo tube door is open as it was on June 4, 1944, when the *U-505* fired a final desperate (and luckily ineffective) T5 acoustic torpedo shot at the American task group.

Groups of a dozen or so can enter the submarine for a docent-led tour from one end to the other. Inside, they squeeze into the amazingly cramped space where fifty-nine men once lived and worked. They see what those men saw: for the first time since the end of World War II, the *U-505* is now painted in the original colors, with deck plates and lockers and countless valves and pipes in place. Bunks, officers' quarters, the radio room, and the tiny galley all appear much as they actually existed during the U-boat's wartime service. Hear the diesel engines throbbing, the Morse code from the radio room, a torpedoed ship breaking up, and the sounds of depth charges from an Allied destroyer! The *U-505* exhibit of a half century past is now alive as the *U-505* Experience!

The forward torpedo room. *MSI*

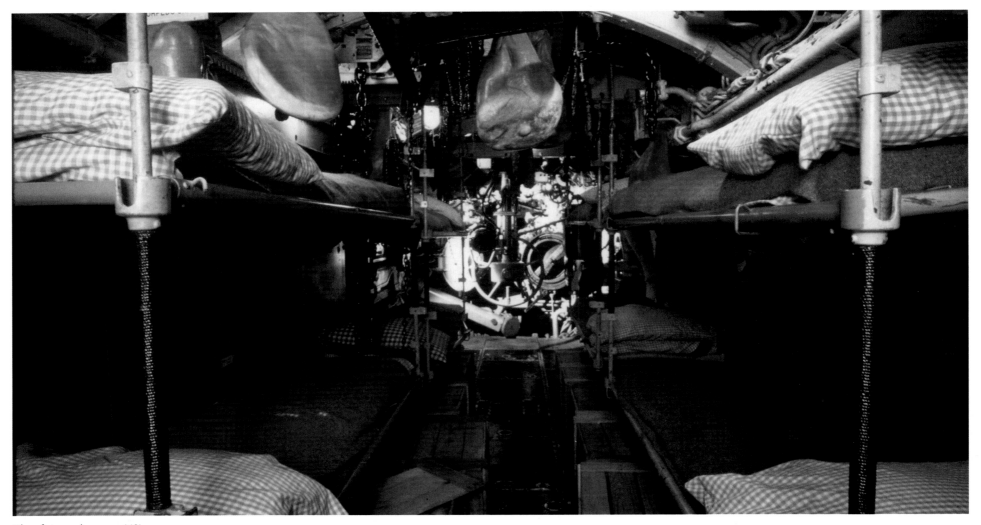

The aft torpedo room. *MSI*

For those too recently born to have known it directly, World War II becomes real, and they come to better understand that freedom is never free. The significance of the *U-505* coalesces in the mind of a ten-year-old boy, or his older sister, or the minds of their parents. As few memorials can, the *U-505* will for many years to come let visitors see and hear and touch the event, then take away new memories and new understanding.

APPENDIX A

Operating and Living on Board the U-505

Once the *U-505* was nestled in a hidden setting in Bermuda, U.S. Navy submariners and intelligence personnel, using information gained from interrogation of the boat's survivors, familiarized themselves with the structure, mechanisms, and operation of the boat, along with her propulsion system, torpedoes, and detection gear. In addition to acquiring technical data, they wanted to learn firsthand what the living conditions were like for German U-boat crews who spent months at sea in a steel tube traveling great distances to engage an enemy.

U-boat officers and crewmen were considered by the German populace to be an elite group: smart, brave, and adventuresome. They got the best provisions, the most money, and additional pay for diving (1.5 to 4 reichmarks a day if the boat dived at least once) and for deploying to distant operational areas. A German city or town sponsored each boat; Bad

akg-images

Wiessee in the Tegernsee adopted the *U-505*, and her crew vacationed there between patrols, regaining their mental health in a relaxed atmosphere. The Bavarian town was a vacation spot for skiers, and hotels and recreational facilities were at the crew's disposal. During the U-boat "happy times" early in the war, crews enjoyed their share of "wine, women, and song" in these escape settings.

The crew of the *U-505* was a mix of raw recruits and veterans transferred from other boats. After a demanding physical examination, new recruits usually went through ninety days of basic training with one of the naval training detachments located along the coasts of Germany and Holland. After graduation they were sent to specialized schools that trained them in radio, engineering, torpedoes, and artillery.

Those who had volunteered for or were ordered to submarine duty had to pass another rigorous physical examination before continuing to train with the Submarine Training Division at either Pillau (Baltijsk) or Gotenhafen (Gdynia). At the latter training facilities, engine room personnel and torpedomen were grouped in two companies of 90 to 100 men. The remainder was divided into regular seaman classes of about 250 recruits each. Graduates of this intense training were skilled professionals who were likewise instilled with a strict code of discipline that served them well who were likewise instilled with a strict code of discipline that served them well.

A view of the interior of the *U-505* with her bow to the right. Spaces shown are forward torpedo room (1) with a hatch leading into the petty officers' and chiefs' quarters (2); the galley (3) (with ladder up to the deck); the commissioned officers' quarters (4) followed by the captain's quarters (5) opposite the radio and sound rooms (6). The control room (7) is next, with a second ladder leading up to the conning tower interior room (8) and the open bridge (9) above that. Aft of the control room is a hatch leading into the diesel engine room (10), with the electric motor room (11), and the after torpedo room (12) further aft. *MSI*

1. Forward torpedo room
2. Petty Officers' and Chiefs' quarters
3. Galley
4. Officers' quarters
5. Captain's quarters
6. Radio/sound room
   (opposite Captain's quarters)
7. Control room
8. Conning tower interior room
9. Open bridge
10. Diesel engine room
11. Electric motor room
12. After torpedo room

in battle. Their graduation meant immediate transfer to frontline operational U-boats.

Not all men serving aboard U-boats during the war followed an established track. For example, Obermaschinistmaat Werner Karl Reh was serving as a petty officer at a Navy school when Admiral Karl Dönitz and his staff paid a visit to the command. The entire faculty, staff, and students were assembled in full dress, and a colorful parade was scheduled. Reh, who was standing in the second rank, collapsed suddenly during the ceremonies. The commanding offi-cer of the school was so furious at such a showing that he ordered an "imme-diate transfer to the front" for the fallen sailor. Reh had had an attack of diph-theria and was suffering the effects while standing in the parade line. He remembered, "All of a sudden I became weak and saw only legs around me. And, two days later, I got transferred to the *U-505*."

The average age of U-boat crewmen was twenty-two; the officers, of course, were older. Most U-boat officers entered the German Navy as officer cadets of the Seaman Branch. As war loomed in the 1930s, recruitment of U-boat officer can-

Crew members lower or carry food and other supplies through the hatch to be stowed through-out the boat. *Ferd. Urbahns*

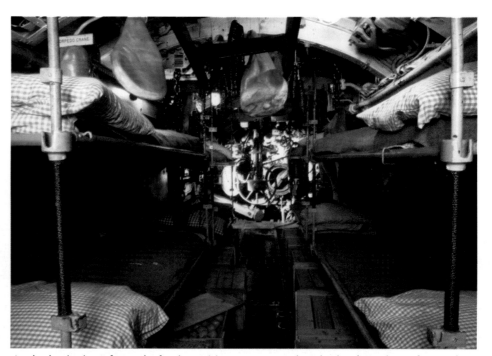

At the beginning of patrols, food provisions were stored under bunks or hung from rafters throughout the boat. *MSI*

didates accelerated. Many recruits came from the surface fleet, and officers who had served on merchant vessels were also ordered to U-boat duty. Surprisingly, a significant number of U-boat commanders came through the ranks.

Officers and enlisted men alike had to learn all the components, systems, and capabilities of their particular boats once they came aboard. To get a glimpse of what the officers and crew of the *U-505* had to learn, and also to see how they operated their equipment and adjusted to life aboard their boats, we'll first glance at the boat from the exhibit floor. Then we'll walk through the boat from forward to aft, that is, from the bow to the stern, looking at the compartments, systems, and crew responsibilities as we go.

The superstructure of the *U-505* was built on top of her outer and inner hulls. Most of the superstructure was covered by a flat, narrow deck, which ran the entire length of the boat. This deck surface provided working space for the crew to handle mooring equipment, to train on and shoot the deck gun, to jostle torpedoes below through a special hatch with the help of a chain hoist, to load food and other supplies aboard, and to refuel the boat. The men could also take a breath of fresh air on the deck when the sub surfaced at sea. An anchor and small mooring fixtures, fueling ports, and a removable lifeline could be seen at various points along the deck.

Originally, a 4.1-inch deck gun had been positioned about a third of the way along the deck back from the bow, just in front of the boat's large conning tower. The deck gun was lost during an early engagement and never replaced, but during the war several antiaircraft guns were added to the boat on and just aft of the conning tower, and they were on the boat when she was captured.

The most prominent part of the boat's superstructure, of course, is her large conning tower. On top of the conning tower was an open-air bridge, the location from which the boat was "conned," or navigated, while on the surface.

The 3.7-cm antiaircraft gun on the *U-505*. This photo is taken from the stern facing forward with a couple of bollards for mooring lines visible on the wooden deck at the base of the gun mount and the conning tower visible beyond the gun mount toward the bow. Note also the twin 2-cm antiaircraft guns facing skyward on the upper platform of the *wintergarten* (the extended platforms behind the bridge used to house antiaircraft guns). Early in the war each of the U-boats also had a large forward deck gun, but when the skies filled with Allied aircraft, that gun was taken off, several antiaircraft guns were added, and gunners became part of the crew. MSI

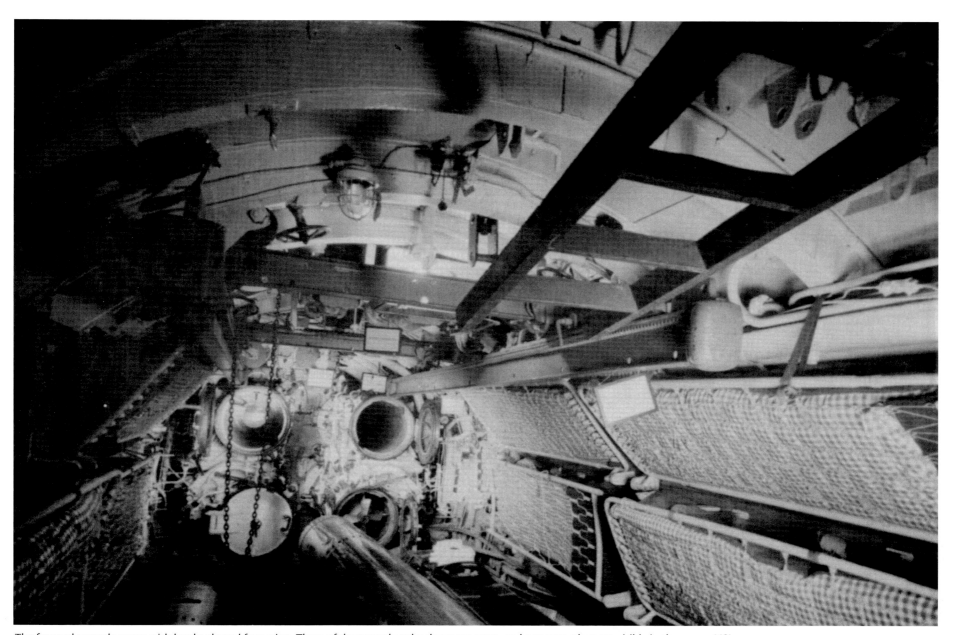

The forward torpedo room with bunks cleared for action. Three of the torpedo tube doors are open, and two torpedoes are visible in the space. *MSI*

Behind the windscreen of the bridge were located the rudder's control box, a targeting stand for torpedo aiming in a surface attack, a gyrocompass, an engine telegraph dial, a "Naxos" radio-location apparatus, and a "Hohentwiel" radar that could be used both as a search device and as a radar detector. Also located on the bridge were wooden platforms for watchstanders, a voice tube, and the tops of two periscopes, although the controls for these periscopes were in the lower enclosed part of the conning tower.

The outer and inner hulls supported all of the boat's superstructure. Within the light outer hull but inside the inner one were several tanks—cells to hold water for ballast (empty when surfaced, full when submerged)—and cells to hold fuel for the boat's diesel engines. These tanks rode alongside the top of the inner hull like sidesaddles. The inner hull is tubular, and it was built to withstand the great pressure of water against the boat when submerged. The *U-505* was designed for a "safe" submergence of 328 feet. The deeper the boat went, the greater the pressure she encountered. The depth to which a submarine could descend was limited by her ability to keep from being crushed by the weight of the surrounding water.

The inner hull of the boat was subdivided, fore and aft, into a number of compartments. These compartments housed the sub's operational equipment, main armament (the torpedoes), and living quarters for her crew. Many of these compartments were constructed so they could be completely sealed off (watertight and airtight) from the rest of the boat, should the necessity arise.

At the forward end of the boat is the forward torpedo room, which has four torpedo tubes. The *U-505* normally carried twenty-two torpedoes when fully outfitted. The forward compartment could accommodate eight torpedoes, with four in the tubes and four in reserve (two in long bunkers below the compartment's deck and two suspended in chain hoists along the compartment's overhead ready for loading). Four more were in the after torpedo room, and ten were stored in pressurized containers topside, five on each side. These containers were lodged in the superstructure just below deck.

U-boat crew members relax on bunks rigged out in the forward torpedo room. The cover to a torpedo tube is visible at the center-left of this photo. *MSI*

The electric torpedoes carried by the *U-505* required constant maintenance. Their batteries had to be kept charged, and their complicated electrical mechanisms required constant attention. Because batteries lose efficiency when cold, provisions were made for warming them.

Large storage batteries supplied electrical power for the boat's motors and electrically operated equipment so the boat could operate quietly while submerged. They were stored in compartments below deck level, one forward and one aft. Each battery had sixty-two cells. Switching arrangements provided for the batteries to be used individually, in series, or in parallel, and voltage variations between 110 to 170 DC and 220 to 340 DC (DC = direct current) were possible. Regulated 110-volt DC was supplied for general purposes other than the main motors. The boat could operate at a maximum speed of 7.5 knots while on battery power, but usually she operated at slower speeds to maximize the time she could spend underwater.

Normal battery charging time was approximately seven hours, and charging was usually done at night while the boat was running on the surface. (The *U-505* had not been refitted with a snorkel; hence, she could not recharge her batteries while submerged.) Maximum speed of the boat while charging at normal rate was 13.5 knots. The batteries were of the pasted plate-side type and had a life of fifteen to twenty-one months.

The greater part of the boat's crew slept, ate, and lived in the cramped forward torpedo room, which measured about seventy-five square feet. The crew's quarters, known as the "Lords" (slang for U-boat ratings), was supposedly

While on patrol, recreation on U-boats was limited to playing cards and other games like chess and checkers, and reading books, papers, and magazines. *Special Collections & Archives Division, Nimitz Library, U.S. Naval Academy*

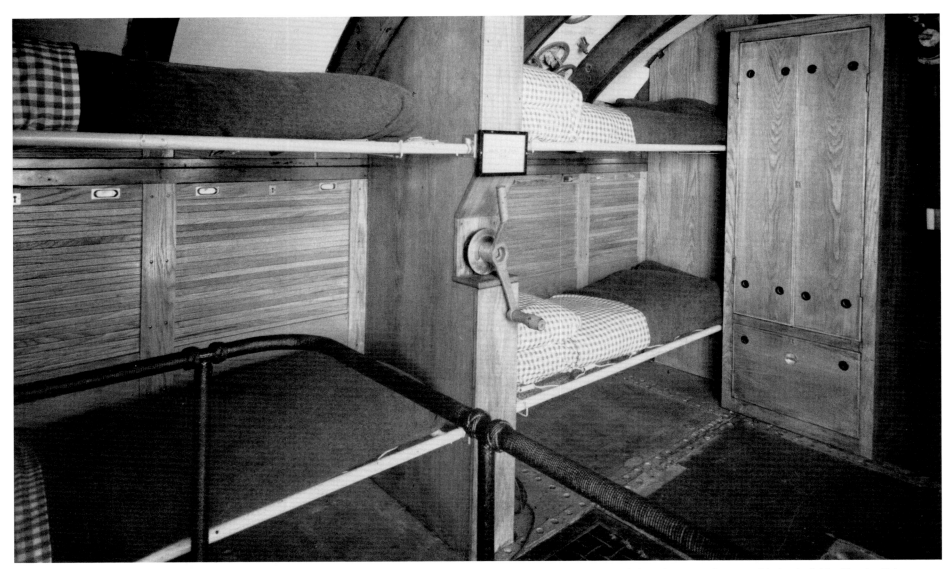

The petty officers' and chiefs' quarters aft of the forward torpedo room consisted of twelve berths, six per side. Senior noncommissioned personnel were entitled to individual bunks. Others were required to rotate use of the berths. *MSI*

named after the British House of Lords. Just aft of the torpedo tubes were ten suspended berths, five on each side, which could be collapsed against the hull to allow for additional storage for torpedoes. Four berths on each side were fashioned as bunks, these lower bunks being reserved for the senior ratings. Although bunks were cramped and valves and pipes took up overhead room, leather-covered horsehair mattresses were provided, as well as blue-checkered sheets and pillowcases.

Lined up along each side of the hull were small wooden lockers for personal possessions and canned foods. Meats and net baskets full of breadstuffs were hung from the pipes overhead. The water closet (bathroom) on the starboard side to the rear of the compartment was also usually filled with food, which inhibited its use as a water closet. The food was inventoried daily for the cook and weighed for the chief engineer, who adjusted the vessel's trim accordingly. After a month or so at sea, when some of the food had been consumed and torpedoes expended, the crew could enjoy more breathing room.

While on patrol, recreation in the *U-505* was limited to card playing, reading books and magazines (the boat had a small library of publications), chess,

and checkers. Studying technical manuals in connection with navigation and submarine operation was a constant necessity. Actually, in addition to their duties while on watch, officers and crewmen had many maintenance and other responsibilities that left little leisure time.

Operatic songs were popular with the crew. Greenhorns (new crew members) had to sing three, preferably women's, roles over the boat's intercom system. The worse they sang, the more jubilant the crew became. On long transits,

The *U-505*'s small galley, between the petty officers' and chiefs' quarters and the commissioned officers' wardroom, was designed to feed fifty men, although on some boats like the *U-505* the cook was required to provide for about sixty men. A soup kettle, a range with three cooktops and two small ovens, and a small refrigerator were found there, along with a small washbasin (on the left, under the voice tube). The washbasin was supplied with hot and cold freshwater and saltwater. Tons of foodstuffs were packed at various locations throughout the sub. The ladder on the right of this photo leads up to a hatch on the main deck forward of the conning tower. *MSI*

if they could tune in no radio stations, crew members played records, preferably English jazz. Smoking was forbidden throughout the boat. Only at night, when the sub was on the surface, could the men enjoy a cigarette.

One of the favorite pastimes of U-boat crews during evening hours was listening to reports of auto races on the Nuerburg or Avus motor racing circuits. The race commentaries were picked up live by the U-boat's radio and passed on to the crew by sailors who used nautical expressions: "Carraciola drives into the starboard bend and races 17 miles an hour along, when suddenly his port diesel breaks down and he has to switch in the E-motors, so that in the meantime he can grind his exhaust gas traps, then he chases on with strong smoke development and giving ample oxyhydrogen sounds. . . ."

Aft of the forward torpedo room are the quarters for petty officers and chiefs. This compartment consisted of twelve berths, six per side. Senior noncommissioned personnel were entitled to individual bunks. The upper berths could be folded against the bulkheads (walls or partitions within a boat) to allow the lower bunks to be used as seating at folding mess tables placed in the center passageway between the lower bunks. Also in these quarters were wooden lockers, larger than those in the forward torpedo room; these were also often used to store food in addition to the men's personal gear. Saltwater mixed with a strong antiseptic lotion flowed from the nozzles of two washbasins.

Still farther aft, between the chiefs'/petty officers' quarters and the officers' wardroom, is the ship's galley, which measured just 59 inches long and 27.5 inches wide. Food in the submarine service was the best that could be had, but the cramped quarters for cooking and storage created menu limitations. Type IXC boats, such as the *U-505*, would carry nearly fourteen tons of foodstuffs for a twelve-week patrol. In addition to what was

The commissioned officers' compartment featured four bunks, two on each side of the sub. When the upper two were folded back, the lower ones became seats. One of three document safes was located on the forward port side of this compartment. *MSI*

stored in the forward torpedo room, canned foods, meats, vegetables, bread, and butter were stowed in odd nooks and corners and even passageways at the start of a voyage. It was not unusual to see sausages and meats dangling from overhead pipes in the crowded central control room.

The galley contained equipment to feed some sixty men three meals a day. There is a small refrigerator, a 40-liter (10.6-gallon) self-heating soup kettle, and an electric range with three hot plates and two small ovens—each with three stages of heat control—that occupied one corner of the galley. A small metal sink provided hot and cold freshwater and hot saltwater. Freshwater supplies at sea were obtained from a saltwater distilling apparatus located under the steps in the rear of the electric motor room. The system could provide 63.5 gallons a day, the use of which was limited to replacement of battery water and drinking and cooking purposes.

Mess gear consisted of individual mess kits for the crew, but officers merited silverware, glass, china, and table linen. Since food was an important factor in the morale and health of the crew, every effort was made to prepare it tastefully within the limits of the sub's equipment and operational conditions. Meals were planned so that crewmen maintained a proper diet and calorie intake. Hot meals were served whenever possible, but if battery power was low, the use of electricity for cooking would be confined to coffee and soup.

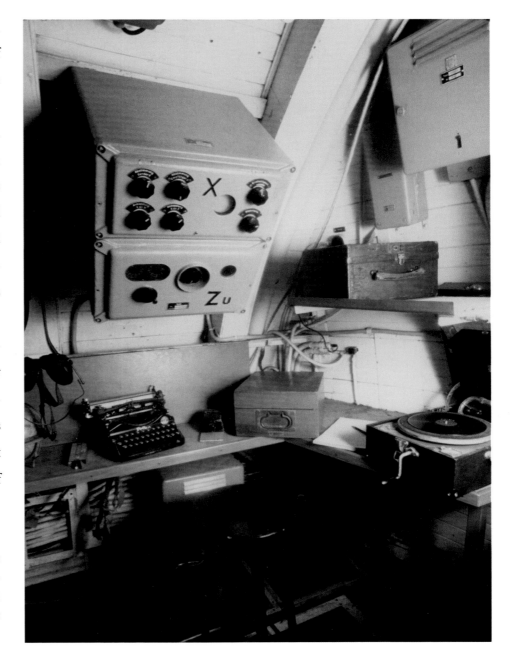

The radio room was crammed with numerous sending and receiving devices. Note on the upper right shelf a box for the typewriter, which is shown on the lower table. Next to the typewriter in the center of the photo is the wooden container for an Enigma machine. If no radio stations could be tuned in, the radioman played records that would sound throughout the boat. The crew's preference was for English jazz and French and German tunes popular at the time. *MSI*

One of the worst problems for crewmen of U-boats was trying to maintain regularity. Castor oil and pills were frequently used, with mixed results. Constipation was caused by the lack of space available for movement and the considerable amount of time spent sitting or resting in bunks. With only one of the two water closets on board the *U-505* regularly available for use (as has been mentioned, the other usually stored food), long lines and the difficulty of working the complicated lever device to flush the bowl made the whole process of relieving oneself a major undertaking.

The commissioned officers' wardroom located aft of the petty officers' and chiefs' quarters just aft of the galley was the most comfortable compartment on the boat. Oak paneling lined the walls, and each of the four under officers (jun-ior in rank to the commander of the boat) aboard had a bunk. The four under officers who served on board the *U-505* during her last patrol were Oblt.z.S. Paul Meyer (1st watch officer and executive officer), Oblt.z.S. Kurt Brey (2nd watch officer), Oblt.z.S. Friedrich Hosenmeyer (doctor), and Oblt.z.S. Josef Hauser (chief engineer). Several lockers in the compartment were used for stowing officers' possessions, food provisions, and sensitive documents and manuals. The officers also shared a small washbasin. A glass cabinet mounted to the starboard side of the passageway contained chinaware, glass, and silverware, part navy issue and part confiscated from restaurants, hotels, and bars visited by the men while ashore.

One of the two Enigma machines recovered from the *U-505* is shown with an attached ticker-tape printing device (above). Four rotors, two of which are shown to the left, fit on the top left of the machine. The serial number of the machine (M7942) is on the small plate below the keys. The Enigma was Germany's primary cipher machine, used by all branches of the military in World War II. However, historians particularly identify Enigma with U-boats because, upon breaking the code, the Allies could listen in on U-boat messages, route convoys around their attackers, and send hunter-killer groups to destroy U-boats. Breaking the Enigma code thus played a crucial part in winning the Battle of the Atlantic. *MSI*

Aft of the officers' wardroom are the radio and sound rooms. The radio room was crammed with numerous sending and receiving devices. A radioman often wore his listening gear with just one earpiece over his ear. In this way he could hear both incoming Morse signals and orders from inside the boat. In addition to messages received by his boat, the radioman carefully logged all messages from headquarters and other U-boats in the boat's war log. When submerged to a boat depth of some sixty or seventy feet, the radioman could still receive long radio waves when the radio aerial antenna was about thirty feet under water. However, short and medium radio waves could not penetrate the sea.

The most important pieces of communications gear aboard the U-boat were the *Schussel M* Enigma machines, also located in the radio room. Outgoing and incoming messages were coded and decoded, and to ensure secrecy, cylinder settings in the apparatus were changed daily in accordance with codebook directives. As we have seen, the British broke the Enigma system early in the war, which proved to be invaluable in winning the Battle of the Atlantic. The British called the intelligence gathered from the Enigma coding machines "Ultra"; the Americans called it "Ice."

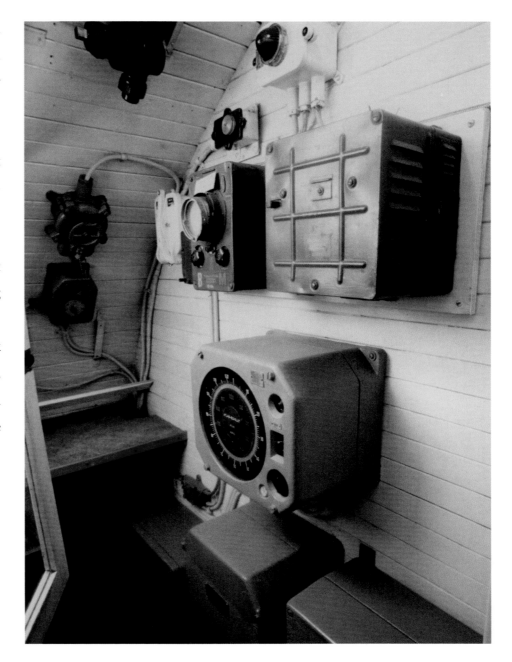

The small sound room just aft of the radio room was manned by a radioman when the boat was in the vicinity of surface vessels or under attack by enemy antisubmarine warships. The boat's hydrophone detector equipment, the "ears" of the boat when submerged, was located on the boat's foredeck. Wearing headphones, the operator could hear the sound of approaching enemy propellers and, by turning a hand wheel, could rotate the detector head to obtain a bearing on the contact. The FuMO 30 radar set was also operated this room. *MSI*

The captain's quarters (visible at the left of this photograph, seen from aft looking forward) provided the captain a folding desktop covering, a wash stand, a couple of cabinets, and a bunk. A curtain could be stretched around this space so that the captain might not be interrupted by crew members using the central passageway to the right. A safe above the captain's bunk was broken open by the boarding party. *MSI*

The radioman manned a second small sound room just aft of the boat's main radio communications room when the boat was in the vicinity of surface ships or under attack by enemy antisubmarine warfare ships. The radioman operated the monitor for the boat's hydrophone detector equipment, which was the "ears" of the boat when she was submerged. Wearing headphones that allowed him to hear the sound of approaching enemy propellers, he turned a hand wheel that would rotate a sound detector head on the boat's foredeck, indicating the bearing of a contact. The equipment was highly sensitive and could detect ship noises from some distance (under ideal conditions, twelve miles for a single ship, sixty for a convoy). During a suspected attack, a U-boat commander would often stand in the passageway outside the sound room to receive verbal reports from the hydrophone operator. When the *U-505* came under attack, the operator could clearly hear the sound of depth charges splashing in the water.

Opposite the radio and sound room is the small space called the captain's quarters. In addition to his bunk and locker, the *U-505*'s captain had a small washstand with a folding top that became a desk. The walls of the submarine here, as in the other officers' sleeping quarters, were covered with oak paneling, which was more comfortable to the touch than cold metal, as well as more

The control room was just below the conning tower and just aft of the radio and sound rooms. Diving and surfacing controls are at the left in this photo. The ladder to their right leads to the conning tower immediately above. The captain gave orders from the conning tower, and the planesmen and other crew members carried them out from here. *MSI*

appealing to the eye. An overhead lamp provided light, and a cloth curtain could be drawn to give the captain some privacy.

The normal number of officers carried by submarines of the *U-505* class was four or five. Under the captain were a chief engineer, who was second in command, and 1st and 2nd watch officers. (While cruising on the surface, a watch officer and four lookouts manned the bridge using 7 x 10 high-powered Zeiss binoculars to scan the horizon for enemy shipping.) A fourth officer, a doctor, was included in the *U-505*'s complement. He tended to the various maladies of the crew and distributed vitamins daily. The health of the crew was important to a submarine's efficiency. And, because every member of the crew

had important responsibilities, when a man was ill, his work fell on another as an additional burden.

Besides a variety of other problems, the crew found it absolutely necessary to take at least some care of their teeth, since there was no dentist onboard. A special tooth powder was used to ward off scurvy. In spite of their efforts, sailors often developed sore gums and loose teeth, which caused considerable pain.

Aft of the radio and sound rooms is the central control room, located amidships. Located just below the conning tower (to which a ladder and hatch provided ready access), the control room was the site where all the important diving, steering, and other controls were situated. One bank of instruments was concerned primarily with diving. Some gauges indicated the depth of the submarine and others her degree of trim or stability. A properly trimmed boat would be riding on an even keel (i.e., floating evenly and level without list). By taking on or removing water ballast from the various tanks, the crew could achieve such stability.

Both trimming the boat and diving were the responsibility of the diving officer acting on directions from the captain. While a boat could be taken down by merely flooding the proper cells with water, this procedure would usually be too slow. Diving and surfacing were accelerated by driving the boat down or up with

The control room also contained a large chart table used by the captain and navigator to plot the course of the boat and plan maneuvers for attacking enemy ships and convoys. *MSI*

her propellers, while simultaneously maneuvering flipper-like diving planes at the bow and stern (outside the hull) that acted like the controls of an airplane. Two planesmen operated the bow and stern dive planes, while a helmsman operated the rudders, which of course turned the boat right or left. The control room included a large chart table used by the captain and navigator to plot the course of the boat and plan maneuvers for attacking enemy ships and convoys.

Also located in the control room is the gyrocompass. The gyrocompass used a gyroscope instead of a magnetic compass because the amount of steel surrounding the boat made a magnetic compass inaccurate. However, a magnetic compass also was provided as a safety measure, and this was housed in an aluminum watertight box located topside. A system of lenses, somewhat like the optical system of a periscope, permitted the magnetic compass to be read from below in the control room as a check against the gyrocompass. The *U-505* carried two periscopes, and the wells for these extended down from the bridge, through the interior part of the conning tower, through the control room, and below it into the lowest compartment. Operation of the scopes was from the conning tower level.

The engine-order telegraph (EOT) telegraphed speed orders directly to the engine room. This device was operated from the sub's control room or from the conning tower when the captain was stationed there, tracking or attacking surface contacts. EOT repeater instruments were placed throughout the boat so crewmen at various stations could see what speed had been ordered up and could determine whether the engines had been ordered to go forward (*voraus*) or be put in reverse (*zurück*). The arrow at the center of this device indicated the engine room's "answer" to the order given. *MSI*

SPEAKING TUBES

Speaking tubes (requiring no power other than the human voice for operation) provided communication from the control room and conning tower to other critical locations throughout the sub. Sound-powered phones also provided for selective communication with individual stations. *MSI*

Command of all of the various systems of communication used in the boat was located either in the control room or in the conning tower immediately above it. While stationed in the interior of the conning tower, for example, the captain could signal the helmsman the desired speed for the boat using the engine-order telegraph. When he moved the handle of this instrument, the needle on the other repeater instruments in various parts of the boat likewise moved to the command indicated on the skipper's. At the same time, a klaxon or horn sounded and continued blowing until all the handles on the repeater instruments matched the needle. Thus, the captain knew that all the required stations had acknowledged his command.

The captain's station, when attacking, was in the conning tower. From there he operated the periscopes (one for attack, the other for surface navigation) and gave maneuvering directions and firing orders.

A hydraulic system activated the periscope hoists and rotation of the fixed eye-level periscope. The captain sat on a powered saddle-like seat that rotated with the periscope and was operated by foot pedals. On one wall of the conning tower were two depth gauges, which indicated the depth of the submarine and the height of the periscope. The amount of wave action on the sea's surface was an important consideration in taking the scope up, as the protruding snout of the periscope and the small wake it created as the sub moved through the water could betray the boat's position.

It was unnecessary to raise the scope far above the waves. While keeping the scope just above the water's surface limited one's vision to when the sub was riding the top of the wave, it also helped keep the sub concealed.

Once the target was sighted and a course plotted, the captain tried to maneuver his boat into the best position for firing her torpedoes. This involved several hours or even days of tracking the target—of getting ahead and lying in wait—or of trying to find an opening in a guarded convoy.

One level above the control room was the sub's conning tower. On the right is the periscope, on the left is the torpedo data computer, and in the center are the preset firing controls. A ladder in this room leads up to a hatch opening on the U-boat's bridge, above. *MSI*

When the sub was finally in the best position circumstances allowed, the captain called the varying data to the torpedo officer, who along with a helmsman, was also in the conning tower.

Data concerning course and speed of the target were set into a computing device that analyzed the information in relation to the torpedo's course. The computer then indicated when the course of both torpedo and target would converge.

In the meantime, the torpedo officer, acting on the captain's directions, set up firing directions on an electrical control panel. Whether the aft or forward torpedo tubes were to be used was determined first; then whether a single torpedo or salvo; finally, the firing order of all tubes. Thus, all the factors were preset on the control board, and down in the torpedo room the same switches had been set (electrically, and also duplicated mechanically by the torpedoman).

When the computer indicated the right moment had been reached, the captain gave the order "Los!" (Fire!), and the torpedo left the sub. The diving officer had the problem of compensating for the lost weight of the fired torpedo by taking on more water ballast.

There was not always time to watch whether a torpedo attack was successful. Sometimes the captain would immediately "take her down" to a safer depth to escape attack by swift destroyers that often protected convoys.

Aft of the control room was the diesel engine room which housed two M.A.N. nine-cylinder, supercharged, four-cycle diesel engines (salt water cooled), each coupled to a dynamotor and to the shaft through appropriate clutches. *MSI*

The sub's most dangerous foes, however, were patrolling aircraft, for the sub was powerless to see or hear a plane acting as an observer to direct surface vessels to attack or one that could drop depth charges itself. As narrated earlier, such a combined operation of planes and surface vessels disabled the *U-505* and resulted in her capture.

Aft of the control room is the diesel engine room. The *U-505* had two 2,170-hp nine-cylinder, supercharged, four-cycle diesel engines (saltwater cooled), each coupled to a dynamotor and to the shaft through appropriate clutches. On the surface, the diesels could drive the boat at a maximum speed of nineteen knots. The *U-505* carried enough fuel oil for a maximum range of 13,450 nautical miles at ten knots.

Air was equally important to operate the diesel engines. When the sub was on the surface, air for the diesels was sucked in through ports or openings on the side of the conning tower; it then traveled through ducts into the engine room behind the engines from which space it was sucked up by the superchargers and fed to the engines. In this way, any water sucked in with the rush of air splashed into the bilges, where it could be pumped out. Exhaust gases from the engines were piped through the hull and released aft under the superstructure. An important part of diving procedures was to close both the intake and exhaust valves to prevent water from pouring into the engine room or the engines.

From various fuel bunkers, oil was pumped to a tank over the engines that fed it to the cylinders. Since the engines were diesels, no spark plugs were necessary to effect combustion. The mixture of fuel and air was ignited by compression.

Each of the diesel engines had its own controls and instruments to provide data needed by the machinist's mate to keep the engines operating; among these were the engine crankshaft tachometers, which indicated how fast the crankshaft was turning. To drive the boat straight, both crankshafts normally were turning at the same speed, while turns in congested quarters could be effected by varying the speed of the port and starboard crankshafts. The temperature of each cylinder was shown on a bank of vertical instruments, and next to these in

Each diesel has its own set of controls, engine-order telegraph, and shaft rpm indicators. The diesels were eventually restored to full operating condition after the boat was brought to the museum. *MSI*

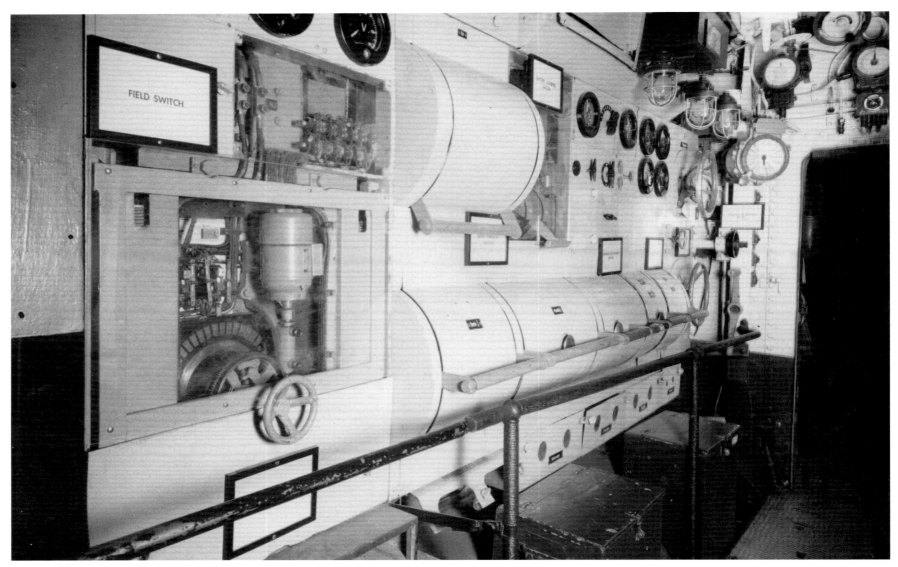

When submerged, the *U-505* was controlled from the electric motor room, located forward on the port side of the electric motor room. Equipment here includes a control board for each dynamotor, engine-order telegraph, shaft rpm indicators, and rudder angle indicator, which is visible at the top right of the picture. Each motor drove one three-bladed propeller. When submerged, the boat had a maximum speed of 7.5 knots but this speed was seldom used because it would exhaust the batteries in a short time. The storage batteries that furnish power for these motors are located in special compartments forward and aft under the deck level and provide a counter balance to the forty-five tons of electric motors in this room. *MSI*

the engine room was the engine-order telegraph repeater—one of many located throughout the boat—that signaled what speed had been ordered.

Large ventilating fans and their ductwork were on either side of the diesel control area and kept air circulating throughout the boat. As the air became fouled with carbon dioxide from the crew's breathing, chemicals purified it by absorbing the carbon dioxide. Oxygen also could be released from bottles to replace that used by the crew, and sometimes the crew members used individual oxygen masks. Another breathing problem for submariners was the amount of moisture the air absorbed. Sometimes this raised the humidity to an uncomfortable degree and thus impaired the efficiency of the crew. It also could cause short circuits in the complicated electrical system.

Another serious problem in connection with the air supply was the danger of gas. When batteries were being charged, hydrogen gas, which is odorless, colorless, and extremely explosive, was released. Precautions had to be taken to prevent explosion. Moreover, if saltwater ever mixed with the acid in the batteries, deadly chlorine gas would form, emitting a pungent odor within the boat. Even relatively small quantities of the gas could be fatal. When crew members found that a compartment was contaminated, they would leave the contaminated compartment and seal it by closing watertight hatches, meanwhile closing off the air lines to that compartment.

The electric motor and maneuvering room houses the boat's electric motors. When submerged, the *U-505* was propelled by her two dynamotors, each rated at 493 hp, one on either side of the passageway in the compartment.

As mentioned before, the storage batteries furnishing power for these motors were in special compartments under the deck level, some forward and some aft.

Each of these motors drove one three-bladed propeller. When submerged, the *U-505* had a maximum speed of 7.5 knots, but this speed was seldom ordered up, as it would exhaust the batteries in a short time. The usual underwater speed was around 4 knots, and the maximum distance the boat could travel underwater on a battery charge was about sixty-three nautical miles. When the submarine was on the surface, her diesel engines drove the boat while simultaneously turning the dynamotors, which in turn acted as generators to recharge the batteries.

Normal practice during wartime in hostile waters was for the submarine to run on the surface only at night, when risk of visible detection was at a minimum. She would operate on her electric motors during the day while at rest or when cruising slowly underwater at relatively shallow depths. While running in this manner, the sub was controlled from back in the maneuvering room.

Controls for the dynamotors were on the port side. They provided for extreme flexibility in switching electrical connections between motors and batteries to perform a variety of functions. A large box-like panel on the starboard side housed the electric welding controls, for the port side main could serve as a generator to produce enough power for electric arc welding. Acetylene welding equipment was also provided aboard.

Also on the starboard side was a four-stage compressor powered by an electric motor. When the *U-505* was on the surface, this compressor filled the various bottles located throughout the boat with compressed air, which would be used to blow water out of the ballast tanks in order to help the boat to surface, to fire torpedoes, and to start the diesels.

On either side of the walkway in the electric motor and maneuvering room were clutches that engaged the electric motors to the propellers.

When the *U-505* was captured, she was running on her electric motors, half submerged. Only the forward motion provided by those electric motors was keeping the sub afloat at the time. It would have been necessary to blow out water ballast to get the boat at surface trim and set her diesel engines operating. But the batteries were almost exhausted, and if the remaining current had been used in an effort to blow out the water, the boat possibly would have sunk before the diesels were turning. On the other hand, continuing to run on the electric motors with what little power was left in the batteries shortly would have resulted in the same end.

Towing the *U-505* solved the problem. As the *Guadalcanal* picked up the tow and made enough speed to keep the boat up in the water, the electric motors were turned off while the boarding party worked on the diesels. When the fleet tug *Abnaki* joined and took over the tow, it was possible to pull the *U-505* fast enough to turn the propellers so that the sub's dynamotors could serve as generators. When the batteries were sufficiently recharged to operate the air compressor, the water ballast was blown, and with the boat at surface trim, the diesels were cut in so the sub could operate on her own again. In a way, one could say the fleet tug's tow provided the power to the boat's batteries, which was needed so that the U-boat's diesels could be jump-started.

Thus, the boarding and capture of the *U-505* were merely the first steps in the hazardous plan to bring her back intact. Until the sub was actually operating under her own power from the diesel engines, she was in constant danger of going down. Had she gone down then, she would have taken with her whichever members of the boarding party happened to be aboard. One marvels again at the successful capture, particularly since only one of the Americans in the boarding parties had ever been in a submarine before, and his experience was limited.

The last compartment astern is the aft torpedo room. Sixteen crewmen shared quarters in this compartment. As was also the case in the forward compartment, crew members used their bunks in shifts, one shift sleeping while the other was on watch (modern American submariners call this "hot bunking"). Torpedo tubes here, like those in the forward torpedo compartment, were kept loaded and were fired on orders from the captain using controls in the conning tower. Prefiring data that determined the order in which torpedoes were fired (singly or in groups) and the depth and course were determined by electric controls for individual torpedoes. At the same time, manual controls were set in the torpedo room as a precaution against electrical failure. When the captain gave the order to fire, a button in the conning tower and another in the torpedo room were pressed simultaneously, again to ensure against failure.

Pressing the firing button released a charge of compressed air that, acting on a piston, ejected the torpedo out of the tube and into the water. The torpedo's electric motor then took over to drive the torpedo toward its tar-

The *U-505*'s after torpedo room is visible through this hatch; bunks are visible both to the left and right of the two torpedo tube doors found here. On the sub's capture, it was this hatch that the American boarding party thought might be booby-trapped, and it was this room that German crew members reported flooded. Calculating that there was no booby trap and there had been no flooding, Captain Galley opened the hatch, walked through, and, with Earl Trosino, put the after steering wheel (seen in the middle of the photograph between the torpedo doors) and rudders amidships. *MSI*

get. The air, which had driven the piston, was not allowed to escape, because if it were allowed to rise to the surface in a bubble, it would give away the sub's position. Instead, it was bled into the sub's interior spaces as seawater entered the torpedo tube. When the tube was again loaded, the water was drained.

The intimacy of submarine life created special problems for those in the service, long-running, continual problems that added to the many sudden stresses of combat. For example, while less military formality was observed aboard the submarine than in other services, the responsibilities of each individual were greater. The *U-505* crew was grouped into two categories: fifteen to twenty seamen and twenty to twenty-five technicians. The seamen (gun and torpedo crews) operated in three shifts of four hours each, while the technicians (radio/sound men and radarmen, engine room and control room assistants, etc.) worked in two shifts of six hours. Off-watch time, if not used for eating, cleaning, sleeping, and lessons, would be used for reading, card games, and listening to records or the radio.

After-watch sleeping might be nearly impossible should heavy seas rock the boat while running surfaced. Often, men were thrown from their bunks onto the floorboards or into the bunks of neighbors. Sometimes, an entire bunk broke loose and went sliding back and forth across the deck, its occupant clinging to his mattress. Vegetables, bread, and tin cans that were stacked in the bow compartment frequently would come tumbling down on men trying to find rest in the lower bunks. A few unlucky ones were drenched in scalding coffee. It was no small wonder that the crew members were a bit frazzled when they woke in the midst such fretful experiences.

Bathing facilities for the crew were limited to an occasional saltwater shower taken in the engine room with an improvised nozzle fed by warm diesel engine coolant. Special soap was used when washing with seawater. It lathered in the water, whereas normal soap did not. When the sub was not in hostile waters and the opportunity afforded, a swim in the open sea was a refreshing luxury. However, during operations in the Atlantic, crewmen could not escape becoming encrusted with dirt. They soon learned that they could make do just by rinsing off their hands and face a couple of times a week with saltwater. Afterward, they splashed eau de cologne on their face and distributed any remaining dirt with ointment, rubbing it vigorously into their skin.

Bridge watch officers and their lookouts were continually exposed to the elements. Their hair and beards would become filthy and matted from the saltwater breaking over the ship, and even the best comb broke when they tried to disentangle the mess. So, it was left as it was and sprinkled with birch water to neutralize the odor, which seemed to differ with each man.

On long patrols that required frequent underwater running, the smell in the boat became almost overwhelming, especially when the sub operated in tropical waters. Diesel fuel fumes, body sweat, the stench of seasickness, water closet

odors, and the smell of cooking food combined to make living conditions hellish. Though the crew complained, they acclimated themselves to the air around them and carried on.

In fact, despite the confined nature of life aboard, U-boat service typically bred a special form of camaraderie. Machinist's mate Werner Reh testified to this when he said of his service in the *U-505:*

> I am aware of nothing that the entire crew . . . experienced . . . that affected life together. Everyone actually—the way I perceived it—fulfilled his duty. Naturally, . . . with pressures of three months of time at sea, without seeing daylight once, . . . there were . . . certain frictions. . . . Someone would pop out of his corset and there were . . . harsh words. I would not contest that. And I would not contest either, that there were things in the chain of command, where you were threatened with punishment, for example, when someone did not fulfill his duty, then "One week long commode duty!" . . . anyone who has never experienced that—there can be nothing at all that's worse. . . . But otherwise I have no examples of any kind at hand, where I could say we were not a sworn community.

German U-boat crewmen on deck of a U-boat while surfaced, this in the early months of the war before Allied planes filled the sky. Small white pennants marked with tonnage of enemy vessels sunk by this boat fly from the navigation scope. After weeks or even months submerged, the smells of diesel fuel, body sweat, vomit from sea sickness, toilet waste and general cooking all combined to make the air very foul. Breathing fresh salt air on deck helped relieve the situation for a while. *akg-images*

Food Provisions

Food Provisions for Type IXC German U-boat for Twelve-Week Patrol

Source: Jobst Schaefer, "Die Ernahrung des U-Bootsfahrers in Kriege" (Ph.D. dissertation, Christian-Albrechts-Universitat zu Kiel, 1943), 156c-d.

4,808 lbs. preserved/tinned meats

3,858 lbs. potatoes

3,428 lbs. other vegetables

1,226 lbs. bread dough

2,058 lbs. preserved breads

2,365 lbs. other fruits

1,728 lbs. powdered milk

494 lbs. fresh and cooked meats

238 lbs. sausages

441 lbs. fruit juices

334 lbs. preserved fish

397 lbs. dried potatoes

463 lbs. rice and noodles

595 lbs. fresh eggs

917 lbs. fresh lemons

551 lbs. butter and margarine

611 lbs. soup ingredients

408 lbs. marmalade and honey

309 lbs. fresh and preserved cheese

154 lbs. coffee

205 lbs. other drinks

441 lbs. sugar

132 lbs. salt

108 lbs. chocolates

Note: Lemons and limes were carried to ward off scurvy, a disease that resulted from a lack of vitamin C in the daily diet and that severely disabled and often killed seamen. In 1747, James Lind, an officer in the Royal Navy, conducted a study on twelve patients who suffered from scurvy. He divided the patients into six groups of two and gave each group a different remedy. Only the group given oranges and lemons recovered. It took Lind forty-one years, however, to convince the Royal Navy to implement his recommendation. Ultimately, the British provided lime juice instead of lemons or orange juice to prevent the disease, and their sailors thus became known as "limeys."

APPENDIX B

The Evolution of the Submarine

The idea of undersea warfare dates back to 332 BC, when divers severed anchor ropes of enemy galleys, setting them adrift to become victims of shifting winds and swirling tides. These vessels often met destruction on rock-strewn shores and hidden reefs. While laying siege to Tyre, Alexander the Great was faced with such treachery, and it has been written that he himself was lowered into the sea in a glass barrel to determine why his ships were suddenly drifting without direction or purpose.

In 20 BC, divers began using primitive drills to bore holes in the hulls of ships, allowing water to enter the vessels, sinking them. During the siege of Byzantium in AD 196, free-swimming divers severed cables and hijacked the ships rather than allowing them to founder. In 1190, a German poem titled "Salman and Morolf" described how Morolf fashioned a submersible out of leather and stayed under

NHC

water for fourteen days by using an air tube. This story is improbable, both because Morolf would have suffocated without a supply of pumped-in air and because it is impossible for the human lung to draw in air through a tube longer than twice the length of the human windpipe without being overwhelmed by carbon monoxide.

Friar Roger Bacon (1214–92), a noted scientist of his time, recorded in his papers the possibility of devising an apparatus that would allow people to walk underwater safely. Leonardo da Vinci (1452–1519) considered a similar idea; however, he dropped the concept because he distrusted man's use of such a destructive device, concerned about "the evil nature of men who practice assassination at the bottom of the sea."

Not until 1587 did someone—Royal Navy gunner William Bourne—conceive a design for a submersible. In his book, *Inuentions and Deuices—Very necessary for all Generalles and Captaines,* or *Leaders of Men as well by sea as by land,* he describes his "eighteenth devise," the first treatise on the concept of a submarine. Bourne envisioned an enclosed wooden hull made waterproof by leather hides. Using flexible air chambers, the craft would sink or rise when the chambers were compressed or released by internal screws. Oars would be used for propulsion while underwater.

Bourne's theory was never tested, and it was not until the early 1600s that Dutch inventor and alchemist Dr. Cornelius van Drebbel modified Bourne's design and constructed a "moving submarine." He used a downward-sloping foredeck as a diving plane, goatskin ballast tanks, and twelve oarsmen who were provided with tubes attached to floats on the surface so they could breathe in fresh air. When Van Drebbel demonstrated his craft to King James on the River Thames in 1626, he was able to take his "submarine" to a depth of twelve to fifteen feet. The king was noticeably impressed. However, while the vessel appeared to have held together during the test dive, large amounts of water leaked into the craft.

The use of an underseas vehicle during warfare dates back to 332 BC. During Alexander the Great's siege of Tyre, enemy divers cut the anchor cables of his warships and set many of his ships adrift. Allegedly he explored the deep waters around his ships in a glass barrel let down by chains from a ship on the surface. The exploit was no doubt one of the many myths that surrounded the famous warrior. *Cyril Field*

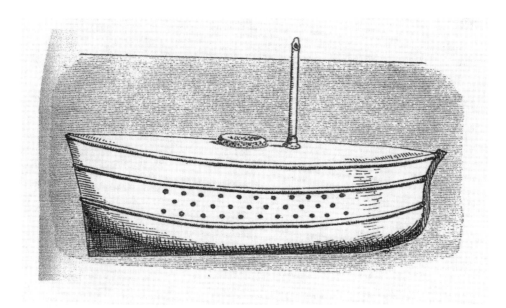

Royal Navy Gunner William Bourne is credited with having worked out and published the first known detailed description of a submarine boat. His design, shown here, never resulted in the construction of an actual vessel, but other designers subsequently used his ideas. *Cyril Field*

Whether Bourne's invention was a diving bell or a submarine is open to question. One aspect of his device, which provided air to submerged crewmen, can be linked to the latter-day snorkel, which did not enter operational service until the German U-boat *U-539* went to sea equipped with such a device in January 1944. Although the British crown supported Van Drebbel's work and provided funds for further experimental work on submersibles, within a year, the government directed that his expertise be used in the development of underwater explosive devices for fire ships. (Fire ships were vessels loaded with ignited combustibles and set adrift to destroy an enemy's ships and shore for-

tifications.) This soon became the focus of his work, and further development of the submarine was abandoned.

Nevertheless, Bourne's work stimulated interest in various other experimental modifications of his submarine. Two French priests, Marin Mersenne and Georges Fournier, designed an underwater craft that would be armed, have wheels for moving about on a seabed, and include a phosphorescent system for lighting. In 1653, another Frenchman, Monsieur De Son, built the first "fighting submarine" in Holland, one that would "kill the English underwater." The vessel contained a mechanical internal paddle wheel positioned amidships. The shape of the craft was similar to a cubicle box, with long pyramids extending fore and aft. A large girder of wood with iron heads on each end ran through the vessel and was used to ram ships under their waterlines. To be effective, the submersible required speed that the paddle wheel device failed to provide. The craft did not fare well in its trials and was discarded.

In 1653 a Frenchman, Monsieur De Son, built a boat in Rotterdam that was generally assumed to have been intended for submarine purposes although it was possible that it was merely to navigate in an "awash" position. The boat attracted considerable attention at the time because it was promoted as a vessel that had the capability to "kill the English underwater." Unfortunately it fared poorly in its trials and was discarded. *Cyril Field*

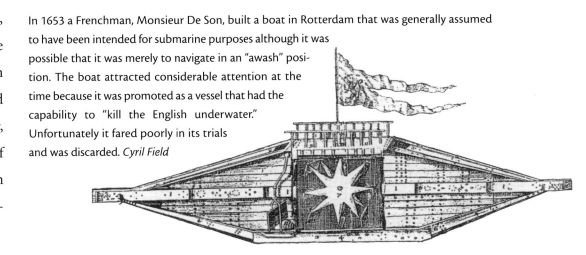

In 1680, another priest, Italian Abbe Giovanni Borelli, published a book of "devices," one of which closely resembled Van Drebbel's vehicle. Borelli's submersible included a hand-operated system that controlled buoyancy by forcing water from leather bottles attached to holes in the bottom of the boat. A sketch of the boat appeared in 1749, and a controversy arose over whether it was Borelli's design or that of an English carpenter, Nathaniel Symons. In any case, Symons actually built such a boat and operated it regularly on the River Dart near Totnes, England. Like many other experimental submersibles, it failed to gain notice, and vanished. Twenty-two years later, however, an inventor known simply as "M.T." published an article in *The Gentleman's Magazine* in 1771 that copied Symons's buoyancy concept using inflated goatskins as ballast tanks.

The first submersible casualty was recorded in 1774, when English carpenter John Day modified a fifty-ton sloop with devices he estimated would set a submerged endurance record. He placed ten tons of ballast inside the boat and attached two ten-ton weights to the ballast with quick-release devices that when a triggered would allow the sloop to surface. He hoped to remain in the craft for twelve hours at a depth of a hundred feet, with no communications. He pro-

By the mid- to late-1770s, designers of submarine-like craft in Europe actually built a number of experimental submersibles; however, most failed to gain notice and vanished. One design (shown here) appeared in *The Gentleman's Magazine*, a British publication, and used inflated goat skins as ballast tanks. The inventor was simply known as "M.T." *The Gentleman's Magazine*, June 1771

vided for a cabin that he stocked with food, water, and comfortable furnishings. He also devised a signaling system to update spectators on his status. The release of a white float would indicate "all was well"; red, "in indifferent health"; and black, "in great danger." Day and his boat, the *Maria,* sank to 170 feet of water in Plymouth Harbor on June 20, 1774. No floats were subsequently released, and Day and the *Maria* were never seen again. Most probably, the hull of the boat was crushed by water pressure as it descended to the bottom of the harbor.

A year following John Day's misadventure, an American inventor, David Bushnell, designed and built the world's first attack submersible during America's War of Independence. Dubbed the *Turtle* because of her pear shape, the boat actually made an attack run on a British warship on September 6, 1776, which established many underwater attack principles that affected the thinking of submersible inventors over the next century.

The *Turtle* was a little more than seven feet long, eight feet deep, and four feet wide. She was made of tar-caulked oak planks secured by iron hoops. A beam in the interior strengthened the hull and doubled as a seat for a single operator. Two hand-cranked propellers maneuvered the boat, one used to move forward, the other to propel the craft upward. A hand-operated rudder bar also was available to steer the submarine in a straight line. Bushnell added 900 pounds of lead ballast to eliminate the boat's positive buoyancy and a small internal ballast tank of water. A foot pedal was used to let water in, and two brass forcing pumps expelled water as required. Two breathing tubes protruded from the top of the boat, allowing the operator to be submerged for forty minutes.

During America's War of Independence, David Bushnell, an American inventor, designed and built the world's first attack submarine. Dubbed the *Turtle* because of her pear shape, the craft attempted to attach a "torpedo" to the bottom of HMS *Eagle*, Admiral Howe's flagship, anchored off Governor's Harbor, New York, on September 6, 1776. An illustration of the *Turtle* beginning her attack is shown here. *NHC*

Sketch of the interior of the *Turtle* with operator at the controls. The attack on the HMS *Eagle* was the first underwater war mission. *USNI*

Next to the tubes were the ship's hatch and a gimlet attached by rope to a 150-pound gunpowder mine affixed to the outside hull.

During an attack, the operator would sight his target through a port and make his approach awash, taking care not to be seen. Once in position, he would submerge his craft and move under the hull. He then would drill a wooden screw tightly into the planking of the ship's hull and detach the mine that was connected to the screw. The operator would escape from under the ship and distance himself before a time-controlled fuse would set off the charge. The result would be a severely damaged and leaking hull that would flood the ship's hold and sink her.

Bushnell was not physically able to cope with the numerous mechanisms of the boat in making an attack, so a twenty-seven-year-old sergeant, Ezra Lee, was recruited and trained to operate the *Turtle*. The boat's first target was the British warship HMS *Eagle*, Vice Admiral Richard Lord Howe's flagship anchored in New York Harbor. Lee successfully maneuvered the *Turtle* beneath the ship but could not insert the wooden screw because he found himself trying to tap into the iron strappings that supported the ship's rudder hinge. Exhausted and running out of air, he escaped and was sighted by the British, who launched a boat to investigate. Lee loosened the mine and it exploded, warding off his pursuers. Although he did not sink the *Eagle*, his action caused the British to scatter their ships, thus weakening their blockade.

A series of experimental submersibles followed until 1879, when the world's first fully powered submarine, the *Resurgam*, was built in Birkenhead, England. Designed and built by a Manchester clergyman, Reverend George Garrett, the thirty-ton submersible used a Lamm closed steam engine, was forty-five feet in length, nine-plus feet wide amidships, and had a sharp conical

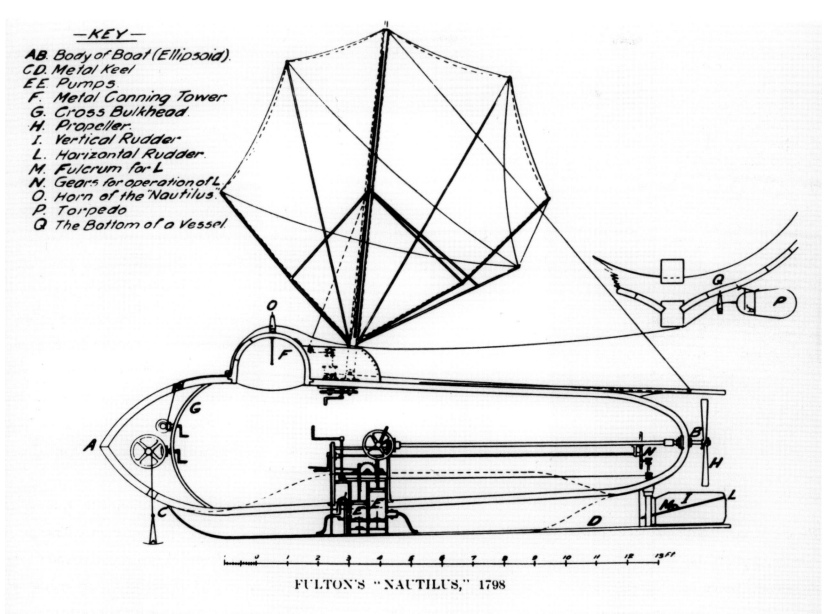

-KEY-

AB. Body of Boat (Ellipsoid).
CD. Metal Keel
EE. Pumps.
F. Metal Conning Tower
G. Cross Bulkhead.
H. Propeller.
I. Vertical Rudder.
L. Horizontal Rudder.
M. Fulcrum for L.
N. Gears for operation of L.
O. Horn of the "Nautilus".
P. Torpedo
Q The Bottom of a Vessel

FULTON'S "NAUTILUS," 1798

American designer Robert Fulton launched the first metal submarine, the *Nautilus*, in 1800. He had been rejected in America, so he took the plans to France in 1797 where they were accepted. She was to become the first submarine built under government contract. Her hull comprised an iron framework covered with copper sheets. A detachable explosive charge attached to her conning tower could be fastened to the hull of an enemy vessel. Although the vessel proved successful during her trials, the French lost interest. Later, the British also lost interest in the unique submarine. Fulton returned to the United States and began building the steam-powered *Mute*. He died before the project could be completed and it was scrapped. *NHC*

bow and stern. The boat was launched in 1879, and Admiralty officials requested her capabilities be demonstrated off Portsmouth. During the transit from Birkenhead to Portsmouth, the three-man crew suffered from the 100-degree heat created by the boiler inside the boat and this, together with fumes from the furnace, sapped the strength of the men to the extent that they decided to be towed to their destination. The *Resurgam* sank in heavy seas when the towrope broke; Garrett and his crew, however, did manage to escape before the boat went under.

Among the early boats was Robert Fulton's first metal submarine, the *Nautilus.* Launched in 1800 and tested successfully, she eventually was rejected by the British and French. Fulton's boat could remain submerged for nearly an hour at a depth of thirty feet. She carried an explosive charge on a spar and sank

a forty-foot French sloop and the British heavy brig *Dorothy.* Nevertheless, the two countries remained unimpressed, and Fulton, an American working in France, returned to his homeland in 1806, where he developed underwater guns for the U.S. government and began construction of a steam-powered submarine, the *Mute.* He died before work was completed on the boat, and the project was scrapped.

The Bauer *Brandtaucher,* Germany's first U-boat, appeared in the early 1800s. Built in Kiel, the stubby, steel-hulled submersible displaced thirty-nine tons and relied on manpower to drive her. Because of a near disaster in February 1851 when the craft plunged to a depth of fifty-four feet and failed to respond to crew efforts to resurface (the three-man crew was about to drown when an air bubble blew the hatch open and they swam to the surface), the *Brandtaucher* was never deployed operationally. However, the incident is recorded as the first submarine escape. The *Brandtaucher* was later raised and renovated. The oldest preserved submarine in the world, she presently is on display at the Deutsches Armeemuseum, Neuer Garten, Potsdam, Germany.

The first German U-boat appeared in 1850 with the launching of the *Brandtaucher,* which was built to ward off the attacks by Denmark on German ships during the war between the two countries (1848–50). Invented by Wilhelm Bauer, the vessel was used to lift the blockade of Kiel. Upon seeing this new alarming war machine, the Danes moved further out to sea, thus opening the port. This submarine, the oldest preserved submarine in the world, is presently on display at the Deutsches Armeemusem, Neuer Garten, Potsdam, Germany. *Cyril Field*

For centuries, naval warfare remained the stimulus for submarine development. The U.S. Civil War continued this trend and accelerated related technologies; the result was submersibles that successfully attacked enemy surface ships. In 1861, the U.S. Navy launched its first submarine, the USS *Alligator*. Designed by French inventor Brutus de Villeroi, the boat was built in Philadelphia. Her mission was to surreptitiously lay mines in Southern ports to destroy Confederate ships and harbor obstructions. In April 1863, while being towed to take part in an attack on Charleston harbor, she was lost in a storm. The wreck of the *Alligator* has never been found. The Union Navy launched a second mine-laying submarine, the *Intelligent Whale*, in 1862. The craft measured thirty-one feet by eight and a half feet by eight and a half feet; she was, in fact, shaped like a whale. She was manned by a crew of between six and thirteen and used hand-cranked mechanisms to power a single screw. A unique innovation of the *Whale* was a hatch through which a diver could deliver a mine while the craft was submerged. Because of numerous diving accidents, the sub's name was changed to *Disastrous Jonah,* and she was abandoned in 1872. The boat was displayed for many years at the Washington Navy Yard until she was moved to the National Guard Militia Museum of New Jersey at Sea Girt. With the failure of these submarines early in the war, the U.S. Navy showed little interest in submersibles for almost two decades.

The U.S. Navy launched its first submarine, the USS *Alligator,* in 1861. It was designed by French inventor Brutus de Villeroi and built in Philadelphia. In 1863 she was lost in a storm and a search for her continues to this day. *NHC*

A second submarine, the *Intelligent Whale*, which was equipped with the time-honored drill for attaching mines to ships' hulls, also carried loaded cannon to be positioned on each side of the conning tower. On either side of the bow was a series of saw-edged horizontal fins that could potentially cut gashes in the bottom of an enemy ship. The boat proved to be a complete failure when she underwent operational trials. She finished her career off Cape Hatteras, where she foundered in a gale. *NHC*

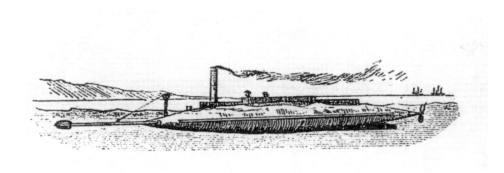

The Confederates countered with steam-powered semisubmersibles called *David* boats. These small cigar-shaped vessels carried a spar with an explosive charge attached. Unfortunately they operated with a smokestack and were easily detected by lookouts on Union ships. *Cyril Field*

The most famous of the Confederate submarines was the CSS *Hunley*. Although the *Hunley* was the world's first submarine to sink an enemy ship, she lost more of her crewmen than did the enemy. In 1864, Union warships tightly blockaded the vital port at Charleston, South Carolina, preventing entry of critically needed supplies. Entering their third year of the war, the Confederates resorted to desperate measures, both to survive and, perhaps, to turn the tide of the conflict.

Up to that point, Confederate use of semisubmersibles and primitive submarines had failed to alleviate the situation. Two New Orleans engineers, James McClintock and Baxter Watson, however, designed a new submersible that appeared to hold great promise. Among the investors who supported the construction of the new vessel was a Confederate naval officer, Horace L. Hunley.

The Confederates, on the other hand, displayed a keen interest in submarines, since the South's harbors and ports were under continual blockade by Union warships. Initially, the South turned to steam-powered semisubmersibles called *David* boats (named after the engineer who designed them, David Chenowith Ebaugh). The forty-foot vessels were cigar shaped and carried a spar with an explosive charge at the end, but they operated with a smokestack that was detected easily by target-vessel lookouts. Another Confederate submarine was the *Pioneer,* homeported at New Orleans and captured when the city fell to Union forces in 1862. The *American Diver* came next; during her construction in 1863, the iron-hulled vessel encountered numerous design and power plant problems. Upon completion, and before her first patrol, she sank in heavy seas while being towed off Fort Morgan.

Confederate States privateer submarine *Pioneer,* 1982. *NHC*

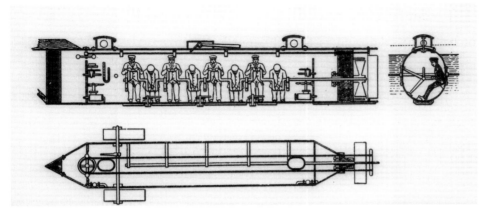

The most famous of the Confederate submarines was the CSS *Hunley.* On February 17, 1864, she sank the Federal sloop steamship *Housatonic.* The Confederate sub failed to return from her mission and was lost. In 1995 the remains of the vessel were found off the coast of Sullivan's Island, South Carolina, and taken to the Warren Lasch Conservation Center in Charleston, South Carolina, where scientists continue to study the artifacts found on the boat. *NHC*

McClintock, Baxter, and Hunley, who helped design the new boat, set up shop in Mobile, Alabama. Their first effort, which resembled the *Pioneer,* sank during testing. Their second model, which was to prove successful, consisted of a cylindrical steam boiler lengthened into an elliptical craft forty feet long. Tapered wedges that could be used as ballast tanks were welded to the bow and stern. The craft was four feet in diameter and had two raised manhole covers with ports to provide the pilot with an outside view, an air box with a breathing tube, and positions for eight men down the middle of the boat to hand crank power to a single screw. While submerged, a compass viewed by candlelight was used as a means of dead reckoning. The flickering light of the candle also warned of a failing air supply. The submersible's armament consisted of a 140-pound charge encased in a copper container at the end of a thirty-foot-long spar. Her surface speed in calm seas was four knots.

Upon completion in August 1863, the boat was taken by railway flatcar to Charleston. On the twenty-ninth of that month, during a test dive, the craft disappeared off the end of Fort Johnson Wharf. Five of her volunteer crew members drowned (the first submariners to die in history). One of the survivors reported that the pilot, Confederate Navy Lieutenant John A. Payne, accidentally stepped on the lever controlling the dive planes, causing the submarine to dive while her hatches were still open. The vessel was raised, and the Confederate Navy was convinced that the sub should be manned by a crew from Mobile familiar with the boat's operations. The boat was prepared for a nighttime attack when she sank during a routine diving test on October 15.

In addition to the entire Mobile crew, H. L. Hunley was lost, as he insisted on being aboard during the test. Although he was not part of the crew, when the submarine was recovered, he was mysteriously found to be at the helm.

The hull was raised once again, and another attempt was ordered to use the craft, now named the *H. L. Hunley* in honor of her dead commander. A new crew included naval personnel and one artilleryman; Lieutenant George Dixon piloted the craft. The *Hunley* made history on the night of February 17, 1864, when she successfully carried out an attack on the new Federal sloop steamship *Housatonic.* The approaching submerged submarine was sighted and fired on by crewmen aboard the ship, but to no avail. Dixon directed the *Hunley*'s newly fashioned twenty-foot pipe harpoon with its deadly charge into the hull of the steamship, and the resulting explosion blew off the stern of the ship. The *Housatonic* sank within three minutes, taking five crewmen with her, the first casualties of a submarine attack.

The *Hunley* failed to return from her mission, however, and was lost for reasons unknown. In 1995, the remains of the submarine were found off the coast of Sullivan's Island. Best-selling author Clive Cussler, who founded the National Underwater Marine Agency, had spent fifteen years searching for the *Hunley.* The rusty hull was raised in 2000 and transported to the Lasch Conservation Center in Charleston, where scientists went to work excavating and conserving the historic vessel and her artifacts.

After three years of meticulous investigation, scientists were able to verify the identities of the eight men who went down with the *Hunley.* Consulting

In 1879 the world's first fully powered submarine, the *Resurgam II*, was built in Birkenhead, England. Her propulsion was by steam on the Lamm fireless principle. Initial trials were promising, and the designer, George Garrett, decided to set up a base on the Welsh coast. However, as the boat was being towed to her new berth in 1880, she sank during a storm. She has never been raised. *Cyril Field*

with an array of scholars, as well as experts from the Smithsonian Institution, and exhuming one crewman's sister for DNA analysis, the team was able to match which skeletal remains belonged to which crewman.

The successful attack of the *Hunley* and the invention of the torpedo in 1865 by Austrian engineer Robert Whitehead made the submarine a potentially dangerous weapon of war. Thus, the undersea vehicle gained the attention of navies around the world. Many submarines built in the latter half of the nineteenth century made provisions for torpedoes to be fired externally or through bow tubes. What remained problematic, however, was an effective method for underwater propulsion.

The next significant advance in submarine technology took place in the Baltic. In 1893, Thorsten Nordenfelt, a Stockholm shipyard ord-

nance expert, constructed a sixty-ton submarine powered by steam and carrying a firing tube for a Whitehead torpedo. He demonstrated the vessel with great success, and Greece, Russia, and Turkey ordered Nordenfelt boats. The boats proved to be laden with operational defects, however, and soon lost their appeal.

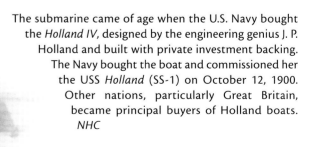

The submarine came of age when the U.S. Navy bought the *Holland IV*, designed by the engineering genius J. P. Holland and built with private investment backing. The Navy bought the boat and commissioned her the USS *Holland* (SS-1) on October 12, 1900. Other nations, particularly Great Britain, became principal buyers of Holland boats. *NHC*

In 1890, the Imperial German Navy took notice of the boat and purchased plans from Nordenfelt to build two boats—*W.1* and *W.2.* The 215-ton steam-powered U-boats were 114 feet in length and had a surface speed of 11 knots and 4-1/2 knots submerged. Using a French design, Krupp arms manufacturer later built a 180-ton boat that used gasoline engines for surface running and electric motors while submerged. When the gasoline engines were replaced by diesels, this propulsion system became the standard for all navies until the arrival of nuclear-powered submarines. Though the German Navy eventually seemed to lose interest in the submarine, Krupp-Germania did not. It continued to build experimental boats, often selling them to other countries. By the early 1900s, German shipbuilders had gained invaluable knowledge in the building and operation of underwater boats.

The submarine came of age when the U.S. Navy bought the seventy-four-ton *Holland IV,* designed and built with private investment backing. Engineering genius J. P. Holland presented her to the U.S. Navy in 1898. Navy officials present at a demonstration of the craft recognized that they were witnessing the world's first practical submarine. The *Holland IV* was fifty-four feet long, ten feet, three inches at the beam, and displaced sixty-four tons on the surface and seventy-five tons submerged. Her running speed was eight knots surfaced and five knots submerged. She carried a crew of seven and was armed with one eighteen-inch torpedo tube with two reload torpedoes. The U.S. Navy bought the boat on April 11, 1900, for $165,000 and commissioned her the USS *Holland* (SS-1) on October 12 of that year. Before Holland could realize any rewards from the U.S. government, however, his company, the Holland Torpedo Boat Company, found itself in financial trouble and was absorbed by the Electric Boat Company. Holland was kept on as a manager, and when he left the company in 1904, he held but one-half of 1 percent of the company.

Before his success with the *Holland IV,* Holland had often found himself in competition with another brilliant U.S. submarine designer, Simon Lake. Though Lake built numerous fine boats, he always seemed to lose U.S. government contract bids to Holland. In 1894, Lake built the *Argonaut,* which was equipped with large wheels to travel along a seabed. In 1901, he built the *Protector,* which bore many similarities to today's boats. She had a periscope, free-flooding tanks, diving planes forward, a small conning tower, and three torpedoes. Lake later sold the *Protector* to the Russians, and designed submarines for the German, Austrian, and Russian navies. In 1912, he founded the Lake Torpedo Boat Company and built submarines for the U.S. Navy; these included the G-class (337 tons) and the N-class (414 tons) long-range submarines.

Other nations became interested in the Holland boat at the turn of the century. Britain, which up to this point had belittled the submarine as a threat to surface navies, built five improved *Holland*s under license between 1901 and 1903. The first to be launched was designated *No. 1* and is now on display at the Royal Navy Museum at Gosport. Britain's First Sea Lord, Admiral Jackie Fisher, wrote in 1904, "It is astounding to me, perfectly astounding, how the very best among us fail to realize the vast impending revolution in Naval warfare and Naval strategy that the submarine will accomplish. . . . It is enough to make your hair stand on end!" Once the Admiralty committed itself to submarines as a weapon of war,

Nordenfelt Submarine Boat — A rigged
When on the journey from Stockholm to
Gothenburg and Copenhagen.

The next advance in submarine development technology were the Swedish *Nordenfelt* boats. These were sixty-ton boats, powered by steam and carrying a Whitehead torpedo. Greece, Turkey, and Russia ordered *Nordenfelt* boats but soon became disenchanted with the submarine because it was found to be laden with operational defects. *NHC*

the Royal Navy started building a fleet of undersea boats with numerical desig-nations. A, B, and C classes (207- to 320-ton submarines) were of *Holland* design. The D class was a 490-ton boat with a surface range of 1,100 nautical miles at ten knots and the 665-ton E class boasted a surface running range of 3,000 nau-tical miles. When World War I began, the Royal Navy had seventy-five submarines in commission and twenty-eight under construction; twenty were long-range overseas service D- and E-class boats (620- to 796-ton submarines), while the A, B, and C classes were coastal boats.

Britain's buildup of its submarine fleet did not go unnoticed by Germany. Though intent on building the Imperial German High Seas Fleet, Grand Admiral Alfred von Tirpitz realized that he had to keep up with the arms race, and thus he authorized the construction of the *U-1*, which was commissioned

At the turn of the century the German naval staff failed to realize the potential of the submarine as a weapon of war, although Britain's buildup of its underseas fleet did not go unnoticed by the Imperial German Navy. The *U-1* was commissioned in 1906. At the outbreak of World War I in August 1914, Germany had twenty-eight U-boats in service. *NHC*

in 1906. The *U-2* was already laid down, and the *U-3* and *U-4* were soon to fol-low. These later German U-boats were more advanced than the British sub-marines. Each had four torpedo tubes, two forward and two aft. They also were equipped with a 37-mm gun that was moved into the hull when the boat sub-merged. The *U-19* was the first of four U-boats constructed with diesel engines, which greatly increased the endurance of patrols. The range of these boats was 7,600 nautical miles while surfaced. Germany now looked beyond a coastal defense strategy for its fledgling U-boat fleet; it realized it possessed the capa-bility to attack enemy merchant ships in time of war.

At the beginning of the World War I, the German Navy had twenty-eight U-boats, four of which were early models slated to serve as training boats. The U-boat arm thus went to war with twenty-four operational boats; these were divided into flotillas and based in the harbor of Hegligoland, a fortified island in the North Sea located north of the River Jade at Wilhelmshaven where the German High Seas Fleet was homeported.

By the beginning of 1916, the Germans began to feel the effects of a British-imposed blockade. British patrols stopped and seized cargoes of more than seven

Last-minute escape from vessel torpedoed by U-boat during World War I. The vessel has already sunk her bow in the waves, and her stern is slowly lifting out of the water. Men can be seen sliding down ropes as the last lifeboat is pulling away. *U-BOOT-ARCHIV*

hundred neutral ships bound for Germany. The situation became so acute regarding the country's food supply that the Germans were faced with the possibility of entering into peace negotiations, even though their army remained undefeated.

By early 1917 the German General Staff realized that the Central Powers were losing the war. German manpower had been drained at Verdun, and the

British blockade continued to deny Germany vital war materials and critical food supplies. All measures had been taken to alleviate the situation, except the unleashing of the U-boat. That changed in 1917, when Germany turned to unrestricted U-boat warfare with the hope that such a campaign eventually would bring Britain to its knees. The German Supreme Command was so confident of Germany's success in launching the campaign that it was not concerned with the likelihood that the measure would possibly bring the United States into the war. For the first six months (February through July), British losses were indeed staggering: 3,813,798 tons of British shipping were sunk.

On March 12, 1917, however, the U.S. steamship *Algonquin* was sunk as she approached the British Isles. A few days later, three more U.S. ships were sunk without warning. On April 6, 1917, the United States declared war on Germany.

Rear Admiral William S. Sims, Commander United States Naval Forces Operating in European Waters, immediately went to England to determine the shipping situation firsthand. Sims championed the British adoption of the convoy system and convinced Prime Minister Lloyd George of its value. On April 30, 1917, the British Sea Lords approved the use of ocean convoys.

Early on, the convoy system showed its worth. As more ships were convoyed, sinkings decreased. The German U-boat arm sent every boat available to sea to wage this decisive battle. An average of forty-five boats were at sea

Prior to America's entry into the war, the German U-boat *U-53* made a brief unannounced call at Newport, Rhode Island, on October 7, 1916. The next day she sank six foreign merchant ships in international waters off the U.S. coast. As can be seen here, the crew was not camera shy during her visit. *NHC*

daily during the summer months of 1917. In July the number peaked at fifty-two. In their haste to wage a swift campaign, however, the Germans neglected to properly maintain and repair their boats. Also, with U-boat sinkings increasing because of improved Allied antisubmarine measures and German cutbacks in new construction, the number of boats at sea declined. In 1917 and 1918, the number of U-boats lost jumped to sixty-three and sixty-nine, respectively.

In the end, it was the Allied victory at the Battle of the Marne that sent the German Army reeling back to the fatherland. At sea, the British naval blockade had taken its toll, and the convoy system defeated the U-boat at sea. Germany was faced with starvation, a mutinous High Seas Fleet, and the possibility of a revolution. The Kaiser abdicated on November 9, 1918, and on November 11, German officials signed the armistice documents.

Although Germany lost 178 U-boats during the war, it still had 171 boats in its fleet at the time of the armistice and another 149 in various stages of construction. The German U-boat war record was astonishing. The underseas fleet had sunk 5,282 British, Allied, and neutral merchant ships and fishing vessels grossing 12,284,757 tons. In addition, they had destroyed 10 battleships, 18 cruisers, 204 destroyers, and 9 submarines.

Even though Germany lost the war at sea, it had introduced the submarine as a feared weapon of war. It developed, built, and operated a highly effective underseas naval arm that sank thousands of vital merchant ships, nearly defeating Great Britain. Its U-boats had both speed and range, and their late war forays into U.S. waters signaled looming danger for any war to come.

Completed in March 1918, the *U-140* was armed with four bow torpedo tubes, one 6-inch gun, and nineteen mines. Far superior to U.S. submarines at that time, the cruiser boat measured 280 feet long, 24 feet abeam, and 25 feet in depth. Two diesel 1,700-hp engines enabled the craft to make 26 knots on the surface. Brought to the United States after the war, *U-140*, together with *U-117*, *U-151*, *U-152*, *U-155*, and *U-156* had operated in U.S. Atlantic waters during the final year of the war. The *U-140* is shown here docked in a U.S. shipyard. *NARA*

WORKS CONSULTED

Further Reading

Alden, John D. *The Fleet Submarine in the U.S. Navy*. Annapolis, Md.: Naval Institute Press, 1979.

Beaver, Paul. *U-Boats in the Atlantic*. Cambridge, England: Patrick Stephens, 1979.

Blair, Clay. *Hitler's U-Boat War: The Hunters 1939–1942*. New York: Random House, 1996.

———. *Hitler's U-Boat War: The Hunted 1942–1945*. New York: Random House, 1996.

Bonansinga, Jay. *The Sinking of the Eastland: America's Forgotten Tragedy*. New York: Citadel Press Books, 2004.

Botting, Douglas. *The U-Boats*. Alexandria, Va.: Time-Life Books, 1979.

Breyer, Siegfried, and Gerhard Koop. *The U-Boat: The German Navy at War 1935–1945*. Vol. 2. Westchester, Pa.: Schiffer Publishing, 1989.

Buchheim, Lothar-Gunther. *U-Boat War*. New York: Alfred A. Knopf, 1978.

Busch, Rainer, and Hans-Joachim Roll. *German U-Boat Commanders of World War II: A Biographical Dictionary*. Annapolis, Md.: Naval Institute Press, 1999.

Chesneau, Roger. *Aircraft Carriers of the World, 1914 to the Present: An Illustrated Encyclopedia*. Annapolis, Md.: Naval Institute Press, 1995.

Churchill, Winston, C. H. *The World Crisis*. New York: Charles Scribner & Sons, 1931.

Decker, Hans Joachim. "404 Days! The War Patrol Life of the German U-505." U.S. Naval Institute *Proceedings* (March 1960): 33–45.

Dobbs, Michael. *Saboteurs: The Nazi Raid on America*. New York: Alfred A. Knopf, 2004.

Doll, Thomas E., Berkley R. Jackson, and William A. Riley. *Navy Air Colors: United States Navy, Marine Corps, and Coast Guard Aircraft Camouflage and Markings*. Vol. 1, 1911–1945. Carollton, Tex.: Squadron/Signal Publications, 1983.

Dönitz, Karl. *Memoirs: Ten Years and Twenty Days*. Annapolis, Md.: Naval Institute Press, 1959.

Field, Cyril. *The Story of the Submarine: From the Earliest Ages to the Present Day*. London: Sampson Low, Marston & Company, LD., 1908.

Gallery, Daniel V. *Twenty Million Tons under the Sea*. Annapolis, Md.: Naval Institute Press, 2001.

———. "Papers including declassified documents, personal papers and correspondence, photographs, etc." Special Collections Archives Division, Nimitz Library, U.S. Naval Academy.

"Gallery Ship Naming Marks 25th U-505 Anniversary." Progress—The Museum of Science & Industry, June 1979.

Gannon, Michael. *Operation Drumbeat*. New York: Harper and Row, 1990.

Gilliland, Herbert C., and Robert Shenk. *Admiral Dan Gallery: The Life and Wit of a Navy Original*. Annapolis, Md.: Naval Institute Press, 1999.

Goebeler, Hans Jacob, and John P. Vanzo. *Steel Boats, Iron Hearts: The Wartime Saga of Hans Goebeler and the U-505*. Holder, Fla.: Wagnerian Publications, 1999.

Gray, Edwyn A. *The Killing Time*. New York: Charles Scribner & Sons, 1972.

———. *The U-Boat War: 1914–1918*. London: Leo Cooper, 1994.

Halpern, Paul G. *The Naval War in the Mediterranean 1914–1918*. Annapolis, Md.: Naval Institute Press, 1986.

Hill, J. H., *Anti-Submarine Warfare*. Annapolis, Md.: Naval Institute Press, 1984.

Högel, Georg. *U-Boat Emblems of World War II*. Atglen, Pa.: Schiffer Military History, 1987.

Humble, Richard, and Mark Bergin. *A World War Two Submarine*. Annapolis, Md.: Naval Institute Press, 1991.

Hutchinson, Robert. *Submarines: War beneath the Waves from 1776 to the Present Day.* London: HarperCollins, 2001.

Jackson, Robert. *Submarines of the World.* London: Friedman/Fairfax Publishers, 2000.

Jordan, David. *Wolfpack: The U-Boat War and the Allied Counter-Attack 1939–1945.* New York: Barnes & Noble Books, 2002.

Kahn, David. *Seizing the Enigma: The Race to Break the German U-Boat Codes, 1939–1943.* New York: Barnes & Noble Books, 1998.

Kemp, Paul. *U-Boats Destroyed: German Submarine Losses in the World Wars.* Annapolis, Md.: Naval Institute Press, 1997.

Konstam, Angus, and Jak Mallmann Showell. *7th U-Boat Flotilla: Dönitz's Atlantic Wolves.* Hersham, Surrey, U.K.: Ian Allan Publishing, 2003.

Messimer, Dwight R. *The Merchant U-Boat: Adventures of the* Deutschland *1916–1918.* Annapolis, Md.: Naval Institute Press, 1988.

Miller, David. *The Illustrated Directory of the Submarines of the World.* St. Paul, Minn.: MBI Publishing, 2002.

Morison, S. E. *History of United States Naval Operations in World War II.* Vols. 1, 10, 15. Boston: Little Brown, 1975.

Museum of Science & Industry. *The Story of the U-505.* Chicago, 1978.

Navy Department, Office of the Chief of Naval Operations, Naval History Division. *Dictionary of American Fighting Ships.* Vol. 3. Washington, D.C.: U.S. Government Printing Office, 1977.

Niestlé, Axel. *German U-Boat Losses during World War II: Details of Destruction.* Annapolis, Md.: Naval Institute Press, 1995.

Padfield, Peter. *War beneath the Sea.* New York: John Wiley & Sons, 1995.

Paterson, Lawrence. *Second U-Boat Flotilla.* Yorkshire, Great Britain: Leo Cooper, 2003.

Pope, Stephen, and Elizabeth-Anne Wheal. *The Dictionary of the First World War.* New York: St. Martin's Press, 1995.

Potter, E. B. *Sea Power: A Naval History.* Annapolis, Md.: Naval Institute Press, 1954–1961.

Pridmore, Jay. *Museum of Science and Industry.* Chicago: Harry N. Abrams, 1997.

Rohwer, Jurgen. *Axis Submarine Successes, 1939–45.* Annapolis, Md.: Naval Institute Press, 1983.

Roskill, S. W. *The War at Sea 1939–1945.* London: HMSO, 1954–1961.

Savas, Theodore P., ed. *Hunt and Kill: U-505 and the U-boat War in the Atlantic.* New York: Savas Beatie LLC, 2004.

Showell, Jak P. *U-Boats under the Swastika.* Annapolis, Md.: Naval Institute Press, 1989.

Syrett, David. *The Defeat of the German U-Boats: The Battle the Atlantic.* Columbia: University of South Carolina Press, 1994.

Tall, Jeffrey. *Submarines & Deep-Sea Vehicles.* San Diego: Thunder Bay Press, 2002.

Tarrant, V. E. *The U-Boat Offensive 1914–1945.* Annapolis, Md.: Naval Institute Press, 1989.

Truman, Ben C. *History of the World's Columbian Exposition.* Chicago: Mammoth Publishing, 1893.

"U-505 Captain and USN Captor Meet 20 Years Later." Progress—The Museum of Science & Industry, June 1974.

"U-505 Captor Host to Students." Progress—The Museum of Science & Industry, June 1974.

"U-505 Crew and Americans Have Reunion." Progress—The Museum of Science & Industry, June 1989

Vaeth, J. Gordon. *Blimps & U-Boats: U.S. Navy Airships in the Battle of the Atlantic.* Annapolis, Md.: Naval Institute Press, 1992.

Watts, Anthony J. *The Royal Navy: An Illustrated History.* Annapolis, Md.: Naval Institute Press, 1994.

Weir, Gary E. *Forged in War: The Naval-Industrial Complex and American Submarine Construction, 1940–1961.* Washington, D.C.: Naval Historical Center, Department of the Navy, 1993.

White, John F. *U-Boat Tankers, 1941–1945.* Annapolis, Md.: Naval Institute Press, 1998.

Wiggins, Melanie. *U-Boat Adventures: Firsthand Accounts from World War II.* Annapolis, Md.: Naval Institute Press, 1999.

Williams, David. *Wartime Disasters at Sea.* Somerset, England: Patrick Stephens Limited, 1997.

Williamson, Gordon. *Grey Wolf: U-boat Crewmen of World War II.* Oxford, U.K.: Osprey Publishing, 2001.

———. *Kriegsmarine U-boats, 1939–45.* Vol. 1. Oxford, U.K.: Osprey Publishing, 2002.

———. *Kriegsmarine U-boats, 1939–45.* Vol. 2. Oxford, U.K.: Osprey Publishing, 2002.

———. *U-Boat Bases and Bunkers, 1941–45.* Oxford, U.K.: Osprey Publishing, 2003.

Winters, Andrew J. *Ministry of Defence, German Naval History: The U-Boat War in the Atlantic 1939–1945.* London: HMSO, 1989.

Wise, James E. Jr. "The Dawn of ASW." U.S. Naval Institute *Proceedings* (February 1964): 91–103.

———. "U-Boats off Our Coasts." U.S. Naval Institute *Proceedings* (October 1964): 84–103.

———. "Enter the U-Boat." *Our Navy Magazine,* July 1965, 6–7; 42–43.

———. "The Sinking of the *UC-97.*" *Naval History* (Winter 1989): 12–17.

Y'Blood, William. *Hunter-Killer: U.S. Escort Carriers in the Battle of the Atlantic.* Annapolis, Md.: Naval Institute Press, 1983.

Official Sources

Commander Task Group 23.3, USS *Guadalcanal* (CVE-60) Action Report, "Capture of German Submarine *U-505*," dated June 19, 1944, with following enclosures:

(A) Reports of Units involved in Action
    (1) Commander Escort Division Four
    (2) USS *Chatelain* (DE 149)
    (3) USS *Pillsbury* (DE 133)
    (4) USS *Pope* (DE 134)
    (5) USS *Flaherty* (DE 135)
    (6) USS *Jenks* (DE 665)
    (7) Composite Squadron Eight
    (8) Statement by the Captain of *U-505*
(B) Chronological Narrative of Action
(C) Track Charts
    (1) Track Chart of *U-505* Action
    (2) Track Chart of *U-505* and T.G. 23.3 showing U/B estimates
(D) Radio Log
(E) List of Prisoners
(F) List of Boarding Parties
(G) Photographs (60)
(H)
    (1) Intentions for Night Signal for May 17
    (2) Plan of the Day for June 4
(I) Complete A/S cruise report

Roll Call Logs for USS *Guadalcanal,* USS *Chatelain,* USS *Pillsbury,* USS *Pope,* USS *Flaherty,* USS *Jenks* for June 4, 1944. National Archives and Records Administration (NARA II), College Park, Md.

Still Photographic Print Division. National Archives and Records Administration (NARA II), College Park, Md.

Navy Department, Office of the Chief of Naval Operations, Naval History Division. *Dictionary of American Fighting Ships.* Vols. 1–8. Washington, D.C.: U.S. Government Printing Office, 1977.

Navy Department, Office of the Chief of Naval Operations, Naval History Division. *Axis Submarine Losses.* Washington, D.C.: U.S. Government Printing Office, 1963.

Records Relating to U-Boat Warfare 1939–1945: Guides to the Microfilmed Records of the German Navy 1850–1945. No. 2. Washington, D.C.: National Archives and Records, 1985.

Oral Histories

"Reminiscences of Rear Admiral D. V. Gallery, U.S. Navy, Ret." U.S. Naval Institute. June 19, 1976.

"Recollections of Lieutenant Commander Dudley S. Knox, USNR, on Destroyer Escort USS *Chatelain* (DE-149), of the Sinking of German Submarines *U-515* and *U-68* off Madeira Island on 9 and 10 April 1944." Box 18 of World War II Interviews, Operational Archives Branch, Naval Historical Center.

Interviews with the Following American/German Submariners Involved in Capture of *U-505* on June 4, 1944. Interviews were conducted at the Chicago, Illinois, Museum of Science & Industry on April 18, and March 1–5, 1999.

German: Maschinmaat Karl Oscar Springer

Maschinmaat Karl Werner REH

Mechanikeroberge Freiter Wolfgang Gerhardt Schiller

Horst Bredow—Director U-Boat—Archiv, Cuxhaven, Germany

(Interviewed at U-Boot Archiv/Museum, Berlin, Germany, April 18, 1999)

American: Albert Rust, Survivor of Liberty Ship *Thomas MacKean*

Captain Edwin Harvey Headland, Commanding Officer, USS *Pope* (DE 134)

Don Carter, SM2C, USS *Guadalcanal* (CVE-60)

Lieutenant D. F. Hampton, Senior Watch Officer, USS *Guadalcanal* (CVE-60)

Commander Earl Trosino, Chief Engineer, USS *Guadalcanal* (CVE-60)

Coxswain Phil Trusheim, USS *Pillsbury* (DE-133)

Radarman Joseph Villanella, USS *Chatelain* (DE-149)

W. M. Pickles, BM2C, USS *Pillsbury* (DE-133)

Zen Lukocious, MOMM1C, USS *Pillsbury* (DE-13)

Joe Hill/Jim Sisson, Members of American Navy crew that operated *U-505* during her war bond tour of U.S. port cities

Lieutenant (junior grade) Ritzdorf, TBM Pilot, Composite Squadron Eight (VC-8)

Lieutenant Jack W. Dumford, Communications Officer, USS *Guadalcanal* (CVE-60)

Sonarmen L. Watts and M. Chapman, USS *Chatelain* (DE-149)

Internet Sources

The Battle of the Atlantic: Allied Naval Intelligence in World War II. *Punching the Convoys Through: "Hunter-Killers" in the Atlantic, 1943–1945.* At http://www.mariner.org/atlantic/gg01.htm.

The Battle of the Atlantic: Allied Naval Intelligence in World War II. *An American Capture: U-505.* At http://www.mariner.org/atlantic/hh01.htm.

The Battle of the Atlantic: Allied Naval Intelligence in World War II. *Using Special Intelligence.* At http://www.mariner.org/atlantic/ii01.htm.

Capture of U-505 on 4 June 1944. At www.history.navy.mil/faqs/faq91-1.htm.

Moving the U-505. At www.msichicago.org/exhibit/U505/moving.html and www.msichicago.org/exhibit/U505/gallery/gallery_move.html.

Museum of Science & Industry U-505 Submarine: Follow Construction of the New Exhibit Pen and the Move. At http://www.hydepark.org/parks/jpac/submove.htm.

Photo Gallery: U-505 Ceremony. At www.msichicago.org/exhibit/U505/gallery/gallery_ceremony.htm.

Rose, Julie. "The World's Columbian Exposition: Idea, Experience, Aftermath." At http://xroads.virginia.edu/-MA96/WCE/title.html

Task Group 23.3 Reunion Information. At http://505.dnsdata.com/reunion.htm.

U-505. At http://www.msichicago.org/exhibit/U505/U505home.html.

U-505 Personal Diary. At http://www.history.navy.mil/library/special/U505_personal_diary.htm.

U-505 Restoration. At www.msichicago.org/exhibit/U505/restoration.html.

USS Gallery (FFG-26). At http://navysite.de/ffg/FFG26.htm.

USS Knox (FF-1052). At http://navysite.de/ff/ff10952.htm.

USS Pillsbury DER-133 Memories. At http://pillsburyder133.tripod.com/M5.html.

USS Pillsbury Memories pages. At http://pillsburyder133.tripod.com/M5.html.

ABOUT THE AUTHOR

James E. Wise Jr. became a naval aviator in 1953 following graduation from Northwestern University. He served as an intelligence officer aboard USS *America* and later as the commanding officer of various naval intelligence units. Since his retirement from the U.S. Navy in 1975 at the rank of captain, he has held several senior executive posts in private-sector companies in the Washington, D.C., area.

A resident of Alexandria, Virginia, Wise is the coauthor of many books published by the Naval Institute Press, including *Shooting the War: The Memoir and Photographs of a U-Boat Officer in World War II, Stars in Blue, Stars in the Corps, Stars in Khaki,* and *International Stars at War,* which he coauthored with Scott Baron. His other books include *Sole Survivors of the Sea, Sailor's Journey into War,* and *James Arness,* an autobiography that he helped Arness write.